Teacher Evaluation Policy

SUNY Series, Educational Leadership

Daniel L. Duke, Editor

Teacher Evaluation Policy

From Accountability to Professional Development

edited by
Daniel L. Duke

State University of New York Press

Published by
State University of New York Press, Albany

For information, address the State University of New York Press,
State University Plaza, Albany, NY 12246

Production by Christine Lynch
Marketing by Fran Keneston

Library of Congress Cataloging-in-Publication Data

Teacher evaluation policy : from accountability to professional
  development / edited by Daniel L. Duke.
      p.   cm. —(SUNY series, educational leadership)
    Includes bibliographical references and index.
    ISBN 0-7914-2792-7 (pbk. : acid-free). — ISBN 0-7914-2791-9 (cl.
    acid-free)
    1. Teachers—United States—Rating of. 2. Teachers—Great
  Britain—Rating of. 3. Educational accountability—United States.
  4. Educational accountability—Great Britain. I. Duke, Daniel
  Linden. II. Series: SUNY series in educational leadership.
  LB2838.T42 1996
  371.1'44'0973—dc20   95-11832
                                                           CIP

10   9   8   7   6   5   4   3   2   1

To RICKY STIGGINS with gratitude
for taking time from fishing to involve me in the quest
for better teacher evaluation systems.

Contents

1

The Move to Reform Teacher Evaluation

Daniel L. Duke

The 1980s witnessed a concerted effort at the national, state, and local level to improve public schooling in the United States. Similar attempts to promote educational reform occurred in other countries, most notably Great Britain. Policymakers left few aspects of education unaddressed. School goals, governance, finance, curriculum, graduation requirements, and testing all received attention. No area received more scrutiny, however, than the quality of instruction and those employed to deliver it. Summing up the period, Darling-Hammond (1990, p. 18) noted that the public "has come to believe that the key to educational improvement lies as much in upgrading the quality of teachers as in revamping school programs and curricula."

The desire to ensure that young people are served by competent teachers led reformers to rethink teacher preparation and certification, staff development, recruiting and hiring practices, remuneration and benefits, supervisory practices, and personnel evaluation. In the sphere of teacher evaluation, policymakers examined the purposes of evaluation, performance standards, the relationship between evaluation and professional growth, merit pay, and career ladders, among other issues. Much of this work took place at the local level—in board meetings and at bargaining tables. New teacher evaluation systems were negotiated in school districts from Florida to Washington State. As Darling-Hammond (1990 p. 18) points out, however,

. . . the development of teacher-evaluation practices in local school districts does not occur in a vacuum. State policies often define some of the key features of evaluation.

The purpose of this book is to present relatively detailed accounts of the formulation and implementation of teacher evaluation policies in selected states and Great Britain, particularly England and Wales. Reform always occurs in context. It is impossible to understand fully how a local teacher evaluation system develops without knowing about the broader policy context. Sometimes interactions take place between local and state or national contexts, causing policy intentions at each level to be moderated or compromised. Sometimes the traditional top-down flow of policy influence is reversed as local developments shape state policy. Studying the development of teacher evaluation policy in different contexts may help readers to appreciate local variations in policy and assess the extent to which consensus exists regarding particular aspects of contemporary practice in teacher evaluation.

Restless Contexts and Conflicting Choices

Studying the formulation and implementation of teacher evaluation policy requires historical perspective along with a sense of context. Policy does not happen at one point in time. It is best thought of as evolving gradually. As policy is formulated and refined, however, its context does not necessarily remain stable. Political leaders leave office and are replaced by new leaders who may have different views and priorities. Economic conditions fluctuate. New concerns surface, displacing existing policy initiatives or relegating them to the political "back burner."

Changes in policy context present policymakers and those expected to implement policy with daunting challenges. It is difficult enough to develop new policy without the uncertainties of changing circumstances. Gaining agreement among competing interest groups is always hard work. Trying to accomplish the task amid contextual changes at times may be virtually impossible. The feat is analogous to hitting a moving target from a moving vehicle.

Making policy is, in essence, a process of making choices. Policymakers choose which problems merit attention, how to define them, how to address them, and often how to implement the policies that result from their deliberations. Practitioners also engage in policy-related choices, deciding how to interpret policies and the extent to which they will comply with policy expectations. These choices are influenced to varying degrees by people's understanding of context and their attitudes toward change. Individuals do not always agree, for example, on a set of assumptions regarding the likely course of future events. They also may disagree about the past, disputing the conditions that are claimed to have given rise to the need for policy in the first place.

To make matters more complex, how people choose to interpret the same events may change over time. Policymakers frequently reexamine and revise policies as the meanings of policies are perceived to change in light of subsequent events. Affirmative action policies, for instance, do not necessarily mean today what they meant when they initially were introduced (Steele 1990). As a result, it is probably best to think of policymaking as a continuous process rather than one with a well-defined beginning and end.

Necessity, of course, dictates that the accounts of the formulation and implementation of teacher evaluation policy in this book must conclude at some point in time. The authors, however, have been careful to note that the policies about which they write continue to evolve in the face of changing circumstances and reconsidered choices.

Deborah Stone, in her pathbreaking book *Policy Paradox and Political Reason* (1988), maintains that choice-making invariably entails politics. Stone rejects the view, which she associates primarily with classical economics, that policy results strictly from rational decision making. Such a viewpoint holds that policy emerges from a logical process in which 1) goals are identified, 2) determinations are made regarding why goals have not been achieved and 3) means for achieving goals are selected. Preferences are presumed to be relatively stable. Countering this view, Stone observes that policymakers may not always begin with goals. Sometimes they start out, for example, with a politically attractive solution and then search for a goal for which it might be appropriate. Furthermore, they may ignore research and evaluations that offer explanations concerning why goals previously have not been achieved. Preferences turn out to be unstable, often changing in unpredictable ways.

Stone sees policymaking rooted in the social construction of reality, a perspective which maintains that reality only can be known through an understanding of how individuals choose to categorize it, name it, and invest it with meaning. At the base of all policymaking, she contends, is political struggle over the categories of thought that will guide and define the process. Participants in policymaking contest policy causes, purposes, evaluation criteria, consequences, and underlying values, among other things. Stone (1988, p. 306) concludes that,

> Reasoned analysis is necessarily political. It always involves choices to include some things and exclude others and to view the world in a particular way when other visions are possible.

The heart of politics, and policymaking, according to Stone, is the struggle over ideas. J. D. McNeil (1981, p. 272) captures the flavor of this struggle in the area of teacher evaluation policy:

Conflicts over the proper bases for evaluating teachers are numerous. Individuals and groups have different concepts of the desirable characteristics, institutional contributions, community services, and instructional effectiveness of teachers. They also have different purposes for evaluating teachers: instructional improvement, personal growth, and accountability and control. . . . Each value base has its supporters and detractors, who use political techniques to broaden their position. At times evaluation procedures reflect the intents of employers, who use evaluation for the purpose of promotion or dismissal. At other times, assessment plans, involving peers and union representatives, are aimed at the improvement of teaching performance.

The accounts in this book reveal some of the central ideas related to teacher evaluation over which policymakers have been struggling during the past two decades. These ideas include accountability, professional development, professionalism, and performance pay. Those engaged in the "struggle" include politicians, business people, citizens' groups, teachers, school administrators, school board representatives, and educational researchers.

Accountability

A buzzword in education since the early seventies, accountability often is invoked to justify the need for teacher evaluation. Critics of public schools argue that teachers must be held accountable. They sometimes point to private schools as exemplars of accountability, presumably because dissatisfied parents can withdraw their children and choose another school. Since this option is unavailable to many parents of children in public schools, mechanisms must exist, they argue, to ensure that teachers are doing their job. But what does "doing their job" really mean? R. B. Wagner (1989, p. 1) points out that accountability implies a set of questions: "accountable to whom, for what, in what manner and under what circumstances?" Should teachers, for example, be held accountable for performing functions specified in their job descriptions? Meeting specific performance standards? Seeing that students attain designated levels of achievement?

Questions such as these are frequently debated in the process of formulating teacher evaluation policy. In addition, concerns surface regarding the most appropriate unit of accountability. Should the focus of accountability-based evaluation be individual teachers, groups of teachers, or schools? Student success rarely is the result of one teacher's efforts. Then, too, parents and students themselves play a role in the educational process. Should they be held accountable as well and, if so, for what and by which mechanisms? What should be the relationship between parent, student, and teacher accountability?

Two concerns are often at the center of demands for accountability-based evaluation of teachers. One involves the fear that incompetent teachers will be allowed to remain in classrooms. Almost every person, it seems, can cite at least one unpleasant story concerning a teacher who harmed them or someone close to them. These people question why action was not taken to discipline or remove the accused. They wonder whether anyone evaluated the performance of the teacher. The second concern involves money. Schooling is big business, and taxpayers complain that costs keep rising without commensurate gains in student achievement. They expect to see tangible improvements for their increased contributions, and when these improvements are not forthcoming, they frequently question the process by which teachers are evaluated.

The desire for accountability does not always match the capacity to collect the information necessary to reach judgments about accountability. Researchers point out that the data on which accountability decisions are based often are invalid and unreliable. Teacher advocates contend that the due process rights of teachers are jeopardized by misguided policies and inadequate evaluation practices. They criticize policymakers who believe that new evaluation systems can be implemented without new resources for training and assistance. Even when reasonable evidence of inappropriate professional practice has been gathered, school officials may be reluctant to press for teacher dismissal. The problem is the cost of litigation. In an article in the March 1, 1995, issue of *Education Week*, reporter Joanna Richardson described how a school district in California spent eight years trying to remove a high school teacher. School administrators documented more than 400 reasons why the teacher was unfit to teach, reasons that included ignoring student questions and belittling students. By the time the teacher exhausted her last appeal, her dismissal had cost the district more than $300,000! Cases such as this one have prompted some policymakers to abandon conventional accountability strategies and attack teacher-tenure laws.

Professional Development

According to McNeil (1981, p. 283), there are two conflicting views of teacher evaluation. The first, or "controlling view," is represented by demands for greater accountability. The second, or "noncontrolling," view holds that teacher evaluation should downplay "the crushing pressure of judgments from supervisors, principals, students, parents, and peers" and concentrate on "instructional improvement." Advocates of the noncontrolling view consider the vast majority of teachers to be competent. They contend that resources, therefore, should be focused on helping good teachers become better rather than removing a few incompetent teachers. They cite evidence to indicate that many experienced teachers derive little or no benefit from accountability-based evaluations (Stiggins and Duke 1988).

Teacher evaluation for the purpose of professional development has steadily gained in popularity during the late 1980s and early 1990s. Besides enjoying the support of teachers' organizations, such evaluation has won praise from administrators' groups (Duke and Stiggins 1986). The latter regard growth-oriented teacher evaluation as a way not only to improve relations between teachers and supervisors, but also to free administrators in order that they can spend more time with the few teachers who need intensive assistance. Many teacher evaluation systems that focus on professional development are based on individual goals that permit competent teachers to grow in unique and meaningful ways. School systems often provide resources in the form of release time, tuition credit, and conference fees to support professional development efforts.

A debate has developed around the issue of whether accountability-based and growth-oriented teacher evaluation can coexist in the same evaluation system (Duke 1990; McLaughlin and Pfeifer 1988; McNeil 1981). One position holds that both purposes can be served in the same system. The other maintains that accountability and growth may be compatible in theory, but in practice too much confusion and role conflict arises to allow a functional blending of purposes. Those who argue the latter position point out that growth often entails trust and risktaking, factors which may be undermined by concern for accountability. One point on which advocates for each position agree is that teachers should be held accountable for professional development. How this is best accomplished, though, is disputed.

Professionalism

Professionalism can mean different things to different people. When administrators and legislators use the term, they often think of adherence to rules and policies. Teachers, on the other hand, frequently associate professionalism with a reasonable degree of autonomy—in other words, freedom from excessive constraints. It is impossible to think about teacher evaluation policy without considering what it means to be a professional.

According to sociologists who study occupations, professions differ from other endeavors along a number of dimensions (Myers 1973). One dimension concerns evaluation. Professionals are evaluated according to performance standards which they themselves help to establish. If people who are not members of the profession determine the bases upon which professionals are evaluated, serious questions can be raised regarding the extent to which the occupation represents a true profession.

The 1970s and 1980s saw considerable effort at state and district levels to develop research-based performance standards to guide teacher evaluation. In most cases, teachers played important roles in the identification of these standards. Toward the end of the 1980s, however, questions surfaced concerning the limitations of performance standards. "Standardization" of practice might be important for accountability purposes, but it did not inspire professionals to pursue excellence. Research on expertise revealed that the most capable professionals were not bound by the standard practices and rule-governed behavior of their less accomplished colleagues (Berliner 1994). If an important dimension of professionalism involved continuing efforts to improve practice, new forms of evaluation would be needed.

Once again, issues of autonomy and control arose. Traditionally, opportunities and resources for teacher development were controlled by school administrators. Teachers, individually and through their organizations, began to insist on greater influence over their own professional development. Restructured teacher evaluation systems in the late 1980s and early 1990s reflected this desire.

Pay for Performance

The fourth idea over which policymakers have struggled in recent years concerns pay for performance. Known variously as merit pay, incentive pay, and career ladders, pay for performance was pushed by admirers of private enterprise who believed that a key to the success of American business involved differential remuneration. They maintained that a profession with more than two million practitioners must be characterized by a wide range of performance. The most capable teachers should be rewarded, advocates reasoned, lest they lose interest and leave teaching.

Teachers' organizations have tended to oppose most forms of pay for performance. Among their stated concerns are the qualifications of those charged with making judgments about merit, and the instruments used to collect the data upon which such judgments are based. Fears also have been expressed that attempts to differentiate between more and less skilled teachers might undermine faculty morale.

Pay for performance schemes surfaced in the 1970s when school enrollments were shrinking and districts were forced to reduce how many professional employees they employed. At the time, concerns existed that, if seniority was the primary criterion by which reductions were made, some of the best teachers might be lost. When enrollments eventually stabilized and large numbers of teachers no longer faced job loss, pay for performance seemed less crucial. Fiscal conservatives questioned whether school systems could afford to offer financial incentives to the best teachers. In some areas, school officials complained that weak teachers must be retained because no pool of replacement teachers existed. Incentive pay systems based on the premise that poor performers can be easily replaced obviously were less appropriate in these situations.

While pay for performance proposals declined for awhile, they did not disappear completely. There currently is evidence of a new push to link evaluation and pay. Vice-President Albert Gore has suggested pay for performance as part of his campaign to "reinvent" government. Business roundtables in some states have been promoting merit pay in discussions of new teacher evaluation policies and practices.

Ideas such as pay for performance, professionalism, professional development, and accountability lie at the heart of the struggle to restructure teacher evaluation. Understanding what these ideas mean to different interest groups and how these meanings influence the formulation of teacher evaluation policy are central concerns of this book.

Overview of the Book

Following this introductory chapter, Professor Emeritus Richard Brandt, of the University of Virginia, offers an excellent review of developments during the 1980s to link teacher evaluation and career ladders, incentive pay, and related pay-for-performance schemes. In the process, he also surveys the status of accountability-based teacher evaluation, examines some of its technical problems, and describes the growing interest in moving beyond minimum competence to professional excellence. Brandt identifies some of the political difficulties encountered in implementing pay-for-performance policies and their origins.

North Carolina's Teacher Performance Appraisal System is the focus of Chapter 3. David Holdzkom of the Durham Public Schools and Richard Brandt review the development of the Teacher Performance Appraisal System in the early 1980s, efforts to pilot test the system in selected school districts, and subsequent revisions. In Chapter 4, Ed Iwanicki of the University of Connecticut and Douglas Rindone from the Connecticut Department of Education recount the story of Connecticut's efforts, beginning in 1974, to restructure teacher evaluation. This initiative eventually led to a unique blending of teacher evaluation, professional development, and school improvement. Beatrice Baldwin of Southeastern Louisiana State University follows in Chapter 5 with an account of the Louisiana Teacher Appraisal System, a system that started out with an accountability focus, but subsequently underwent major adjustments in light of teachers' concerns. The resulting system provided ample opportunities for teachers to focus on professional development.

The last two case studies deal with efforts to develop policies focusing primarily on professional development. In Chapter 6, a team from the Washington Education Association collaborated with the editor to study the creation of Washington State's Professional Growth Option, an alternative to conventional evaluation for teachers with a history of competent performance. Agnes McMahon of the University of Bristol offers in Chapter 7 a chronicle of the introduction of teacher appraisal in England and Wales. Her fascinating account traces the growth of Tory interest in appraisal in the early 1980s, the role of teachers' and administrators' organizations in shaping policy, and passage of the Reform Act of 1988, a bill which fostered more comprehensive educational restructuring than anything yet attempted in the United States. McMahon then describes the initial efforts to interpret and implement teacher appraisal policy at the local level.

The book concludes with a cross-case analysis of the case studies and speculations on future directions for teacher evaluation. Chapter 8 identifies similarities and differences in teacher evaluation reforms and the processes by which new policies were formulated over the last two decades. Of particular interest are the obstacles encountered by reformers and the strategies employed to overcome them. The final chapter considers new developments in education that could affect teacher evaluation and whether the evaluation of individual teachers is the best mechanism to ensure educational accountability.

A Note to Readers

Change can be studied from many perspectives. In their highly original *Reframing Organizations*, Lee Bolman and Terrence Deal (1991) describe how organizational change can be understood in terms of structural, human relations, political, and symbolic frameworks. The primary framework adopted in this book is the political. This perspective regards change as the consequence of conflict and choice. The teacher evaluation policies described in this book resulted from complex negotiations and maneuvers by various interest groups concerned with school reform, the cost of public education, the welfare of teachers, and other issues. Bargaining and compromise are the lifeblood of politics. Readers should be alert to the decision points along the road to teacher evaluation policy—points at which policymakers were compelled to choose between competing alternatives. Understanding why particular choices were made is a critical part of trying to make sense of policy formulation.

In order to understand why particular choices were made, a knowledge of context is essential. Policy choices are not made in a vacuum. They are influenced by the party in power, current events, economic conditions, the past experiences of key individuals, and a host of other factors. What makes the study of policy formulation especially challenging is the fact that context is rarely stable. As context changes, the status of policy can change. A policy that seemed reasonable during a time of budget surpluses may appear extravagant when retrenchment sets in. When the context changes, policy is then subject to reconsideration and revision. To this extent, policy is never completed. The accounts in this book illustrate how teacher evaluation policy continues to evolve, even after it has been adopted and implemented.

References

Berliner, D. C. (1994). Expertise: The Wonder of Exemplary Performances. In J. N. Mangieri and C. C. Block eds. *Creating Powerful Thinking in Teachers and Students.* Fort Worth: Harcourt Brace, pp. 161–186.

Bolman, L. G., and Deal, T. E. (1991). *Reframing Organizations.* San Francisco: Jossey-Bass.

Darling-Hammond, L. (1990). Teacher Evaluation in Transition: Emerging Roles and Evolving Methods. In J. Millman and L. Darling-Hammond eds. *The New Handbook of Teacher Evaluation.* Newbury Park, Calif.: Sage.

Duke, D. L. (1990). Developing Teacher Evaluation Systems That Promote Professional Growth. *Journal of Personnel Evaluation in Education,* 4:131–144.

Duke, D. L., and Stiggins, R. J. (1986). *Teacher Evaluation—Five Keys to Growth.* Washington, D.C.: National Education Association.

McLaughlin, M. W., and Pfeifer, R. S. (1988). *Teacher Evaluation: Improvement, Accountability and Effective Learning.* New York: Teacher's College Press.

McNeil, J. D. (1981). Politics of Teacher Evaluation. In J. Millman ed. *Handbook of Teacher Evaluation.* Beverly Hills: Sage.

Myers, D. A. (1973). *Teacher Power.* Lexington: Lexington Books.

Richardson, J. (March 1, 1995). "Critics target state teacher-tenure laws. *Education Week,* p. 1, 13.

Steele, S. (1990). *The Content of Our Character.* New York: St. Martin's Press.

Stiggins, R. J., and Duke, D. L. (1988). *The Case for Commitment to Teacher Growth: Research on Teacher Evaluation.* Albany: State University of New York Press.

Stone, D. A. (1988). *Policy Paradox and Political Reason.* Glenview, Ill.: Scott, Foresman.

Wagner, R. B. (1989). *Accountability in Education: A Philosophical Inquiry.* New York: Routledge.

2

Teacher Evaluation for Career Ladder and Incentive Pay Programs[1]

Richard M. Brandt

The impetus for much of the wave of reforms in teacher evaluation that swept the United States in the 1980s derived from intense interest on the part of politicians and business leaders in applying private sector solutions to public sector problems. Nowhere was this interest keener than the application of incentive pay schemes. It is fitting, therefore, that a volume dealing with recent developments in teacher evaluation policy begin with a review of efforts to implement career ladders, incentive pay programs, and related accountability systems. Paying teachers based on performance requires high quality data, lest accusations of discrimination and unfair treatment be directed at school officials. The quest for "objective" data that led many states and school systems to re-assess their teacher evaluation policies and practices at times took on a highly technical character, as will be seen in the accounts to follow.

Taking a New Look at Teacher Evaluation

The most widely recognized immediate effect of the career ladder/incentive pay movement that marked the 1980s was an overhaul of traditional teacher evaluation practices. Scales for rating general traits were replaced by behaviorally specific instruments consisting of carefully selected, research based, precisely defined instructional variables. Teacher manuals described the variables to be studied, indicators to look for, examples to follow, and forms on which to record observational data systematically. The principal was joined by other school personnel, including teachers, in the role of evaluator. Evaluators were given training in the correct use of rating and low-inference coding systems. Sources of data other than direct classroom observation, including parent and student surveys and student performance data, provided some of the information used for judging the quality of teaching.

In those school districts where school boards asked that only truly superior teaching be rewarded, the design of appropriate evaluation mechanisms proved especially challenging. Traditional evaluation instruments were considered to be notoriously weak. The four- or five-point rating scales that had been used for decades to rate teachers on several dozen general traits or behaviors ("makes good decisions," "is well organized," etc.) lacked both the discriminating power and validity to be used to identify superior teaching. Rating distributions on such scales typically showed two-thirds of the teachers received top scores in most categories, while all but two or three percent received nothing below the top two steps on the scale in anything.

Summative evaluation of experienced teachers (i.e., assessments of the quality of teaching of those who had achieved continuing contract status) was both limited and unsystematic in the early 1980s. Principals typically rated their experienced teachers each year on a number of teaching dimensions and general characteristics after only a few, and, in some cases, no classroom visits. Precise records of teaching practices were seldom attempted. What observational instruments were being developed in a number of places (e.g. Florida, Georgia, and later, Virginia) were being used primarily for assessing the minimal competency of beginning teachers. For experienced teachers, formative evaluation was considered more appropriate under a clinical supervision model in which teachers themselves were allowed to decide what aspects of their teaching were to be observed and improved.

Until the recent reform movement shifted the target from minimum competency to the excellence end of the spectrum, little attention was devoted to how outstanding teaching should be identified. Newly designed scales in the early 1980s focused on basic teaching practices that all teachers must be able to use with reasonable competency and not necessarily on the total scope and quality of superior teaching. Even now the lack of valid, well accepted measures of outstanding, as contrasted with professionally competent, teaching remains the biggest stumbling block to a successful response to the public's desire to reward good teachers. The National Board for Professional Teaching Standards has struggled for almost a decade to formulate requirements for a national teaching certificate for advanced competence.

According to one report (Wuhs and Manatt 1983), twenty-six states had laws requiring the evaluation of teachers by the time *A Nation At Risk* was published. Two years later, thirty-six states had enacted such leg-

Risk was published. Two years later, thirty-six states had enacted such legislation (National Education Association 1985). Stated purposes behind most of these laws included both formative and summative evaluation, for example, to improve teachers and assist with personnel decisions. Most of the new laws did not specify precise guidelines for local districts to follow. In many states, the actual design and operation of teacher evaluation procedures was left to school districts (Stiggins and Duke 1988, p. 10). In several states (Florida, North Carolina, Tennessee, and Texas), however, career ladder or master teacher plans were tied to evaluation instruments designed and mandated by the state.[2] In some states (e.g. Alabama, Delaware, and Oklahoma), early interest in incentive pay programs led to the funding of research and development on new teacher evaluation systems. State support for incentive pay schemes, however, did not result from these efforts. South Carolina and Utah, on the other hand, provided general guidelines and approved locally developed district appraisal systems for incentive pay purposes.

Development of Summative Systems

Many issues may arise in the development of a summative evaluation system for use with incentive pay or career ladder schemes. What criteria are appropriate for judging good teaching? What means of measurement and data sources shall be used? How shall standards be set? Who should do the judging? How can teachers receive fair and equal consideration given vast differences in teaching assignments, grade-levels, and subjects? To capture some of the complexity of the teacher evaluation reform initiatives that marked the 1980s, each of these issues will be examined.

Criteria

The new evaluation systems were supported by specific expectations about how teachers should perform both inside and outside the classroom. These performance expectations became the variables on which teacher behavior was to be judged. The primary means of assessment was observation of classroom teaching behaviors and recording and rating how well they were manifested. In many systems, variables selected for assessment were those that, according to research, promoted student learning.

Not all of what teachers do, of course, can be observed during classroom teaching. Important job expectations also included the quality of planning, collegiality with other teachers, and professionalism outside as well as inside the classroom. A survey (Brandt and Gansneder 1987,

p. 36) of eleven Virginia districts revealed use of the following criteria for determining whether or not an award or promotion was justified:

Quality of lesson plans	8
Quality of teaching	8
Kind/extent of professional development	6
Professionalism in attitude behavior	6
Attendance of teachers	5
Collegiality with other teaching personnel	5
Leadership qualities	4
Graduate work taken or degree received	3
Amount of extra curricula supervision/activity	3
Other	2

The two superintendents who checked "other" indicated that "student achievement" was the sole criterion they used. Among the other nine districts, the quality of lesson plans and the quality of teaching were among the criteria in all but one instance. For this one district, in lieu of assessing the overall quality of teaching, teachers were observed as they attempted to demonstrate one set of designated teaching practices at a time, up to three sets a year. Although nine out of eleven school districts paid a supplement for graduate degrees or course work, these accomplishments were counted toward merit awards or promotion in only three. Similarly, all but one district paid extra money to those who sponsored clubs or activities. These activities counted as part of the overall teacher assessment criteria in only three districts.

One finds many of the same general criteria included in the state evaluation systems, but some differences as well. In Tennessee, for example, all of the general criteria listed for the Virginia plans were included in the state evaluation system in one way or another, except for teacher attendance. In addition, professional knowledge and minimum reading and writing skills were assessed by requiring teachers to take tests in these areas. Student achievement was added to the assessment criteria in 1988.

In North Carolina the eight major functions of the Teacher Performance Appraisal System included five related to the quality of teaching, as assessed through classroom observation, and three that covered planning, maintaining, and using student records; interacting with colleagues, students, and parents; and performing noninstructional duties. The latter encompassed adherence to established laws and policies and evidence of growth in pursuing a professional development plan. Neither leadership nor attendance were included as specific criteria.

The Texas appraisal instrument contained fourteen performance criteria, ten of which focused on the quality of teaching and were assessed through classroom observation. (Texas is currently in the process of revising its teacher evaluation policy.) The other four criteria related to how teachers engage in professional development, communicate with parents, comply with policies, and evaluate student growth. Teacher attendance, collegiality, and leadership (except for career ladder level IV, which was never implemented) were not included as performance criteria.

Performance criteria for the former Florida Master Teacher Program included, in addition to teaching practices assessed through direct observation, knowledge of teachers' primary teaching subject. To be selected as master teachers, candidates were required to take a standardized test in their teaching field and to score in the top quartile of the performance distribution on both this test and the observation instrument.

In the development of evaluation systems, decisions must be made not only about what general characteristics of teachers' work are to be included but also which specific aspects of teaching and related activities as well. The former may be referred to as domains (e.g. "Instructional Strategies" in the Texas system) or major functions (e.g. "Instructional Presentation" in the North Carolina system). The latter may be called specific functions, performance indicators, basic skills, or performance criteria.

Together the general teaching characteristics and the subordinate, more behaviorally specific teaching functions constituted the criteria on which the new evaluation systems were based. The development of a system typically started with the selection of performance criteria. Criteria were described in precise behavioral language with definitions and examples cited for each. The following example from the Mesa, Arizona, Public Schools Career Ladder evaluator handbook illustrates how even specific teaching practices—in this case one of forty performance criteria in the evaluation system—required explanation and description of what should be looked for in judging how well they were accomplished:

Explaining objectives, learning tasks, performance expectations, and assessment plans.

INTENT: *To determine the clarity and preciseness* of the teacher's communication about the nature *of the academic tasks in which students will engage.* Research suggests that students spend as much as 50% of their time attempting to "figure out" what the teacher considers as acceptable performance. Teachers who structure and communicate the task demands for students, increase the probability that the students will be successful. INDICATORS: The evaluator will base the bulk of the evaluative decision on classroom observation data. Did the teacher state or write the goals or objectives of the presentation? Did the teacher avoid ambiguous phrases or pronouns? Did the teacher give explicit step-by-step directions or present an outline when the material was complex? Did the teacher explain how the academic work would be assessed? Did the vast majority of the students appear to understand the nature and degree of the academic task demands? Or, Did the students spend considerable time "negotiating" or clarifying the nature of the academic work?

Measures

Following specification of performance criteria, measures were selected or, more often, adapted from other systems. Because most of what teachers do is in the classroom, systematic observation, recording, and judging of regular teaching activity were the primary procedures employed.

Observational methodology has advanced considerably over the past decade due to (a) increasing emphasis on classroom research, and (b) greater reliance on observation in both formative and summative teacher evaluation. Two kinds of observation systems have been employed for summative evaluation purposes, one much more common than the other. The least common are low inference category systems designed around instructional variables that research studies have indicated affect student learning.

The Florida Performance Measurement System was a prime example. Observers who had been trained to recognize selected teaching behaviors recorded their frequency in tally form as they visited classrooms. They did not attempt to evaluate teaching, but only to record each instance in which these behaviors occurred. The record was scored elsewhere, based on the frequencies and patterns of occurrence of the selected teaching practices during a given period of instruction. Several studies reported significantly greater learning for students whose teachers have high rather than low FPMS scores (Peterson, Micceri, and Smith 1985, pp. 63–77; Peterson 1986).

Although the Florida master teacher program is now defunct, the instrument developed for it is still being used with beginning teachers. A low-inference category system, developed by Don Medley and his colleagues, was, until recently, used with beginning teachers in Virginia as a basis for awarding continuing certification. Career ladder legislation in Alabama also led to the development of a low-inference coding system, with the assistance of Homer Coker, Don Medley, and Robert Soar, among others. The career ladder program itself, however, was not funded.

Most incentive pay/career ladder programs have required the use of high-inference observation instruments which required observers to evaluate, not just record or tally what they have seen. Although evaluators made high-inference judgments of what they saw, rating procedures and instruments differed substantially from those used previously. As with low-inference coding systems, many of the teaching variables to be assessed in high-inference systems stemmed from literature on effective teaching. They were carefully specified in manuals and included indicators and examples of what to look for. Rating scales often were behaviorally anchored with brief descriptions of superior, satisfactory, and unsatisfactory practice. For example, descriptors of one of the practices monitored in the Danville, Virginia, evaluation system are shown below. (This system was substantially revised in the early 1990s.) They helped distinguish between the categories of outstanding, professionally competent, needs improvement, and unsatisfactory:

> *Provides Immediate and Frequent Feedback to Students in Simple Clear Language.* Feedback refers to verbal behavior that assists students in learning. Teachers may give feedback by narrowing the focus of student attention by cuing, promoting or giving hints; informing students that answers are wrong and giving substantive information; and using questions that assist students in discovering and correcting errors and inaccuracies.

O = The teacher gives feedback in a timely and effective way. Student responses are used to probe and expand ideas and concepts. Questions are used as a feedback technique along with cues, prompts, and hints. The teacher gives feedback so that learning takes place at a higher cognitive level.

P = The teacher gives feedback so that the correctness of student responses is not in doubt. The teacher asks questions and gives examples that assist students in the learning process. The teacher is consistent in providing feedback to students.

I = The teacher is inconsistent in providing feedback to students. Feedback is overly general, little, and too late.

U = Feedback is ineffective and unclear. Students are not informed about the correctness of their responses.

In considerable contrast to earlier procedures, observers were instructed and trained to write low-inference narrative descriptions (what Madeline Hunter has called "script tapes") of teaching activity and student responses to provide a relatively objective running record of the visit. Immediately after classroom observations, the observer retreated to a quiet office to reread the record and add details. The rating scale then was filled out with careful attention to how closely various teaching acts matched scale and variable descriptions.

In North Carolina, this process was formalized with two discrete products from each visit. The Formative Observation Data Instrument (FODI) constituted a cleaned up, readable script tape, that is, a judgment-free running record of what the observer saw and heard. A Formative Observation Data Analysis (FODA) then was completed by (a) coding statements in the running record to indicate the teaching functions they represented, (b) summarizing one's judgment from the FODI about the quality of performance of each of the five major teaching functions, and (c) listing specific teaching practices that were considered strengths and those in need of improvement.[3] These products were used to provide feedback to teachers after an observation for formative purposes. For each teacher, the FODAs and FODIs from all visits also were reviewed at the end of the year as a basis for making summary ratings.

Observation of classroom teaching was not the only source of performance data on teaching. The exhibit below shows the kinds of data used in eleven Virginia school districts (Brandt and Gansneder 1987).

	1	2	3	4	5	6	7	8	9	10	11
Self-evaluations		x			x	x					
Obs. by Administrators	x	x	x	x	x	x	x	x			
Obs. by other teachers	x		x	x	x				x		
Student performance	x	x		opt			x			x	x
Student ratings	x										
Parent ratings	x										
Teacher records	x	x	x	x	x	x	x	x	x		

Other than two systems that depended solely on student outcome data,[4] districts relied on at least two data sources. In general, the more selective the incentive pay/career ladder scheme (i.e. the lower the percentage of teachers receiving extra pay or promotion), the larger the number of data sources and the amount of information considered. While administrators' observations played a key role in eight of the systems, lesson plans and other teacher records were used just as frequently. Student learning and performance data were required in five districts and optional in one another, and observations by other teachers played a role in the evaluation process in five school districts. Self evaluation served as a source of data in three districts, but only one of these districts was highly selective. Although self-evaluation can be helpful in formative evaluation, its utility in summative evaluation is questionable, especially when decisions about merit pay or promotion are entailed. The teacher may face a conflict of interest between providing accurate information and receiving an award. Only one system included the opinions of parents and students. It remains to be seen how valuable student and parent ratings are in the assessment of teaching and, particularly, how well they agree with other data sources.

Perhaps the country's most comprehensive experiment in summative evaluation was that associated with the Tennessee career ladder. Displayed below is a list of sources and instruments used in assessing a teacher's performance under the system (French, Malo, and Rakow 1988):[5]

Data Sources	Instruments
1. Teacher	1. Professional development and leadership summary
	2. Observations (6)
	3. Dialogues (3)
	4. Tests:
	Written test of professional knowledge
	Written tests of reading and writing skills
2. Students	5. Student questionnaires (elementary and secondary forms)
3. Principal	6. Principal questionnaire
4. Peer evaluator team (three persons)	7. Consensus rating (based on patterns developed over daylong visits by each evaluator)

A team of three highly trained peer evaluators from outside the district was responsible for conducting six observations of and three dialogues with level II and level III candidates and providing a consensus rating from their daylong visits. An integrated scoring system that combined data from the several sources on weighted indicators made sharp and relatively objective distinctions between levels I, II, and III teachers (McLarty 1987).

In the development of Tennessee's system, a number of critical issues arose. Those that were particularly noteworthy included the following:

Will outside observers be used, which is more costly and difficult to arrange but adds a degree of objectivity and neutrality, or can inside evaluators be sufficiently well trained to perform the critical data gathering interpreting tasks?

How many observations of classroom teaching are needed to provide a representative sample of teaching performance?

Should visits be announced so teachers can be optimally prepared to put on their best lesson or should they be unannounced—more representative sample of daily performance?

How can necessary information be collected to provide fair and comprehensive assessment without overloading teachers, administrators, and evaluators with excessive paperwork?

What is the proper role for principals in the summative evaluation process and how will it affect their role in providing formative assistance?

What is the proper role for teachers in the summative and formative evaluation of their colleagues?

How can inconsistencies in collecting and interpreting information be minimized between and among evaluators?

Evaluation systems used for incentive pay purposes have varied from one locality to another because of substantial differences in the way issues such as those above have been resolved. Despite such differences, the overall trend has been to rely on several kinds of data and more than one individual to collect data and/or provide the final evaluation. Performance has been assessed using a variety of measures, some of which teachers themselves have helped select. In several Arizona and Utah districts, for example, teachers had a choice of the types of data by which they would be evaluated. In the use of student outcome data in other localities (e.g. Danville, Virginia, and three South Carolina districts), teachers selected not only several teaching objectives but also the measures to be used in determining how well they were achieved.

Standards

Developing an incentive pay or promotion system requires decisions not only about criteria and data, but about standards as well, that is, the number of outstanding ratings, points, or scores to be achieved. In the Virginia incentive pay plans, standards typically were specified (a) as a certain proportion of teacher evaluation variables that must be rated "exceptional," with none judged below the competency level, or (b) for those based on student achievement, average test scores or the percentages of children who passed designated tests. No district plan was based on comparisons made among teachers.

The avoidance of direct comparisons of teachers has been one of the most distinguishing features of personnel practices in schools, as contrasted with those in business and industry. Commissions, bonuses, and promotions in the private sector frequently go to those with the best performance records. Comparing performance records and ranking people from best to worst is a common practice in business and industry. In education, ranking people is almost tabu. Quotas also are frowned on as an arbitrary limitation on how many can be considered "best."

One of the major dilemmas school systems have faced in creating a merit pay or career ladder system stems from philosophical differences between education and industry. Evaluation practices that might provide the clearest, most discriminating performance data, that is, information obtained by ranking individuals, making forced choices, or using sociometric techniques, run counter to longstanding educational traditions. No Virginia plan could be found where teachers were compared directly with each other.

In order to achieve a degree of discriminatory capability at the positive end of the performance continuum, raters in some evaluation systems (e.g. Texas) were instructed to specify teaching behaviors that led them to assign above average ratings. Special documentation was required for many variables. Precise descriptors of exceptional teaching patterns, as contrasted with good and poor teaching patterns, also were provided in most plans. In one Virginia system, principals were asked, in recommending career candidate applicants, to indicate if they were among the best, second-best, and so forth of all the teachers they had ever seen with respect to each variable. Such a requirement is designed to minimize the ceiling and halo effects of traditional rating scales, and to encourage valid identification of those who perform better than the average. To repeat the point above, however, if evaluation schemes have failed to single out "the best teachers," it probably has been due, in part, to a tradition that discourages the use of assessment methods that discriminate between professionals.

Special Features and Aspects

Compared with earlier evaluation systems, those developed for incentive plan purposes have been more *explicit, objective, comprehensive,* and *discriminating.*

Being explicit implies fairness, since the criteria, the measures, and the standards by which teachers are judged are clearly prescribed. Objectivity is increased through systematic observations, narrative recordings of teaching practice, and other carefully gathered information. Judgments about teaching are kept separate from the records on which they are based. It is therefore possible to assess the accuracy of data by having two observers record classroom activity simultaneously but independently. Lynchburg, Virginia evaluators have done this routinely. Comparing the ratings of one evaluator with those of another also is done to estimate inter-rater reliability and to determine successful accomplishment of an evaluator training program. Where summative judgments have been appealed, records have been independently reevaluated to determine the similarity of the two sets of ratings.

It is fallacious, of course, to think that an objective appraisal system removes the need for human judgment. An evaluation system, by its very nature, always contains an important element of subjectivity. It may be manifest in the performance ratings or the selection of particular measures and standards on which to concentrate. A relatively objective system, however, separates what is record from what is judgment and seeks considerable agreement about the actual record.

Discriminating between solid, effective teaching and categorically outstanding teaching has proved a challenge for many new evaluation systems. Those that have done it best, such as Tennessee's, depended on a variety of measures and judgments. The principal was involved, but so were other observers and evaluators. Teachers were not accustomed to being graded; and with at least half of them considering themselves among the best ten percent of the teachers in their districts, summative ratings that suggested otherwise needed to be based on a lot more than the principal's impression (MGT of America 1989).

Thorough and effective training of all evaluators in the methods of data-gathering and interpretation has been essential to the implementation of new evaluation systems. Evaluators have needed to be tested for competency in their role. Without consistency among and between evaluators, both within and across schools, incentive plans can be unfair and lack credibility.

Principals were found to be particularly in need of such training. They tended to have many responsibilities besides instructional supervision and evaluation. In many instances, they lacked the background of teaching the particular grades and subjects they were expected to assess. New evaluation systems required principals to spend much more time in classrooms watching teaching, gathering data, and assisting teachers with instruction.

In many systems teachers were also involved in the evaluator role. In Tennessee, they were released from their own districts for a year or more to serve as outside evaluators to other school districts. In North Carolina, pilot districts received extra state money to employ selected teachers as observer-evaluators for one or more years. In districts elsewhere, teachers continued with their own classes while serving in a limited observer-evaluator role, visiting classrooms during their own free periods or when substitutes were available.

In North Carolina pilot districts, teachers observed, recorded (complete FODIs), and analyzed lesson reports (complete FODAs) for the major teaching functions. Principals did the same, but additionally had responsibility for rating the three nonteaching functions and constructing the final summative evaluation. The latter was based not only on their observations, but also on the FODIs and FODAs of the peer evaluators. Peer evaluators were asked by some principals to help achieve a consensus judgment about final ratings.

One positive outcome from the operation of summative evaluation systems for incentive programs has been more sharply focused formative assistance and staff development activities. The North Carolina legislature, for example, provided $500 grants to any of its teachers who attended a training workshop on the new appraisal system. Almost all teachers in the state took advantage of the opportunity. Districts continued inservice programs, often under the leadership of the peer evaluators, on one or more of the specific teaching functions. Teachers who served as peer observers frequently indicated how much their own teaching had benefited from the opportunity to work with other teachers.

Many new evaluation systems have emphasized student learning. In several states and districts, student learning has been written into career ladder/incentive pay legislation and other policy directives as a major criterion for assessing teacher performance. Arizona, South Carolina, and Utah required student achievement data to be used for making decisions about career ladder advancement. Texas insisted that teachers assess their own students' learning as part of their summative evaluation procedure; although the data was not scored or used in the final assessment process. School incentive plans, similar to the South Carolina campus model in which the teaching staff received bonuses if their schools scored at or above predicted achievement test targets, already were operating or had been proposed in Florida, Georgia, Kentucky, Louisiana, and Texas. Information about student progress eventually was added to the list of data collected on Tennessee career ladder candidates.

Two kinds of plans have been associated with data on student outcomes. One was the previously mentioned school-based program in which schools received extra instructional resources if their students met established targets. Teachers also received individual bonuses on an equal basis, if any other individual criteria, such as attendance, were met.

The other type of plan was one in which teachers were judged individually and given bonuses if their students met or exceeded specific learning or performance targets. In many, but not all programs of this sort, teachers (a) established their own goals and selected appropriate measurement processes early in the year, and (b) provided data near the end of the year documenting how well goals had been met. Ratings of the significance and amount of student learning were made by peer-controlled panels.

Most incentive programs that have included student data for judging individual teacher performance were of this second, goal-based variety. Teachers initially needed assistance in selecting and refining goals for their particular classes and in designing plans for documenting how well those goals had been achieved. District or outside test experts sometimes were used to provide inservice training in how to specify goals in measurable ways, and to help with the administration and scoring of performance instruments. In some cases, districts designed their own criterion referenced tests or used commercial test item banks to construct pre and post-measures for particular grades and subjects.

In Aiken, South Carolina, for example, alternate test forms were constructed annually from a commercial test bank. Teachers expressed teaching objectives in the form of specific percentage gain scores for their classes. Similar measures were selected and administered by other parties for all teachers of similar subjects and grade-levels. According to the program coordinator, teachers were glad to have assistance in designing and conducting the measurement of student outcomes. They liked the objective, impartial administration and computerized scoring process. A panel of teachers helped oversee the design of the tests to ensure appropriate coverage and judge the significance of the target objectives and results.

Problems and Concerns

Experiments with incentive pay schemes have revealed a variety of practical problems. First of all, the generic teaching skills derived from the effective teaching research typically were insufficient to capture the full range of criteria needed to identify outstanding teaching. While the teaching practices typically included were important and supported by research findings about the teaching of basic knowledge and skills to students from low socioeconomic backgrounds, they rarely took into account the demands of particular subject matter or teaching specialties. They comprised essential functions that must be mastered by all teachers, regardless of subject or age-group. But they did not necessarily promote growth beyond competence, the kind that must take into account each teacher's unique circumstances and subject matter assignments. Ability to conduct effective lessons patterned on cooperative or mastery learning models, for example, was not likely to be measured well if generic teaching skills were the primary focus. Yet solid research findings have indicated the effectiveness of both of these teaching models.

A second problem with evaluation criteria and measures was that they did not distinguish clearly and consistently between good performers and those who were truly outstanding. Ultimately, the solution might lie in requiring a broader range of criteria at the highest performance levels. Such criteria could include monitoring and other leadership skills, capability in various styles of teaching, and demonstrated effectiveness with different kinds of students or in various teaching contexts. Difficulty in achieving consensus about the criteria for level III caused a postponement in the scheduled implementation of the advanced teaching component of the North Carolina career ladder program.

A third problem concerned the fact that no measure is perfect. All are subject to distortion. The stakes were high in incentive pay schemes. Individuals were challenged to put their best foot forward; some might even have been tempted to cheat. Sending certain children out of the room when tests were given; setting student objectives no higher than what they already knew; bribing children to behave properly when observers were present; and reteaching lessons in which students as well as teachers had rehearsed their parts all were reported to have been tried as ways of improving performance ratings. To the extent that these practices worked and the teachers involved succeeded in achieving promotions or rewards, they undermined morale and threatened the credibility of the system. Human failings being what they are, it is important that steps be taken to secure measures and establish whatever safeguards are needed to ensure the system is operating as fairly as possible.

Many objections have been raised in the education community about the fairness and validity of basing the assessment of teaching on student performance. The use of standardized achievement tests as the basis for judging student performance also has been attacked (Berk 1988). One primary reason for concern has been the tests' lack of curricular validity, that is, inconsistency with what teachers are responsible to teach. The American Federation of Teachers took the St. Louis School District to court over a policy that put teachers on probation if half of their students did not achieve at the national norm on the California Achievement Test and attain one month's learning progress for each month in the classroom. A comparative analysis of the test, the curriculum guide, and assigned textbooks for the four grades studied showed only a 9.5 percent overlap of all content items (*Education Week*, 6/3/87).

Where a single test is used year after year, especially with bonus money attached to it, test security can become an issue. We have heard instances of cheating, that is, not just teaching to the test, but teaching actual test items and correct answers. Another commonly recognized problem stems from the instability of average pupil-gain scores from one class to another and one year to the next. How much students learn from one time to another can vary dramatically for reasons unrelated to the quality of their teaching.

Because of differences in what teachers are responsible to teach and the instability of pupil-gain scores, many incentive programs that have required the use of standardized tests have been of the school-based variety. To take into account variations in student ability and other population characteristics that are known to influence test results, schools should be matched on selected demographic variables so that only schools with similar socioeconomic characteristics and student backgrounds are compared.

A major problem with setting individual student outcome goals for teachers has been the lack of local norms and common standards to help interpret teacher achievement. Typically, teacher panels have examined goals and rated the difficulty and importance of the learning targets. For example, in various Arizona, Utah, and South Carolina districts, teacher goals received points which, when combined with points for other components of the evaluation system, provided an overall ranking of individual performances for incentive pay purposes.

So far, few programs have been developed where student outcome data for individual teachers was the sole basis for determining whether or not incentive pay would be awarded. An exception has been some South Carolina districts. When learning goals were met by most of the applicants and the numbers of applicants did not exceed the money available, bonuses were allocated.

Flowing Wells, Arizona, provides another example of the early cautious use of student outcome data for performance-based pay decisions. Of 878 candidates reviewed for career ladder promotion in 1987–1988, only five did not receive the full ten points allocated for their student achievement results. We were told much the same story in Amphitheater, a neighboring district.

Finally, the costs in time, resources, paperwork, and attention to procedural detail can be considerable if summative evaluation for incentive purposes is to be done fairly and well. Wherever incentive pay/career ladder programs were tried in the 1980s, complaints were registered about the time principals and others spent in classrooms, and the time teachers devoted to documenting student learning and noninstructional activities. Streamlining procedures, wherever possible, is important, but it can be carried only so far without jeopardizing the validity of the assessment process. In the long run, summative evaluation must be seen as an important activity that is instrumental in the accomplishment of such major school objectives as improved teaching and learning. Otherwise the time and resources so critical to high quality assessment are unlikely to be available.

Teacher Acceptance of Summative Evaluation

The costs in lowered morale may be substantial when new evaluation systems are introduced in connection with incentive programs. At best, reactions are initially ambivalent. Teachers have acknowledged that evaluation procedures in many cases are much better—fairer, more objective, more precise—than they used to be. By the second or third year of use, they often say that principals and other evaluators have improved in their consistency and accuracy. At the same time, teachers continue to question how well these systems distinguish between good and superior teaching. Although the multisource, multijudge procedures featured in most plans are a considerable improvement over observation-based evaluations done by principals alone, they may still vary in quality from one school to another and one district to another. The reliability of ratings across settings may still seem too low for many teachers to be satisfied.

Teacher skepticism regarding the quality and intent of new evaluation schemes has been a real deterrent to participation in some career ladder programs. In one Virginia district, a majority of teachers chose to be evaluated formally only every other year even though it meant giving up the option of applying for the career ladder. Eligibility depended on two successive and successful annual evaluations. In programs where limits are set on how many teachers can be promoted, the numbers of those volunteering to participate are often no larger than the number of openings available or awards that are expected to be made.

Almost everyone likes extra pay for extra work opportunities. The extended contract and job enlargement options available to teachers continue to be very popular. These innovations have not required rigorous evaluation. When rigorous and systematic judgments about the quality of work performance must be made, however, teachers have hesitated to embrace change. Performance evaluation can be both stressful and disturbing. It threatens longstanding, comfortable egalitarian relationships. It can reduce the freedom and autonomy teachers long have prized. Trust between teachers and administrators can be undermined. Temporarily at least, it may work against teacher empowerment. For these reasons and perhaps others, many good teachers have chosen not to participate in incentive programs.

On the other hand, teachers who either have decided to participate or were required to do so and who subsequently attained high ratings and rewards frequently have felt much more positive about the new evaluation process. In general, administrators also have liked incentive programs and accompanying changes in evaluation procedures. They credit these innovations with improvements in a whole range of things from teacher attendance and planning to teaching and learning (MGT of America 1989). The heavier evaluation burden they often must carry because of these programs, of course, clearly has complicated their lives. Still, they seem inclined to assume the extra responsibility. In some cases, they have received help they never enjoyed in the past. Most principals in South Carolina pilot districts, for example, welcomed the involvement of teacher-led committees in making judgments about student-outcome plans. More than 60 percent of the principals also indicated that both peers and administrators should be involved in conducting TIP participants' performance observations (MGT of America 1988).

Assessing the 1980s

While *A Nation At Risk* and other national commission reports called for programs that would pay bonuses or promote teachers whose performance and productivity were clearly outstanding, these turned out to be the programs most strongly resisted in the education community. The early demise of the Florida Master Teacher program and the relatively low ratings given the performance component of the Utah programs were two of many examples of the failure of merit pay to receive strong endorsement from educators. The great majority of plans under development or consideration in the late 1980s emphasized features such as extended contracts and enlarged responsibilities, while avoiding such controversial matters as pay for performance. Extra pay for extra work, not extra pay for better work, became the guiding principle.

If incentive schemes are to enjoy strong professional support, large numbers of teachers must be able to participate in one way or another. Rewarding a minority of teachers for superior performance is unlikely to be acceptable. According to one report, Georgia lawmakers failed to appropriate the $11 million needed to start an incentive plan in 1989 that had already been tested in several districts because it would benefit fewer than half the teachers. This action followed strong lobbying by teacher groups for across-the-board raises before giving bonuses to a few. What remains unclear is whether, in the long run, efforts to make incentive schemes palatable to teachers will result in loss of support from policymakers and the general public.

A second trend has been the growing popularity of school-based incentive programs. School-wide goals in the form of student achievement targets increasingly are being set. All teachers in a school receive similar bonuses or additional instructional resources if school goals are met. Tracking the performance of schools is technically easier and more justifiable, according to many statisticians, than monitoring the performance of individual teachers, especially if the primary assessment data are derived from measures of student learning. In addition to programs in Florida and South Carolina that have been operating for several years, legislation establishing school-based incentive programs was passed in Louisiana and Colorado, and proposals were made in Arkansas, Kentucky, and Texas in 1989 (Cornett 1989).

The new evaluation systems that were initiated in the 1980s had a profound influence on both the monitoring of classroom instruction and the search for ways to improve it. Classroom doors were opened as never before. Principals, assistant principals, and peer evaluators visited classrooms to observe teaching much more frequently than they had previously. These were not just casual drop-in visits, either. Continuous, precise tallying and note taking of what was occurring provided lengthy descriptive records for later analysis and formative feedback. Those who did the observing were carefully trained in how to observe and record, how to analyze and report, and how to confer with teachers so they would be helped, not hurt. Teachers were compelled by the assessment process to reflect on the teaching practices on which evaluations were based. In school systems all over the country thousands of teachers participated in workshops and other staff development activities in order to examine the generic teaching practices contained in their evaluation systems.

It is this author's judgment that the advent of incentive pay and related accountability schemes caused summative evaluation to be taken more seriously than in the past. Until teaching had to be evaluated for differential pay purposes, there was little reason to spend much time and energy on developing and operating such elaborate systems. It can be predicted that if the need for rigorous, valid, and discriminating teacher appraisal is eliminated as a consequence of the disappearance of performance-based pay and promotion practices, use of summative instruments will decline as well.

Notes

1. This chapter was adapted from a manuscript prepared for the Southern Regional Education Board. Permission to use it in this book is gratefully acknowledged.

2. Texas used local evaluation instruments while a system was being developed.

3. A thorough description of the development of the North Carolina Teacher Performance Appraisal Instrument can be found in the next chapter.

4. After the survey was conducted, a revenue shortfall kept one of these programs from being funded.

5. Student learning as assessed through dialogues with teachers was added to this list in 1988.

References

Berk, R. A. (1988). Fifty Reasons Why Student Achievement Gain Does Not Mean Teacher Effectiveness. *Journal of Personnel Evaluation in Education* 1:345–363.

Brandt, R. M. (1990). *Incentive Pay and Career Ladders For Today's Teachers.* Albany, NY: State University of New York Press.

Brandt, R. M., and Gansneder, B. M. (1987). Teacher Incentive Pay Programs in Virginia. Charlottesville, VA: Curry School of Education, University of Virginia, p. 36.

Cornett, L. (1989). Funding Performance Pay Plans—April 1989 update. Atlanta, GA: Southern Regional Education Board.

French, R. L., Malo, G. E., and Rakow, E. A. (1988). What We Have Learned From Tennessee's Career Ladder Experience. *Education Leadership,* p. 70–73.

McLarty, J. (1989). Career Ladder Instrumentation: The Tennessee Experience. Paper presented at the annual meeting of the American Educational Research Association, San Francisco, March 1989.

MGT of America. (1988). An Evaluation of the Teacher Incentive Program 1987–1988 Pilot-test Implementation. Report submitted to the South Carolina Department of Education, Tallahassee, FL, June 10, 1988.

National Education Association. (1985). *School Personnel Evaluation Manual.* Washington: National Education Association.

Peterson, D. (1986). Teaching Skills as Observed With the Florida Performance Measurement System. Paper presented at the annual meeting of the American Educational Research Association, San Francisco, April 1986.

Peterson, D., Micceri, T., and Smith, B. O. (1985). Measurement of Teacher Performance: A Study in Instrument Development. *Teaching & Teacher Education* 1 (no. 1):63–77.

Stiggins, R. J., and Duke, D. L. (1988). The Case For Commitment to Teacher Growth: Research on Teacher Evaluation. Albany, NY: State University of New York Press, p. 10.

Wuhs, S. K., and Manatt, R. P. (1983). The Pace of Mandated Teacher Evaluation Picks Up. *American School Board Journal* 170 (4):23.

3

From Accountability to Professional Empowerment in North Carolina

David Holdzkom and Richard M. Brandt

The educational literature of the past decade contains considerable discussion of the reform movement and its predecessor, the accountability movement. Often such discussion is conducted from a national perspective and thus obscures significant features of these movements, which, when viewed from the perspective of individual localities and states, often takes on a very different complexion. Indeed it is difficult to generalize about these movements, unless individual variations are taken into account. In this chapter, we will discuss the accountability movement as it unfolded in one state. In the process, we will focus primarily on evaluation of teaching performance and how the political and technical issues that swirled around efforts to create accountability in classrooms led to some curious outcomes. As an example of the influence of policymakers on the day-to-day life of institutions, it would be difficult to find a clearer example than that offered by North Carolina.

As in many southern states, government authority in North Carolina is highly centralized for a variety of historical reasons. This centralization, with its roots in the Reconstruction Period of our nation's history, has spawned a climate that fostered the growth of a mixed economy highly favorable to business (Foner 1990). A combination of relaxed tax laws, antiunion sentiment, and a reluctance to interfere in relations between corporations and workers led to the development of industries that did not rely upon highly skilled labor as much as upon a dependable labor force willing to work for low wages (Hall et al. 1990). This condition was exacerbated by a reluctance to permit government to play an active role in the advancement of the condition of African-American citizens.

Rather, government was expected to maintain the social status quo while keeping taxes low, thereby limiting funds for social services.

Today, North Carolina relies on an income tax, supplemented by a sales tax, to generate the revenue needed to pay for social services. While property is taxed, the bulk of the state government's income is derived from non-property-based sources. By paying for many services that in other states are funded locally, the government has been able to provide a modicum of service, regardless of local wealth. In exchange, the state government has acquired enormous power to make policy on issues that are local matters in other states. Thus, for example, the vast majority of educators are paid from state funds (NC Department of Public Instruction 1993). Accountability for dispensing those funds and for the services that are purchased is a state concern even more than it is a local matter. In this chapter, we will explore the consequences for teacher evaluation of this division of responsibility between the state and local boards of education. Of particular concern will be the development of teacher accountability practices and the emergence of policies and laws that have, in the last five years, placed increasing amounts of power in the hands of teachers and principals.

Background

In order to know how the accountability movement evolved in North Carolina, it is important to understand some of the basic politics and economics of the state. Historically, North Carolina has often been considered a poor state. With an economy largely based on fishing and farming, diversification of the economy in the early part of the twentieth century was seen as an important goal. With a relatively poorly educated workforce, North Carolina was hospitable to the development of textile mills where workers performed highly repetitive tasks that did not require extensive training (Hall et al. 1990). Moreover, the willingness of legislators to enact laws highly favorable to mill owners made it relatively easy to prevent efforts to unionize industrial workers in the state. The industry that was attracted to North Carolina did not depend on a highly skilled, economically independent work force. Education requirements for earning a living were relatively low. One segment of the population that especially valued education, particularly a classical academic education, was the newly freed African-American population (Anderson 1988). The state and local governments, however, were unwilling to provide such education for the children of former slaves.

With the realization that the economy increasingly would depend on a highly skilled work force, North Carolinians in the second half of the twentieth century began to rethink their approach to public education. It became clear that attracting high-tech industries would be difficult unless the quality of public schools could be improved.

Education in North Carolina has always reflected an uneasy balance between local and state desires. Since the Civil War, the state has been expected to pay the major costs of education. Local communities have demonstrated repeatedly that they are reluctant to tax themselves sufficiently to pay all the costs of quality schools. State financial support for schools has usually been accompanied by a desire to control spending and insure that funds are well spent.

Costs of Education

In North Carolina, almost 70 percent of the costs of K–12 education are paid by the state through its biennial budget process (NC Department of Public Instruction 1993). Over the last fifteen years, that share has actually increased, as federal contributions and the local share have declined from 13 percent and 24 percent to 8 percent and 23 percent respectively. If funds for child nutrition are excluded, the federal share drops to 5.4 percent. Moreover, most of the state's share is used to pay salaries and benefits for school district employees, leaving very little discretionary money for other purposes. These salaries are established by a state-wide salary schedule that educators from local districts are compelled to use when paying staff, whether those staff members are paid from state funds (as are the majority), or from local funds. Typically, local funds are used to pay the ancillary costs of education, for example, supplementary instructional materials, additional teachers, technology and so on. Therefore, state-level policymakers have a keen interest in the quality of performance that is being paid for with "their" money.

North Carolina is a "right-to-work" state in which unionizing of public employees is illegal. While estimates vary according to the source, perhaps two-thirds of North Carolina's teachers belong to the North Carolina Association of Educators (NCAE), an affiliate of the National Education Association (NEA). While NCAE members may neither bargain collectively nor strike, they are able to wield considerable influence in the election of legislators. This influence affects not only the setting of salary schedules for educators, but also decisions regarding other education-related issues.

As a result of these relationships among state lawmakers, local boards of education, and teachers, many issues that are contract stipulations in other states are embedded in state law in North Carolina. For example, The Fair Employment and Dismissal Act is a law that provides due process for teachers in any dismissal action by a local board, once that board has granted the teacher "tenure." Moreover, the law specifies that, while a board need not grant an individual tenure, the board cannot continue to employ individuals after their third year without granting tenure (North Carolina General Assembly 1992). The statutes of the state also spell out the responsibilities of teachers, principals, superintendents, and boards of education. The performance evaluation requirements imposed on local boards are codified in the statutes, as is responsibility for fixing hours of school, school holidays, determining the length of teachers' contracts, providing professional liability and health insurance, establishing retirement programs, and granting sick and annual vacation leaves.

The Umstead Commission: An Early Accountability Effort

The story of the accountability movement in North Carolina begins at least as early as 1946, when Governor R. Gregg Cherry established the Umstead Commission, a legislative committee whose charge was to determine whether some practical means for differentiating the salaries of teachers based on performance quality could be found (The Commission on Merit Rating of Teachers 1946). The commission engaged a professor from Columbia University to assist in this task. Professor William McCall attempted to determine what teacher characteristics, if any, accounted for differences in student learning. Anticipating later researchers, McCall determined that several personal characteristics, popularly believed to influence teaching effectiveness, did not, in fact, account for performance differences among teachers. McCall ruled out gender, age, race, university degrees, and years of experience as contributors of teacher effectiveness. He also sharply criticized the existing teacher salary schedule, which was based on race, gender, years of experience, and earned degrees (McCall, 1952). Despite Professor McCall's recommendations, no policy directives emerged from the Umstead Commission's report (or Professor McCall's research) and, to the present day, teachers' salaries in North Carolina are differentiated by degrees held and years of experience; race was ruled illegal in the 1960s.

Although the North Carolina General Assembly did not actually establish accountability measures based on the Umstead Commission's work, the notion that one should be able to distinguish among teachers and pay those who were most effective more than other teachers was an idea that refused to die. Moreover, the General Assembly's 1946 initiative confirmed its right to impose accountability standards that school boards and educators would be expected to meet.

The centralization of important controls, as well as funding, had become a fact of educational politics in the state by the early 1960s. No organized voice existed that could counter the General Assembly's efforts to assert its control over the schools of the state. The General Assembly served as the chief engine of both accountability and, increasingly, educational reform. In some very subtle ways, this meant that responsibility for change and improvement of education had passed from educators to lawmakers. The Governor, the State Department of Public Instruction, and the State Board of Education also played key roles. As we shall see, problems of a technical nature became hopelessly entangled with the political process at levels increasingly far removed from the classroom.

In 1961, the General Assembly authorized the establishment of an experiment in merit pay in three school districts. The first challenge was to determine the basis upon which "merit" would be judged. Each of the three districts developed, using a consensus method, an evaluation checklist that articulated the expected behaviors of all teachers (Holdzkom and Kuligowski 1993). For example, one criterion by which teachers would be judged was: Does a teacher show tolerance and patience in situations where these qualities are needed? Not surprisingly, the three sets of criteria were remarkably similar, since each was based on the practical knowledge and experience of school-level educators. No systematic procedure was developed, however, for specifying when and how to observe these criteria or even discerning what they would look like. Merit would be determined on the basis of the quantity of those behaviors, with more equaling better. The experiment lasted for three years and gained a measure of acceptance in the participating districts. It was under constant attack, however, by teachers in other districts and the superintendents of the three experimenting districts, who preferred a free hand to spend the extra salary money as they saw fit (NC Department of Public Instruction 1965).

During this period in the early 1960s, North Carolina was widely regarded as having an inferior precollegiate education system. Teachers' salaries were low by national standards, students' measured achievement on national examinations was low, dropout rates were high, and the tension created by the United States Supreme Court's *Brown* decision kept attention focused on school segregation rather than on improving the general level of education. Throughout the 1970s the integration of North Carolina schools remained the primary item on the education agenda for both the legislature and the local school districts. As formerly segregated systems were merged, it became clear that money would be needed to achieve parity in terms of physical plants, books, educational equipment, supplies, and the salaries of black and white teachers.

Continuing Efforts at Creating Accountability Structures

The accountability movement in North Carolina schools regained momentum with the election of Governor James B. Hunt in 1980. A number of Southern states at that time elected "education" governors and, at least initially, Hunt was widely regarded as one. Recognizing that teachers' salaries lagged behind those of teachers across the nation, Hunt and his associates in the General Assembly engineered a trade: there would be an immediate salary increase, with a teacher evaluation program to follow within two years. This deal represented a compromise in the time-honored position of the NCAE, which held that accountability systems, and especially any form of merit pay, could not be instituted until educators' salaries achieved a "living wage" level. The focus on salary improvements now was too tempting for the association to pass up. Indeed, over the next four years, the teacher salary schedule received annual attention from Governor Hunt and his staff. Often, this attention was focused on adding more steps and grades to the salary schedule; sometimes, it was a system for combining annual salary increases with step promotions. During this period, teachers received on average 11.5 percent per annum salary increases. Only during 1982 was there no change in teachers' salaries. A teacher receiving $1,000 per month on June 30, 1980, was earning a little more than $1,500 on July 1, 1984. Salary improvements, however, were not the only legislative actions that affected teachers. Efforts to improve education and increase accountability included a new focus on student testing, with the introduction of a requirement that all students in Grades 3, 6, and 8 would participate in a nationally normed test of basic skills. Additionally, new curriculum standards were developed at the state level for implementation locally, a review procedure for selection of text books was established with purchases restricted to books on the adopted list, kindergarten programs were established state-wide, and teacher assistants were employed for every K–3 classroom, with salary costs borne by the state.

The first efforts at development of a state-wide teacher evaluation system also were launched at this time. Characterized by the use of a consensus process to identify appropriate criteria for evaluation, educators were surveyed and forums were held to identify those skills that educators, themselves, believed would be reasonable performance expectations (Inman 1982a). The criteria proved relatively easy to identify, perhaps because of widespread cultural expectations about what teachers were supposed to do. The lack of research-derived information about teaching practice essentially meant that, other than personal experience, there was no alternative basis on which an evaluation system could rest.

The development of uniform implementation procedures, however, was another matter. People did not agree on the nature of evidence, the system for the collection of data on which judgments could be based, or the relative importance of the views of the evaluator and the evaluatee (Inman 1982b). Using an industrial model of supervision, teachers and principals assumed from the start that evaluation was the responsibility of management, in this case, the principal, despite the fact that no legislative authority for principal evaluation of teaching existed. Given the widespread assumption that many principals were hired for political reasons, some teachers were skeptical that the evaluation system could be implemented effectively. Nevertheless, there seemed no reasonable alternative, given the unwillingness of teachers to evaluate one another and the financial inability of the state to hire external teams to evaluate teachers.

Finally, it was agreed that, while the criteria would be uniform, each district would be free to develop its own implementation procedures and standards. This was a fairly innocuous decision, but, pragmatically, it served as a tacit acknowledgment that the evaluation system was unlikely to produce any important decisions. That is, there was no system of merit pay, there was no real connection between evaluation of teachers' performance and the granting of tenure (a local board prerogative highly susceptible to the influence of local politics), and there was no commitment to using the evaluation outcomes for teacher dismissal proceedings. In short, the teacher evaluation system was perceived as a token accountability system, lacking real enforcement mechanisms. Indeed, evaluation outcomes were never collected for aggregation at the state level, nor was there a directive that the data be used at the local district level.

As might be expected, early efforts at implementing the evaluation system were uneven. Some principals and superintendents believed that the system provided a means of improving the quality of instruction and recognizing teachers who were performing at high professional levels. Many other people, however, viewed the evaluation of teaching less positively. The loose implementation standards made it easy to avoid serious evaluative activity. More than one teacher found an evaluation form in his/her mailbox with a note, asking the teacher to "please complete this, and return it to the office." Such practice was tantamount to inviting the teacher to do his or her own evaluation. Within eighteen months of instituting the new evaluation system, the State Department of Public Instruction staff undertook a review which reached several conclusions: (1) accountability was generally regarded as an appropriate concern of the state and of the profession; (2) the development of uniform procedures and standards for implementation was perceived as important; and (3) a desire to continue to recognize teacher evaluation as a local concern (since local boards employed and dismissed teachers) was expressed along with a belief that evaluation guidelines should be articulated at the state level.

In addition to these general conclusions, widespread dissatisfaction with the criteria was noted. Educators began to ask whether a better standard for inclusion of a behavioral expectation than "everyone knows" could be found. The general sense that "better" criteria existed contributed to the next important development in the North Carolina teacher evaluation system. Sentiment also began to grow at this time for overhauling the entire system of school personnel management.

A number of initiatives, launched at the state level during the years 1980–1985, were intended to raise the quality of educators working in the state's schools. Loosely linked under the rubric of the Quality Assurance Program, these efforts included: (1) a reexamination of the "program approval" procedure used by the State Board of Education to certify the quality of teacher preparation programs at all universities in the state; (2) establishment of an executive training program, based at the University of North Carolina—Chapel Hill, for upgrading the skills of all principals; (3) an overhaul of the teacher certification system, with the result that an Initial Certificate Program for teachers in the early years of their careers was launched; (4) the development of a mentor program intended to link experienced teachers with teachers holding an Initial Certificate; (5) increased funding for local district staff development activities with an average of $100 per teacher per year allocated for staff development; and (6) an extensive review of the course and program requirements that teachers would be expected to complete before being granted a teaching certificate.

Many state legislators were convinced that there was a general problem with the quality of teachers and other educators employed in the state. The solution to this problem was felt to lie in a multifaceted program of improvements in all aspects of the personnel management system, ranging from preparation to employment, with checkpoints (certification and recertification requirements, annual performance evaluation, annual staff development) built into a comprehensive Quality Assurance Program. While all of these programmatic efforts were intended to act in a complementary way to ensure high quality performance by educators, it is clear that the amount of control being exercised at the state level was significantly increased. It should be remembered, of course, that the legislature that enacted these accountability measures also bore the cost of implementation.

EXHIBIT 3-1. Practices and functions of the North Carolina Teacher Performance Appraisal Instrument

---

1. Major Function: *Management of Instructional Time*
   1.1 Teacher has materials, supplies, and equipment ready at the start of the lesson or instruction activity.
   1.2 Teacher begins the class quickly.
   1.3 Teacher gets students on task quickly at the beginning of each lesson or instructional activity.
   1.4 Teacher maintains a high level of student time-on-task.

2. Major Function: *Management of Student Behavior*
   2.1 Teacher has established a set of rules and procedures that govern the handling of routine administrative matters.
   2.2 Teacher has established a set of rules and procedures that govern student verbal participation and talk during different types of activities—whole-class instruction, small-group instruction, and so on.
   2.3 Teacher has established a set of rules and procedures that govern student movement in the classroom during different types of instructional activities.
   2.4 Teacher frequently monitors the behavior of all students during whole-class, small-group, and seat work activities and during transitions between instructional activities.
   2.5 Teacher stops inappropriate behavior promptly and consistently, yet maintains the dignity of the student.

3. Major Function: *Instructional Presentation*
   3.1 Teacher begins lesson or instructional activity with a review of previous material.
   3.2 Teacher introduces the lesson or instructional activity and specifies learning objectives when appropriate.
   3.3 Teacher speaks fluently and precisely.
   3.4 Teacher presents the lesson or instructional activity using concepts and language understandable to the students.
   3.5 Teacher provides relevant examples and demonstrations to illustrate concepts and skills.
   3.6 Teacher assigns tasks that students handle with a high rate of success.
   3.7 Teacher asks appropriate levels of questions that students handle with a high rate of success.
   3.8 Teacher conducts lesson or instructional activity at a brisk pace, slowing presentations when necessary for student understanding but avoiding unnecessary slowdowns.

3.9 Teacher makes transitions between lessons and between instructional activities within lessons efficiently and smoothly.

3.10 Teacher makes sure that the assignment is clear.

3.11 Teacher summarizes the main point(s) of the lesson at the end of the lesson or instructional activity.

4. Major Function: *Instructional Monitoring of Student Performance*

   4.1 Teacher maintains clear, firm, and reasonable work standards and due dates.

   4.2 Teacher circulates during classwork to check all students' performance.

   4.3 Teacher routinely uses oral, written, and other work products to check student progress.

   4.4 Teacher poses questions clearly and one at a time.

5. Major Function: *Instructional Feedback*

   5.1 Teacher provides feedback on the correctness or incorrectness of in-class work to encourage student growth.

   5.2 Teacher regularly provides prompt feedback on assigned out-of-class work.

   5.3 Teacher affirms as correct oral response appropriately, and moves on.

   5.4 Teacher provides sustaining feedback after an incorrect response or no response by probing, repeating the question, giving a clue, or allowing more time.

6. Major Function: *Facilitating Instruction*

   6.1 Teacher has an instructional plan that is compatible with the school and system-wide curricular goals.

6.2 Teacher uses diagnostic information obtained from tests and other assessment procedures to develop and revise objectives and/or tasks.

   6.3 Teacher maintains accurate records to document student performance.

   6.4 Teacher has instructional plan that matches/aligns objectives, learning strategies, assessment, and student needs at the appropriate level of difficulty.

   6.5 Teacher uses available human and material resources to support the instructional program.

7. Major Function: *Communicating Within the Educational Environment*

   7.1 Teacher treats all students in a fair and equitable manner.

   7.2 Teacher interacts effectively with students, coworkers, parents, and community.

8. Major Function: *Performing Noninstructional Duties*

   8.1 Teacher carries out noninstructional duties as assigned and/or as need is perceived.

8.2 Teacher adheres to established laws, policies, rules, and regulations.

8.3 Teacher follows a plan for professional development and demonstrates evidence of growth.

A Research-Based Evaluation System

As part of its Quality Assurance Program, the North Carolina General Assembly enacted a bill requiring annual performance evaluation of educators in the state. The bill required that local boards of education adopt performance standards established by the State Board of Education. In 1982, a contract was offered by the Department of Public Instruction (DPI), acting in its capacity as staff to the State Board of Education, to a consortium of education professors at the University of North Carolina to identify "research-based" evaluation criteria. The "Group for Effective Teaching" (as the university group was called) included a number of individuals who were experienced in both laboratory experimentation and field work. Moreover, the group was aware that many of the federally funded education research studies were appearing in the professional literature. Criteria were established to guide the group as it looked at the results of education research (The Group for Effective Teaching 1983). According to the criteria, teaching skills had to be:

1. identified in at least two different empirical studies as leading to increased student achievement and/or increased time on task.
2. associated with success in more than one grade or subject area.
3. both observable and alterable.

In all, the group examined more than 120 studies covering twenty-eight skills. These skills were divided into five general teaching functions:

1. Management of Instructional Time
2. Management of Student Behavior
3. Instructional Presentation
4. Instructional Monitoring
5. Instructional Feedback

Much of the research base on which the group depended derived from "process/product" studies that had been reported during the late 1970s and early 1980s. These efforts primarily focused on correlating specific teacher behaviors and student achievement, usually as measured by improvements on norm-referenced tests of basic skills. Thus, a particular view of both teaching and learning was built into the review system developed by the group.

Having identified the target skills of teachers, group members conducted field tests in three school districts and, simultaneously, developed and tested protocols for data collection, analysis, and reporting (The Group for Effective Teaching 1985a). It should be noted that the members of the group were primarily researchers with fairly limited experience in teaching or school administration. Not surprisingly, the methods for data collection and analysis that they developed were somewhat foreign to practitioners.

Exhibit 3-1 presents the entire set of practices developed for the five teaching functions. The function, Managing Instructional Time, for example, consisted of four separate practices:

1.1 The teacher has materials ready at the beginning of class.
1.2 The teacher begins the class quickly.
1.3 The teacher gets students on task quickly at the beginning of the lesson or activity.
1.4 The teacher maintains a high degree of time-on-task.

With respect to Practice 1.3, for example, a teacher might demonstrate a variety of different behaviors. Before explaining a task or activity, a teacher could encourage all students to face her/him. Also a teacher might circulate among the students to ensure that everyone's book is open to the right page before beginning to discuss the outlined task. The teacher might wait silently until all students are settled down before starting to explain the next task. Each of these observable behaviors must be noted by the evaluator as being related to Practice 1.3.

The formative aspect of the evaluation cycle occurred when judgments in the form of narratives were reported to teachers during the course of conferences scheduled within a few days of classroom observations. Formative evaluations were not reduced to quality point designations. The formative aspects of the evaluation system resembled the data collection and analysis methods used by qualitative researchers. In the course of post-observation conferences, teachers and observers were expected not only to discuss narratives and supporting data, and to certify that the data was accurate and complete, but also to identify alternative interpretations.

The summative aspects of the evaluation system were intended to allow organizational decisions (promotion, tenure, contract renewal, and staff development programs) to be made on the basis of observed conditions of practice. Summative evaluation was based on the assumption that most people teach in habitual ways. That is, it is possible to generalize about the quality of teaching performance if one has a reasonable number of behavioral examples. Class observations were required three or four times per year. Based on these observations, evaluators tried to describe the general level of performance demonstrated by the teacher for each of the functions. For the sake of convenience, a quality number also was assigned to each of the functions. The six steps on the rating scale included:

6. Superior
5. Well Above Standard
4. Above Standard
3. At Standard
2. Below Standard
1. Unsatisfactory

Each teacher's annual performance evaluation, then, was reduced to a series of numbers representing separate functions. These were never combined to create a composite number, since a skill level in one function did not necessarily predict skill levels in other functions. Each function was considered a necessary, but not a sufficient condition of teaching practice.

The new evaluation system entailed several changes for principals, the primary evaluators of teaching performance. First they needed to allocate their time differently. Estimates of the time needed to complete observations, data analyses, conferences and evaluation averaged about eight hours per teacher per year. This was a vastly greater amount of time than most principals had been accustomed to spending. Moreover, the observation requirements required principals to spend between thirty and fifty-five minutes (an entire class period) conducting the observation. Being confined in one place for this long was a difficult adjustment for many principals. Furthermore, few observers could conduct more than three observations per day. Even with excellent script-taking skills, observers reported that they had completely forgotten the first observed lesson on a given day by the end of their third observation.

The evaluation process also required expertise that most principals did not possess. Three kinds of skills or knowledge were required by the new evaluation system. The evaluator had to know the research base that supported the evaluation system and recognize the surface behaviors when they were presented. Second, he or she had to be very skilled in both analytic and synthetic thinking. That is, the observer needed to divide the complex act of instruction into its component parts. Additionally, the observer had to recognize patterns in the individual teacher's behaviors that may be presented at different points within the lesson, as well as in different lessons. The evaluator finally had to possess communication skills, both oral and written. Not only does the script taping require good writing skills, so that a usable record can be constructed, but the narrative must be written so that it accurately reflects the displayed behavior. The evaluator must communicate the outcomes orally, in an environment that could be highly charged emotionally, especially if the teacher is receiving a negative evaluation. Few training programs addressed all three of these areas.

Having completed the terms of their contract, the group turned its findings over the NC Department of Public Instruction (The Group for Effective Teaching 1985b). DPI officials immediately recognized that the work was limited to one aspect of the performance of teachers: the work conducted in classrooms with children present. Believing that teachers' jobs included more expectations than just what was observable in classrooms, DPI officials added three other functions for evaluation:

1. Facilitating instruction (planning and use of test data)
2. Communicating within the educational environment
3. Performing noninstructional duties

Thus was created the North Carolina Teacher Performance Appraisal System (NCTPAS). DPI commissioned the development of training programs for both teachers and principals to facilitate implementation of the new evaluation process. *Effective Teaching Training* was a thirty-hour program planned for presentation over a five-day period. The program presented each of the eight teaching functions evaluated by the NCTPAS in operational terms. Associated skills were defined, the research base was presented, and opportunities were provided for trainees to discuss and practice each skill. Moreover, videotape vignettes of teachers demonstrating the skills were included in the training packages. Beginning in the summer of 1985, training was presented in centralized locations throughout the state. By the end of 1987, more than 60,000 educators in North Carolina had participated in the thirty-hour program. The General Assembly authorized and funded a stipend of $250 for every participant. This $15 million fund was in addition to other salary payments.

A twenty-four hour training program for evaluators also was developed. Prospective evaluators were trained to collect data in classrooms, analyze data, and rate the quality of demonstrated skills. At the conclusion of the training, a practical exercise was completed that allowed trainees to demonstrate their competence. Trainees were required to analyze a teacher's performance on videotape and evaluate it. The results were compared to a standard that had been established for the videotaped episode. Although the competence of trainees was not certified at the end of training, superintendents were informed by DPI of all persons in their district who had been trained and what their performance scores were. Any principal or supervisor who failed to demonstrate acceptable levels of performance was identified, along with his or her score, and a recommendation was made to the superintendent that the person not be permitted to evaluate teaching without undergoing additional training.

Two Tests of the Teacher Evaluation System

In July 1985, DPI implemented a pilot test of the evaluation system in twenty-four school districts. The twenty-four systems represented the diversity of the state's population and included both large and small districts drawn from all parts of the state. While no incentives were offered for participation in the pilot study, some districts were hopeful that their cooperation in this effort would lead to future opportunities to test a merit pay scheme that was being planned simultaneously with the field testing. At the end of the pilot period in July of 1986, DPI conducted a program evaluation to determine how well the performance appraisal system had been implemented.

The results of the study (Stacy, Holdzkom, and Kuligowski 1989) indicated widespread acceptance of the criteria among both teachers and evaluators, a belief that the rating system could be used to distinguish incompetent from competent teachers, and the general perception that the system was of value for summative appraisal purposes. The study also showed, however, that most people did not value the improvement aspects of the evaluation system, either because people lacked time to implement the formative procedures and the necessary follow-up training, or because of a lack of confidence in the prescriptions resulting from the observations. This finding was extremely disheartening for several reasons. First, the DPI staff had believed that performance evaluation in which the evaluatee played a prominent role would lead to greater acceptance of the findings, especially when the system supported performance improvement. The findings of the evaluation suggested that little value had been derived from the formative aspects of the system. Second, it was clear that, while the primary purpose of evaluation from the perspective of the General Assembly was summative, the system developers had hoped to emphasize the performance improvement aspects of the evaluation system. Indeed, the most widespread reason for teacher performance evaluation had been found to be instructional improvement (Kuligowski, Holdzkom, and French 1993). The steps needed to bring about instructional improvement, however, were not being carried out in the new evaluation system. Evaluators, especially principals, complained that the data collection system was too time-consuming. The appraisal system was estimated to require about eight hours per teacher per year, a figure perceived to be too high given other demands on administrators' time.

Despite the low ratings given to the formative aspects of the NCTPAS, DPI recommended to the State Board of Education that the new teacher performance evaluation system be adopted for optional use by local boards of education from July 1, 1986, to July 1, 1987, at which time the system would be made mandatory. This recommendation largely rested on the positive reception given the NCTPAS' summative process. All local boards adopted the new evaluation system well before the mandated deadline. Early adoption led staff to push forward the training calendar so that all evaluators could be prepared to implement NCTPAS. Adopting a turnkey model for training, the DPI staff worked with local district educators to develop a system that would place training responsibility increasingly on school districts. Once the turnkey model was adopted, DPI staff abandoned all efforts at quality control.

At the same time that the evaluation system was being piloted, the General Assembly authorized another pilot program intended to encourage greater accountability while simultaneously making teaching more attractive. The Career Development Program (CDP) represented the carrot, while the new evaluation system was seen as the stick. The General Assembly insisted that superior teachers should be identified and rewarded. While many people immediately termed the new program a "merit pay" plan, the goals of the CDP were more diverse.

It has long been recognized that teaching is one of the few professions without some kind of promotion system (Lortie 1975). A teacher has essentially the same responsibilities on the day before retirement that he/she had on the first day of practice. For many persons, this lack of career growth and a corresponding system of rewards is a frequently cited reason for discontent and departure from the profession. The CDP was seen by some legislators as a means to make teaching more attractive, both to those new to the profession by offering rewards based in part on individual merit, and to experienced teachers by creating mechanisms for increasing salaries and professional responsibilities.

The Career Development Program

The CDP encompassed a four-year pilot designed to provide immediate salary increases to those individuals demonstrating teaching skill above expected levels. The details of the program were codified in law (North

Carolina General Statute 115C–363). The CDP entailed three performance levels. When newly licensed, a teacher in North Carolina would be designated an "Initially Certified Teacher" (ICT). During the first two years of teaching, the ICT was assigned a mentor teacher who helped the young teacher attain a level of professional competence designated as "At Standard." During the third year of employment, the teacher became a candidate for Career Level I. Based on observations of the teacher, the evaluator recommended the teacher for Career Level I if performance in classes was acceptable. Career Level I, when awarded, brought a pay increase of 5 percent over the appropriate salary step. During the third year on Career Level I, the teacher could declare candidacy for Career Level II. Initially, Career Level II was reserved for teachers who demonstrated a high level of competence, as measured by the NCTPAS. A "high level" was considered to be ratings of at least 5 (on a scale from 1 to 6) in each of the eight standards of the evaluation instrument. In addition, the candidate was expected to prepare a portfolio that contained evidence of professional growth, good attendance, and certification appropriate to assignment. Later these requirements were scaled back, with the portfolio entirely eliminated. Henceforth, the rewards of the CDP would be based entirely on measured performance. The award for attaining Career Level II was significant, a salary increase of 10 percent above schedule, along with the original 5 percent for attaining Career Level I. At the time of the CDP's implementation, the average teacher salary for all teachers in North Carolina was $27,000 per year. Thus, 15 percent for Career Level II represented, on average, $4,050. During initial planning, a Career Level III was proposed, but it never became a reality. The Career Level III salary differential would have added a 10 percent increment, based on performance evaluation.

In addition to salary awards, the CDP offered a variety of additional professional opportunities to teachers. Eligibility for these opportunities was to be limited to Career Level II teachers in the original plans for the CDP. Though written into the authorizing legislation, the provision became a serious point of contention between the legislature and the participating districts throughout the pilot period. Extra duties included serving as a mentor teacher, department chair or grade-level team leader, planning and conducting staff development activities, teaching in a summer school program, and planning and developing curriculum. The CDP, therefore, offered both additional responsibilities during the school year and the opportunity for extended employment during the summer. While it was hoped that teachers would take advantage of these opportunities, the authors of the legislation were careful to point out that participation had to be entirely optional.

Because the stakes involved in the new evaluation system were relatively high, the legislation included a number of features intended to insure that evaluation was conducted competently. The creation of a new position—that of the observer/evaluator (O/E)—was mandated for school systems. Over the years, individual legislators had been told by teachers that some principals were not competent to evaluate teaching, no matter how elevated their skills might be in other areas of school management. The O/E was intended, therefore, to be a teacher who was held in high professional esteem by his/her colleagues (NC DPI 1985). This person was responsible for conducting in-class observations on at least two occasions for every candidate for promotion. The results of observations were to be shared with the teacher by the O/E, who would also be required to suggest ways in which the candidate's performance could be improved. Each district was allocated one O/E for every ninety-six teachers. In addition to the two observations by an O/E, the principal or his/her designee had to conduct two observations, bringing to four the number of performance samples to be used in each summative evaluation. The observer/evaluator also was expected to provide staff development for teachers throughout the district. Persons serving as O/E's were paid on the supervisor's salary schedule, and the normal certification requirements for placement on the supervisor's schedule were suspended for them.

Each participating school district also was given funds to hire a project coordinator, and, after the first year of the pilot study, a halftime secretary. The Career Development Program legislation stressed the new reward structure and the resources needed to implement the pilot program. Specifics concerning evaluation criteria, processes for data collection, and similar technical questions were not codified, but were intended to be developed by DPI staff. An important provision of the law required DPI "to consult" with the participating boards of education during the course of the pilot, which was authorized for a four-year period.

Other provisions of the law are worth nothing. For example, no quotas for participation or awards could be established. From the viewpoint of teachers, this meant that there would be no need for competition, since all qualifying teachers could earn the promised awards. In addition, evaluators were relieved of pressure to hold down evaluation ratings in order to keep the number of teachers earning the rewards low.

Another feature of the law had a major impact on the pilot. It had been anticipated that career-level eligibility would rest both on demonstrated performance and years of experience. Because the pilot was intended to run for four years, however, a decision was made to declare teachers eligible for Level I in the first year of the pilot if they possessed at least three years of experience in teaching. Since Level II criteria would be implemented in the second year of the pilot, it also was agreed that teachers with six years of experience would be eligible for Level II candidacy in that year. Thus, a fast-track for career advancement was established. Many teachers with the requisite years of experience could earn salary increases of up to 15 percent in a relatively short time period, while simultaneously receiving whatever across-the-board raises the General Assembly chose to give to all teachers.

The law's specification that the pilot would run for four years also was important, since it precluded early decisions to extend the pilot to include other school systems (as Governor James G. Martin would urge after the first year of the pilot) or to abandon the effort (as would be recommended by the state leadership of NCAE after the first year of implementation). Career Development Program implementers were assured of a reasonable amount of time to implement and finetune the new scheme before being required to recommend state-wide implementation or abandonment.

In July 1985, sixteen school districts across the state were invited to participate in the CDP pilot. Two districts were chosen from each of the state's eight legislative districts and, in combination, the districts represented the diversity of characteristics found in the state's school systems. The largest district—Charlotte-Mecklenburg—successfully argued that it should be granted autonomy from all state regulation during the pilot period, since it was already in the second year of its own pilot program. The other fifteen districts accepted the basic state-designed plan for the pilot; some local variation was allowed. While the evaluation system, reward structure, and use of O/Es was required for the fifteen districts, the criteria for selection and deployment of staff was a local decision. Each district created a local steering committee to monitor the pilot, though there was no requirement that they do so. The selection of members of the committee, as well as its charge, varied from district to district. In one district, for example, members were appointed by the superintendent; in another district, each school faculty elected its own representative to the committee. The first year of implementation was marked by efforts to provide appropriate training for teachers and evaluators, while the first round of evaluations were being conducted. This year was complicated by the fact that virtually all the teachers who were eligible for participation in the pilot elected to do so. About six thousand teachers and six hundred and fifty other educators were enrolled at the start of the pilot. This figure represented about 98 percent of those employed in the fifteen districts (Division of Personnel Relations 1986).

The pilot was managed by DPI staff in conjunction with the local career development coordinators and superintendents. In order to carry out the law's mandate "to consult" with participating educators, as well as monitor and assist in implementation efforts, DPI staff established a state steering committee for CDP. Each district was invited to send its superintendent, one teacher, and one principal to participate on this committee, which met monthly throughout the four-year pilot period. In addition, the CDP coordinators from each district met monthly with DPI staff to discuss and resolve implementation problems and act as staff to the state steering committee. This group later became an important political force as the debate about state-wide implementation was joined. It is important to note that a representative of NCAE was invited to observe the meetings of the state steering committee, as were representatives of the North Carolina School Boards Association and the North Carolina Association of School Administrators.

The legislation required that a report of pilot activities be prepared for the General Assembly annually. During the months when the Assembly was not in session, authority to deal with the pilot was vested in a four-person committee representing both the House and Senate. Members of the committee included the Senate Budget Committee Chairman and the House whip, a close associate of the speaker. The other members of the committee included a senator who had been superintendent of schools in a large urban district in the state, and a younger member of the House who would ultimately be elected state superintendent of public instruction. This influential committee met regularly with DPI staff and members of the state steering committee and agreed to sponsor amendments to the original CDP legislation that the steering committee determined would allow smoother implementation of the pilot. Chief among these changes were adjustments in the evaluation standards required for movement to Career Level II (these were changed twice: once being relaxed, and once being tightened) and alterations in the extra duties provision to allow local administrators a freer hand in assigning teachers.

Legislative Efforts to Evaluate the Project

While legislators were willing to write a blank check for implementation of the CDP pilot, they insisted on an independent evaluation of the program and the NCTPAS. The history of the relationship between the General Assembly and the elected state superintendent of public instruction, who was administratively responsible for DPI staff, was sufficiently contentious that members of the legislature were not willing to rely solely on DPI's internal assessment of the pilot. In order to obtain independent judgments of the work being conducted by DPI, the General Assembly, acting through the committee overseeing CDP, offered two contracts for third-party evaluations in 1988. One contract provided for a review of the NCTPAS, while the second called for a major study of the CDP implementation process.

In the spring of 1988, a four-member panel of national experts in teacher evaluation was convened and charged with reviewing the NCTPAS to determine its validity and reliability when used to distinguish among different levels of teaching competence. The panel, under the direction of Richard Brandt from the University of Virginia, spent several weeks reviewing documentation provided by DPI officials and participating districts. The panel's report, prepared for submission to the Legislature, noted that the North Carolina Teacher Performance Appraisal System was a sound system for performance evaluation and could be used to make defensible decisions about teaching for several purposes, including certification, job retention, and differentiation between basic and advanced teaching. The panel was unconvinced that the instrument should be used for the identification of teaching at the highest level. The need for additional criteria and evaluation processes was expressed as well (Brandt, et al. 1988). The report was presented to the General Assembly at its summer session in 1988 by the panel's chairman.

The first third-party evaluation contract also required a review of the two-stage appeals process prescribed by the North Carolina General Assembly for candidates whose performance evaluations resulted in either no promotion or demotion (Brandt 1988). Of the sixty-five cases (about 7 percent of those who had failed to attain Career Status II) that had been appealed to special panels of trained evaluators, only one-fifth were overturned. Of almost two dozen that were appealed further to local boards of education, half were overturned. The report concluded that, despite the small number of appeals, potential problems loomed ahead. If not resolved, they threatened to undermine the NCTPAS and the CDP. The report indicated that either the final appeal should remain with trained professionals, that is, the first-stage panel, or school board members should receive specific training in the performance evaluation process (Brandt 1990a).

The second major study that the North Carolina General Assembly commissioned was a third-party evaluation of the implementation of the CDP pilot. As part of this evaluation, the investigators studied the distribution of teachers along the six points of the rating scale, the reliability of evaluators in each of the districts, and the opinions of participating teachers, principals, superintendents, and local board of education members about the pilot program. They found that the pilot had been implemented well, that most of the evaluators had demonstrated reliability, and that, by and large, almost all participants in the pilot, without regard to employment status, were satisfied with the fairness and quality of implementation of both the evaluation and rewards systems. While greater degrees of satisfaction were observed in some school districts than in others, in no case did a majority of teachers or other staff in any district advocate abandoning the Career Development Program or the associated NCTPAS (Furtwengler 1988).

The NCAE, which had spent the four years of the pilot criticizing the CDP, now brought its considerable political weight into the fray. The specific motivation of NCAE has remained unclear to many observers of the political fight that was joined in 1988–89. Certainly, the NCAE's parent organization, the National Education Association (NEA), had long opposed efforts to link teacher evaluation and merit pay. NCAE realized that the funds for the "merit pay" plan (budgeted at $48 million for FY 1989 alone) could be used for across-the-board pay increases. Moreover, the cost of the CDP might be used by legislators as a reason for not funding a new salary schedule. The use of the performance appraisal system was never in question, however. Only the more narrow question of tying rewards to the outcome of teacher evaluation was at issue.

While DPI's external evaluators supported most aspects of the NCTPAS and the CDP, the NCAE leadership managed to use the third-party evaluations to advance their position as well. While ignoring the central finding in the evaluation of the performance evaluation system (namely, that the instrument was well-suited to its purposes), NCAE focused on the relatively minor suggestions for improvement made in the report, claiming that these suggestions reflected the NCAE's own concerns. Further, in numerous polls of both the general membership and of the local leadership, NCAE found widespread support for abandoning the CDP and the evaluation system (NCAE 1986; Bunch 1988). This finding came primarily from those districts not involved in the CDP pilot effort and contravened the opinions of most teachers with actual experience with the NCTPAS and the CDP. A letter addressed to one of the NCAE's officials, sent on the letterhead of the National Education Association's division of Instruction and Professional Development, stated: "A good rule of thumb for reviewing these questions is 'Will I get any information that will allow NCAE to get some evidence to modify or kill the evaluation system?'" (NEA 1988). Clearly the issue of teacher evaluation and merit pay had become politicized. And it would be in the political arena that the issue would be resolved.

Another voice of dissent was raised at this time. The North Carolina Public School Forum was a lobbying group that brought together business leaders and politicians to push for educational programs. Headed by a former executive director of the NCAE, this group represented an effort to harness the power of business in order to bring about political change. During the early 1980s business people had been fairly quiet in the discussion of performance evaluation of teachers (Boyd 1994). Now, however, they weighed in on the side of district autonomy rather than a state-run evaluation and rewards program. The Forum suggested a less costly alternative to the Career Development Program based on the "lead teacher" concept.

The General Assembly Strikes a Compromise

In addition to the two third-party evaluations, the North Carolina General Assembly had received periodic reports on the CDP's implementation and results. One report prepared by DPI staff analyzed student achievement levels in the fifteen CDP pilot districts and found that, when compared to students from fifteen similar districts, the CDP students posted greater academic achievement gains over the four-year pilot period (Holdzkom, Stacy, and Kuligowski 1990). It was becoming apparent from the increased budgets and salaries in pilot districts, however, that state-wide implementation of the CDP would be very costly, with some estimates reaching "a billion dollars by the end of the century." Clearly the General Assembly was reluctant to make such a commitment during an economic downturn. Moreover, a state-wide election was being held in which a new governor and a new state superintendent of schools would be elected. The General Assembly found itself on the horns of a dilemma: on the one hand, a substantial body of evidence showed that the NCTPAS and the CDP had achieved some success; on the other hand, the NCAE was clearly opposed to expansion (or even continuation) of the CDP and the cost of doing so seemed prohibitive.

The compromise that eventually was worked out illustrated that education policy is never developed in a vacuum. The CDP and the NCTPAS had been initiated at a moment in history when the quality of public education was under serious attack. *A Nation at Risk* had been published in 1983 just as the teacher evaluation system was being developed. By 1989, however, the national conversation on educational quality had changed dramatically, with increased emphasis on shared decision-making and decentralized control of work quality. Led by the state Senate, the General Assembly enacted a bill that stressed outcomes over inputs, placed more decision-making control in the hands of local boards of education, and freed educators from many bureaucratic constraints that were perceived to block schools from attaining high levels of quality.

Specifically, the General Assembly declined to expand the Career Development Program to all school districts; although it did allow the pilots to continue into a fifth year in the fifteen districts where they were in-stalled. Moreover, while holding spending on CDP at the 1988–89 level, the legislature allowed participating districts to adjust their program bud-gets to ensure that payments to teachers would not be reduced. This meant that other program elements (staff development, salaries of ob-server/evaluators, funding for extra duties) could be reduced to ensure that awards to teachers would not be reduced. For the remaining school districts, the General Assembly created the School Improvement and Ac-countability Program. This program was voluntary and offered a variety of incentives for districts that chose to participate (North Carolina Gen-eral Assembly 1989). Incentives were of three types: (1) districts could seek relief from state laws, policies, and regulations that were felt to im-pede progress in attaining improved student achievement; (2) some line items in the state budget allocated to the district could be combined and used to support purchases that the district felt would help in attaining specified student achievement targets; and (3) funds were made available for districts to establish a "differentiated pay plan" for certified staff (teachers, principals, and supervisors). Although the pay plan could take a variety of forms, only some of which were specified by the legislation as examples, the legislature agreed to fund the plans in an escalator fashion, beginning at 2 percent in the first year of implementation (the year *after* enactment of the legislation) and rising to 7 percent by 1995. While these percentages stipulated the allotment formula for budget purposes, they did not necessarily translate into a cap on the amount of differentiated pay that might be earned by an individual.

In exchange for these benefits, participating districts were required to establish a plan for improvement on a variety of student achievement measures that were to be adopted by the State Board of Education. These measures included average daily attendance, improvements in average scores on a new battery of tests that DPI was to develop, and improve-ments in average SAT scores. Plans were to be implemented over a three-year period, with achievement benchmarks set for the interim years. The legislation also required that persons eligible to participate in the differ-entiated pay plan be allowed to vote on the plan before it was imple-mented in the district.

The legislation addressed the evaluation of teacher performance in several ways. First, school districts were still required to use the NCTPAS for the evaluation of any teacher not protected by "tenure." That is, Ini-tially Certified teachers, any teacher coming to a North Carolina school from out of state, and some teachers who transferred from one school dis-trict to another would still be subject to the NCTPAS requirements that had been established in the State Board adopted evaluation system. Second, districts could elect to create an "alternative" evaluation system for teachers. Districts were not required to seek authorization or approval of the State Board when implementing their alternative system of teacher evaluation. Thus, the General Assembly retained the state teacher evaluation system for "new" teachers, as an accountability measure, but gave up evaluative control of veteran teachers. Clearly, NCAE had won a major victory in the struggle for control of accountability, including the standards that would be expected for practicing educators. For all intents and purposes, the General Assembly had surrendered its control of educational improvement and accepted an accountability system that, over the next four years, called for the role of teachers and principals in school decision making to grow, in exchange for promises of student improvement. Schools, for example, were not given performance standards that they were expected to meet. Rather, teachers and principals established these targets, based on previous performance of the district schools. The legislation was silent on what would happen if a district failed to achieve its goals, although there was some suggestion that the State Board of Education could prevent a district from further participation if it failed to attain its goals. To date, no such action to exclude a district has occurred, despite the fact that only 54 percent of participating districts attained the improvement goals that they had set under the School Improvement and Accountability Program.

One of the interesting, if little noted, aspects of the negotiations surrounding the legislation concerned the training of teachers to assume the new responsibilities of the bill. Teaching is a highly individualistic—even isolated—profession. Teachers do not routinely work with their colleagues, and they are expected to perform their most important duties outside the view of other adults. The School Improvement and Accountability Act, however, required teachers to work in groups, if only to plan for improvements. It was recognized by some people that skills in teamwork, consensus-building, and group dynamics would need to be developed by teachers, if they were to meet successfully the expectations of the new law. Early in the hearings on the bill, $250,000 had been included in the budget to provide just this kind of training. When the bill was brought before the legislature for adoption, however, the funds were deleted by the committee sponsoring the bill. The funds were never restored. A number of districts eventually diverted some of their regular staff development funds to pay for this training. In recognition of its error, the General Assembly did permit spending for such staff development the next year, but these funds were deducted from the differentiated pay plans that were intended to reward teachers financially for participating in the school improvement activities.

Epilogue

The General Assembly has continued to tinker with the School Improvement and Accountability Act, eventually spawning the Performance Based Accountability Program, which increased the degree to which teacher and parent approval was required in the crafting of school improvement plans. Whereas under the School Improvement and Accountability Act, the improvement plans were generated at the district level, under the Performance Based Accountability Plan, school faculty, staff, and parents are responsible for creating the improvement plans. Local boards cannot reject a school's plan unless they provide a specific reason for such rejection. Building plans must specify which waivers from state law, if any, are desired. While the NCAE backs this legislation and the degree of site-based management has increased in North Carolina schools, it is too early to tell whether improvements in educational outcomes will result.

While educators in North Carolina and elsewhere around the country are being given an opportunity to waive state regulations in lieu of improved outcomes, surprisingly few of them have taken advantage of this option (Olson 1990). In North Carolina, for example, the relatively few waivers sought by school districts have tended to focus on reductions in operational standards. Thus, waiver requests have asked for elimination of class size limits, removal of teacher certification requirements, reduction in required observations in the NCTPAS, and relaxed procedures for the identification of gifted children (Kuligowski and Holdzkom 1991).

The road from accountability to teacher empowerment has been a long one in North Carolina. The struggle to use teacher evaluation as a means of improving the quality of education has been difficult and costly. The North Carolina Teacher Performance Appraisal System represents one of the most extensive state-wide efforts to design and install a fair and research-based teacher evaluation system to improve the quality of education. It moved from drawing board to full-scale field-testing over a period of several years in a variety of school districts. The number of supporters grew as "hard evidence" began to accumulate that children whose teachers were involved were learning more than those with teachers who had not participated in the pilot program.

When the NCTPAS began to be used as a basis for decisions in the CDP, however, new challenges—and difficulties—arose. Teacher evaluators had to be selected, trained, and given new assignments observing in classrooms and working with teachers. Principals had to spend much more time in classrooms watching instruction and conferring with teachers. Careful records had to be kept and reviewed and new funds accounted for.

But are not such challenges and difficulties what we should expect from real reform in education? What a shame that shifting political winds brought it all to a stop! So much had been accomplished, and the promise of more success lay ahead. From early reports, the transfer of responsibility to teachers and principals called for by the School Improvement and Accountability Act has not had the desired effects, at least on student achievement. Perhaps teachers and principals now feel more empowered in North Carolina schools than they did in the old days of state-focused, centralized control. Whether children are learning more or better remains an open question, however.

References

Anderson, J. (1988). *The Education of Blacks in the South: 1960–1935*. Chapel Hill, NC: University of North Carolina Press.

Ayers, E. (1992). *The Promise of the New South: Life After Reconstruction*. New York: Oxford University Press.

Boyd, R. (1994). A personal conversation with Holdzkom, April 25.

Brandt, R. (1988). *An Evaluation of the Career Development Pilot Project Appeals Process*. Raleigh, NC: Education Subcommittee of the Joint Legislative Committee on Government Operations, North Carolina General Assembly.

Brandt, R. (1990a). *A Close-up Look: Third-party Evaluation of Program Components*. Paper presented at the Annual Meeting of the American Educational Research Association, Boston, MA.

———. (1990b). *Incentive Pay and Career Ladders For Today's Teachers: A Study of Current Programs and Practices*. Albany, NY: State University of New York Press.

Brandt, R., Duke, D., French, R., and Iwanicki, E. (1988). *A Review with Recommendations of the North Carolina Teacher Performance Appraisal Instrument*. Raleigh, NC: North Carolina General Assembly.

Bunch, M. (1988). *Career Development Plan Pilot Project Survey: Final Report*. Raleigh, NC: North Carolina Association of Educators.

Commission for the Study of Teacher Merit Pay and Implementation of a Revised Public School Curriculum. (nd). *Final Report*. Raleigh, NC: North Carolina General Assembly.

Commission on Merit Rating of Teachers, J. W. Unstead, Chairman. (1946). *Report*. Raleigh, NC: North Carolina General Assembly.

Division of Personnel Relations, NCDPI. (1986). *The Career Development Pilot Program: A Status Report*. Raleigh, NC: North Carolina Department of Public Instruction.

Finn, C. (1990). The Biggest Reform of All. *Phi Delta Kappan*, 584–592.

Foner, E. (1990). *A Short History of Reconstruction*. New York: Harper and Row.

Furtwengler, C. (1988). *Evaluation of North Carolina's School Career Development Pilot Program*. Raleigh, NC: North Carolina General Assembly.

Group for Effective Teaching. (1983). *Teaching Effectiveness Evaluation Project: Final Report*. Raleigh, NC: Quality Assurance Program, NCDPI.

Group for Effective Teaching. (1985a). *Carolina Teaching Performance Assessment System: Observer's Manual*. Raleigh, NC: Quality Assurance Program, NCDPI.

Group for Effective Teaching. (1985b). *Carolina Performance Assessment System: Results of a Limited Field Test: Final report*. Raleigh, NC: Quality Assurance Program, NCDPI.

Hall, J., Leloudis, J., Korstad, R., Murphy, M., Jones, L., and Daly, C. (1990). *Like a Family: The Making of a Southern Cotton Mill World*. Chapel Hill, NC: University of North Carolina Press.

Holdzkom, D., Kuligowski, B., and Stacy, D. (1990). *Better Teaching For Better Learning: Student Achievement Results in a 4-year Pilot of the North Carolina Career Development Plan*. Paper presented at the Annual Meeting of the American Educational Research Association, Boston, MA. (ERIC Document Reproduction Service No. ED 333 022).

Inman, W. (1982a). *Reliability of the Teacher and Principal Performance Appraisal Instruments*. Raleigh, NC: North Carolina State Board of Education.

Inman, W. (1982b). *Reactions of Teachers, Principals, and Superintendents to 1981–82 Performance Appraisals*. Raleigh, NC: North Carolina State Board of Education.

Kuligowski, B., and Holdzkom, D. (1991). *A Progress Report on District Proposals for Implementing School Improvement and Accountability Plans*. Paper presented at the Annual Meeting of the American Education Research Association, Chicago, IL.

Kuligowski, B., Holdzkom, D., and French, R. (1993). Teacher Performance Evaluation in the Southern States: Forms and Functions. *Journal of Personnel Evaluation in Education* 6: 335–358.

Lortie, D. (1975). *Schoolteacher: A Sociological Study*. Chicago: University of Chicago Press.

McCall, W. (1952). *Measurement of Teacher Merit*. Raleigh, NC: North Carolina Department of Public Instruction.

National Board for Professional Teaching Standards. (1989). *Toward High and Rigorous Standards For the Teaching Profession: A Summary.* New York: Author.

National Commission on Excellence in Education. (1983). *A Nation at Risk: The Imperative For Educational Reform.* Washington, DC: US Department of Education.

National Education Association. (1988). A letter addressed to Ms. Marian Stallings, North Carolina Association of Educators, dated January 7.

North Carolina Association of Educators. (1986). *Career Ladder Pilot Survey Analysis: A Summary Report of Major Findings.* Raleigh, NC: Author.

North Carolina Department of Public Instruction. (1965). *The North Carolina Merit Pay Study: A Four-Year Experimental Study in Three Pilot Centers.* Raleigh, NC: Author.

North Carolina Department of Public Instruction. (1985). *North Carolina Career Development Plan: Guide for Pilot/Field Test Implementation, 1985–86.* Raleigh, NC: Author.

North Carolina Department of Public Instruction. (1992). *Statistical Profile of North Carolina Schools.* Raleigh, NC: Author.

North Carolina Department of Public Instruction. (1994). *North Carolina School Improvement and Accountability Act (Senate Bill 2): Report of 1993 Performance.* Raleigh, NC: Author.

North Carolina General Assembly (1990). *General Statutes of the State of North Carolina.* Raleigh, NC: Author.

North Carolina Senate. (1989). *Senate Bill No. 2: The School Improvement and Accountability Act.* Raleigh, NC: North Carolina General Assembly.

Olson, L. (June/July 1990). Few Takers for Waivers. *Teacher Magazine* Vol. 1 (9): 16–19.

Ouchi, W. (1981). *Theory Z.* New York: Avon Books.

Schlechty, P., and Vance, V. (1983). Recruitment, Selection, and Retention: The Shape of the Teaching Force. *Elementary School Journal* 83 (#4): 469–487.

Stacey, D., Holdzkom, D., and Kuligowski, B. (1989). Effectiveness of the North Carolina Teacher Performance Appraisal System. *Journal of Personnel Evaluation in Education* 3:79–106.

4

Integrating Professional Development, Teacher Evaluation, and Student Learning: The Evolution of Teacher Evaluation Policy in Connecticut

Edward F. Iwanicki and Douglas A. Rindone

Introduction

Few issues in educational reform have received more attention than teacher evaluation. Teacher evaluation provides information about the quality of instruction; it provides data regarding teachers' professional growth needs; and increasingly, the teacher evaluation process provides feedback on the extent to which teachers are successful in fostering valued student outcomes. Since decisions as to continued employment are made on the basis of information gathered through the teacher evaluation process, it is important that this process be conducted in a consistent, fair, and equitable manner.

Since the mid-1970s, Connecticut has taken leadership in the reform of teacher evaluation practices in schools through three major initiatives:

1. The Teacher Evaluation Act of 1974
2. The Education Enhancement Act of 1986
3. The Systemic Reform Initiative of 1993

The Teacher Evaluation Act of 1974 focused the evaluation process on professional growth and the improvement of the student learning experience. The Education Enhancement Act of 1986 provided the resources for school districts to refine their teacher evaluation practices on the basis of the then current research on teaching, learning, and teacher evaluation. The Systemic Reform Initiative of 1993 led to the integration of professional development, teacher evaluation, and school improvement with a common focus on student learning.

This chapter consists of two parts. Part I contains a description of the three major teacher evaluation policy initiatives which have been implemented in Connecticut over the past two decades. Part II includes a discussion of what we have learned about teacher evaluation practice as a result of these policy initiatives. The discussion of what we have learned about teacher evaluation practice is organized around the following issues (a) teacher evaluation in organizational context, (b) philosophy and purposes of teacher evaluation, (c) evaluation criteria, and (d) evaluation procedures.

I. Connecticut's Teacher Evaluation Policy Initiatives

The Teacher Evaluation Act of 1974

Connecticut began to address the need to make teacher evaluation a more professional process in the mid-1970s. Public Act 74–278, An Act Concerning Teacher Evaluation, became effective on July 1, 1974.[1] This law defined "teacher" to include each employee below the rank of superintendent who holds a certificate or permit issued by the State Board of Education. It required superintendents of schools to evaluate teachers annually and it required the State Board of Education to establish minimum performance criteria for teacher evaluation. School systems were given five years to comply with the requirements of this new law.

An Advisory Committee on Teacher Evaluation, comprised of representatives of various education groups throughout the state, was appointed. With the assistance of this committee, the State Board of Education adopted four guiding principles for teacher evaluation. These guiding principles were critical since they set a new and more professional tone for teacher evaluation which continues in many respects today. In 1974, teacher evaluation was typically a process for describing and rating teaching, too often on the basis of vague criteria. The guiding principles, as presented below, portrayed teacher evaluation as an improvement-oriented process for helping school districts to better achieve their own educational goals. From this point on it was clear that the primary (albeit not sole) focus of the teacher evaluation process in Connecticut would be on teachers' professional growth and school improvement.

The Guiding Principles

I. The primary purpose of teacher evaluation is the improvement of the student learning experience.

II. The local school district establishes its own educational goals. Such goals form the basis of the teacher evaluation program.

III. Ample time is provided for this goal-oriented approach to teacher evaluation.

IV. A fiscal support system is established for the purpose of assisting school districts to prepare for and conduct evaluation.

Two problems were encountered as the new Teacher Evaluation Act and associated guiding principles were disseminated.

> Obstacles in the way of developing a plan based on these principles were the association of teacher evaluation with the Tenure Act and the requirement for minimum performance criteria. The former implied an evaluation system dominated by administrators in a legalistic setting. The latter required the setting of exact standards at the state level and was contrary to the feelings of the Committee [Advisory Committee on Teacher Evaluation].
>
> Members of the Education Committee of the State Legislature were asked to join in a dialogue over these issues. It was mutually decided to recommend changes in legislation; i.e., that teacher evaluation be removed from the Tenure Act; that the State Board of Education establish guidelines for the development of local evaluation plans [rather than minimum performance criteria]. These suggestions were accepted by the Legislature and incorporated in the present act [Teacher Evaluation Act of 1974]. (Connecticut State Department of Education, 1977, p. 2)

With the assistance of the Advisory Committee on Teacher Evaluation, the State Board of Education established eleven guidelines to provide school systems direction in the development of their teacher evaluation plans. These guidelines as presented below were based substantially on the work of McNally (1973).

The Guidelines

I. Each professional shall cooperatively determine with the evaluator(s) the objectives upon which his or her evaluation shall be based.

II. The evaluation program is cooperatively planned, carried out, and evaluated by all levels of the staff.

III. The purposes of the evaluation program are clearly stated in writing and are well know to the evaluators and to those who are evaluated.

IV. The general responsibilities and specific tasks of the teacher's position should be comprehensively defined and this definition should serve as the frame of reference for evaluation.

V. The accountability relationship of each position should be clearly determined. The teacher should know and understand the means by which he or she will be evaluated in relation to that position.

VI. Evaluations are more diagnostic than judgmental. The process should help analyze the teaching and learning to plan how to improve.

VII. Evaluation should take into account influences on the learning environment such as material and professional resources.

VIII. Self-evaluation is an essential aspect of the program. Teachers are given the opportunity to evaluate themselves in positive and constructive ways.

IX. The self-image and self-respect of teachers should be maintained and enhanced. Positive self-concepts can be fostered by an effective evaluation plan.

X. The nature of the evaluations is such that it encourages teacher creativity and experimentation in planning and guiding the teacher-learning experiences provided children.

XI. The program makes ample provision for clear, personalized, constructive feedback.

School systems were given five years to develop and implement teacher evaluation programs which complied with these guidelines. A local education agency (LEA) was required to form a teacher evaluation steering committee for this purpose. Each year this representative committee of teachers and administrators was required to submit a written report to the State Department of Education on the progress it had made in developing and implementing its new teacher evaluation program. Criteria were developed for each guideline to provide more specific direction to school systems as they worked on their teacher evaluation programs. Later these criteria were used to assess the extent to which teacher evaluation programs complied with state guidelines.

During year one, school systems were encouraged to prepare a plan for how the teacher evaluation program would be developed and implemented. Then in subsequent years they simply updated these plans. Forms were developed by the Connecticut State Department of Education to facilitate the planning and reporting process. Plans to comply with the teacher evaluation guidelines were developed using the Activity Analysis approach (Iwanicki 1976). The activities to be pursued for each guideline were listed along with planned starting and completion dates. Also, LEAs provided an overall rating each year of the extent to which each guideline had been implemented using a scale ranging from 0 to 100 percent.

Annual teacher evaluation reports were analyzed each year by the State Department of Education and feedback was provided to LEAs.

LEAs were commended for the things they were doing well; suggestions were made for improvement; and some misunderstandings of the guidelines were clarified. As annual reports were analyzed, every effort was made to identify things school systems were doing especially well so they could be shared with other school systems. When school systems submitted their plans or updates, they were required to include supporting documentation. For example, if a school system said it provided training for all evaluators in classroom observation skills, then it had to provide sufficient documentation of how this was done. If in reviewing such documentation it looked as though the school system trained its administrators in classroom observation skills especially well, then this approach would be "flagged" and shared with other LEAs. Since in the mid-1970s, the literature on more collaborative, professional approaches to teacher evaluation was fairly sparse, this practice was critical. Thus, Connecticut school systems had opportunities to learn from each other's experiences.

It is important to note that the review of annual teacher evaluation reports was more than a paper screening. On the average, about ten school systems were visited yearly by a State Department of Education site visitation team. The purposes of these visits were to review how the LEA was implementing its teacher evaluation plan, to make recommendations as to how this plan might be strengthened, and to identify any exemplary practices that could be shared with other school systems. Such visits included a meeting with the superintendent and teacher evaluation steering committee to discuss the teacher evaluation plan on file with the State Department of Education, meetings with principals and teachers to examine how this plan was being implemented at the school level, and a paper and pencil survey of a random sample of professional staff to determine the extent to which they believed their school system's teacher evaluation process complied with the state guidelines.

During the five year period which school systems had to strengthen their teacher evaluation practices, resources were provided by the State Department of Education to orient school system personnel to new developments in teacher evaluation. Exemplary practices were shared. Workshops were conducted using in- and out-of-state consultants. Guidebooks were developed (Carrano 1978). A needs assessment model was designed for strengthening a school district's evaluation practices, Inservice Training for the Evaluation of Teaching (Capitol Region Education Council 1976).

During the 1978–79 school year, the final year of the five year planning and development period, it was found that about 80 percent of the school systems were implementing new teacher evaluation programs which complied with the state guidelines. The other 20 percent of the school systems were proceeding in good faith to implement such programs during the next school year. During the planning and development period, educators in Connecticut acquired a better understanding of what good teacher evaluation should be and implemented new evaluation procedures consistent with such beliefs. The problem which resulted was that many administrators and evaluators were not comfortable with what they were implementing. As one administrator shared in confidence, "I know this is the way we should evaluate teachers. But while it's better, I don't feel comfortable with it yet. I don't see how I can find the time to do this with all of my teachers."

In reflecting on the impact of the Teacher Evaluation Act of 1974, many educators have noted that it changed people's perceptions of what teacher evaluation should be, but did not have the desired impact on "the improvement of the student learning experience." This was because too many administrators were not implementing the new teacher evaluation practices which were developed in the "spirit" of the state guidelines. What we may not have been sensitive to during this period was that we were doing more than just strengthening teacher evaluation practices. We were changing substantially the role and responsibilities of the principal. The resistance of many principals to the new procedures for teacher evaluation, resistance which took several forms, may have been their way of saying: "This isn't what I opted for when I chose to become a principal." In fact, five principals retired for this reason at the conclusion of a summer workshop on teacher evaluation conducted by one of the authors.

From 1979 to the mid-1980s the Connecticut State Department of Education continued to monitor the implementation of teacher evaluation programs and supported school systems' efforts to extend the development of their programs even though they complied with state guidelines. Any school system could modify its teacher evaluation program, provided such changes were approved by the Department of Education. As attention began to be focused on the reform of schools and teaching in the mid-1980s, the time was right to further strengthen teacher evaluation practices in Connecticut schools.

The Education Enhancement Act of 1986

The Education Enhancement Act resulted from the recommendations of The Report of the Governor's Commission on Equity and Excellence in Education (1985). More specifically, teacher evaluation was addressed through those recommendations dealing with Career Development and Recognition.

The Commission studied the concepts and practices involved in career ladders, differentiated staffing and professional teacher evaluation systems. The Commission believes that, properly planned and implemented systems such as these hold promise for making teaching a more attractive career (p. 17).

The Education Enhancement Act included provisions for establishing a two year Commission on Career Incentives and Teacher Evaluation. The charge to this Commission was to

(1) hire consultants to provide school districts with training and technical services, (2) distribute information regarding teacher evaluation and career incentive plans to all school districts, and (3) adopt regulations for the development of local evaluation and career incentive plans (Commission on Career Incentives and Teacher Evaluation 1986a, p. 1).

In January 1987, Public Act 87–2,[2] An Act Concerning Revisions in the Education Enhancement Act, was passed. Section 10 of this act provided grants to school districts to revise existing and/or to develop new teacher evaluation programs; Section 11 provided grants to assist school districts in the implementation, assessment, and improvement of their revised or new teacher evaluation programs; Section 12 repealed Section 10–151b of the Connecticut General Statutes (Public Act 74–278, An Act Concerning Teacher Evaluation) and required the State Board of Education to review and revise its teacher evaluation guidelines with the assistance of the Commission on Career Incentives and Teacher Evaluation.

In May 1987, the State Board of Education adopted new Guidelines for Teacher Evaluation Programs at the recommendation of the Commission on Career Incentives and Teacher Evaluation. In developing these new Guidelines, the Commission wanted to preserve the strengths and to address the shortcomings of the prior guidelines. Also, it wanted to take advantage of new developments in the field of teacher evaluation. A working draft of *The Personnel Evaluation Standards* (Joint Committee on Standards for Educational Evaluation 1988) as well as the recent Rand Study, *Teacher Evaluation: A Study of Effective Practices* (Wise, Darling-Hammond, McLaughlin, and Bernstein 1984) were included among the primary documents reviewed by the Commission. The Commission was committed to developing a set of guidelines

which would encourage local school districts to undertake supervision for the purposes of improving instruction through teacher development and simultaneously acknowledge the responsibility of evaluators to take prescriptive action in those cases where teacher performance—even with professional development—is not satisfactory (Connecticut State Department of Education 1990, p. P–2).

The nineteen guidelines which resulted from the Commission's work focused on the areas noted below.

I. Statement of Purpose
II. Focus of the Evaluation Plan
III. Guiding Beliefs of the Evaluation Plan
IV. Definition of Teacher and Evaluator
V. Elements of the Teacher Evaluation Plan
VI. Staff Involvement in Development of the Plan
VII. Responsibilities of Teachers and Evaluators
VIII. Verification of Responsibilities
IX. Enhancement of Self-respect
X. Environmental Influences
XI. Allocation of Resources
XII. The Evaluation Period
XIII. Feedback and Evaluation Report
XIV. Recommendations for Professional Growth and Improvement
XV. Training for Evaluation
XVI. Mentorships
XVII. Training for Teachers
XVIII. Coordination with the BEST Program
XIX. Evaluation of the Evaluation Plan

The Guidelines require teacher evaluation plans to be based on three key elements: local district goals, written definitions of each professional position enumerating the general responsibilities and specific tasks of the position and written objectives [focusing in part on the improvement of instruction and student learning in the classroom] shall be developed as a result of the teacher and evaluator working together. Additionally, the Connecticut Teaching Competencies must be reflected in the written objectives whenever the written description of the position indicates the teacher has primary responsibility for teaching. . . . All districts were required to show full compliance with the new Guidelines for Teacher Evaluation Programs by June 15, 1989 (Connecticut State Department of Education 1990, p. P–2).

It is important to note that these developments in teacher evaluation were complemented by Connecticut's reform efforts in the education, certification, and induction of new teachers. Before prospective teachers were granted an Initial Educator Certificate, they needed to pass an essential skills examination (CONNCEPT) as well as a test of subject-matter knowledge (CONNTENT). Before beginning teachers were granted a Provisional Educator Certificate, they needed to complete the Beginning Educator Support and Training (BEST) Program. As part of BEST, teachers needed to pass a classroom assessment based on the Connecticut Competency Instrument (CCI). A teacher cannot be employed in a public school system in Connecticut without an Initial Educator Certificate. Once employed, that teacher has two years to quality for the Provisional Educator Certificate. These new standards enhanced significantly the quality of teachers entering the profession. The extent to which these standards have impacted the education profession is conveyed by the data shared below (Martin 1992, p.2).

- Over 25,000 individuals have taken the Connecticut Competency Examination for Prospective Teachers (CONNCEPT) or received a waiver since 1986.
- Over 6,000 college students have completed their student teaching since 1987 under the supervision of cooperating teachers who have been trained in the Connecticut Teaching Competencies.
- Close to 5,000 CONNTENT exams (subject-area knowledge assessment) have been administered to candidates for teacher certification since 1988.
- Close to 2,000 beginning teachers have participated in the Beginning Educator Support and Training (BEST) Program since 1989: in 1991–1992 there were nearly 800 teachers in the program.
- Nearly 7,000 practicing teachers have been trained as cooperating teachers and mentors since 1986.
- Over 1,000 teachers and administrators have been trained as [BEST] assessors since 1988.
- Cumulatively, over 25 percent of all active teachers, approximately 10,500, have been impacted by the BEST Program as beginning teachers, mentors and assessors.

If ever there were a "Golden Age" of teacher evaluation in Connecticut, the late 1980s was that time. Connecticut's economy was thriving. Salaries were increased to make Connecticut teachers the highest paid in the nation. Ample resources were available to develop and implement state of the art teacher evaluation programs. One million dollars was allocated to support local school districts' efforts to strengthen their teacher evaluation programs. The more enlightened school districts used such monies over the two year developmental period to pilot and refine new, more productive approaches to the teacher evaluation process. Others simply made the necessary modifications in their teacher evaluation programs to "comply" with the new guidelines.

A critical flaw in this effort to strengthen the quality of teacher evaluation was the lack of central leadership. While the Commission on Career Incentives and Teacher Evaluation gave substantial monies to individual school districts to strengthen their teacher evaluation practices, no funds were appropriated for the necessary staff positions at the Department of Education to provide the leadership and coordination necessary for this major initiative. Early on in the planning process, the six regional educational service centers encouraged school systems to fund regional projects for strengthening teacher evaluation practices, but this concept took hold in only one region. Later the Connecticut Institute for Personnel Evaluation was formed. This was a partnership venture between the Connecticut State Department of Education, the Connecticut Center for Leadership in Educational Administration Development (LEAD), the Department of Educational Leadership at The University of Connecticut, and local school districts. The purpose of the Institute was to strengthen personnel evaluation practices in schools through the dissemination of information, training, and research. Membership in the Institute was voluntary. While over sixty school districts became members and participated in the activities of the Institute, these tended to be the smaller school districts which felt that this would be the best way to use some of their limited developmental funds. Teacher Evaluation Program Development Grants ranged from $1,000 for small school districts to over $40,000 for the larger cities. The only stipulation placed on spending these monies was that they could not be used to supplant funds for existing district programs or services. They could be

properly used in a variety of ways, such as: (a) stipends for the development panel, (b) hiring consultants . . . , (c) hiring support staff for the panel and purchasing materials, (d) seminar fees or tuition payments for panel members, (e) travel expenses, or (f) hiring substitute teachers so district staff can visit other districts to view their existing [teacher evaluation] plans (Commission on Career Incentives and Teacher Evaluation 1986b, p. 3).

In addition to these developmental funds, the Connecticut legislature appropriated three million dollars to support the implementation of the new teacher evaluation programs. This was not a one year appropriation, but rather, a continuing appropriation. For example, a moderate-sized community was scheduled to receive a yearly allotment of around $50,000 for the implementation of its new teacher evaluation program as long as this legislation remained in effect. This community planned to use such funds to supplement the salaries of elementary school teachers who were selected as lead teachers. In addition to their classroom responsibilities, these teachers would serve as peer coaches and supervisors. The lead teacher position was created through that district's career incentives program to complement its revised teacher evaluation program by providing the human resources necessary for quality personnel evaluation and supervision.

While most school systems viewed the implementation funds for teacher evaluation as an opportunity to strengthen the quality of teaching and learning in schools, some were leery of making changes for fear that the state would not continue to support these changes in the future. Their fears were not unfounded. Teacher evaluation implementation funds were cut by the legislature during the first year of implementation. The explanations for this action varied. Some have commented that funds were cut because the teacher evaluation programs developed by school districts did not meet the expectations of those who supported the original legislation. The programs lacked effective procedures for removing incompetent teachers from the classroom. Others have attributed this cut to a rumor being circulated among legislators that some superintendents viewed such monies as a "slush fund" and thus, did not really need them. Probably the best explanation for the cut was that the state was running out of money. Over three hundred million dollars in additional funding had been allocated to support the new reforms which resulted from *The Report of the Governor's Commission on Equity and Excellence in Education* (1985). Such reforms were funded through a state surplus, but that surplus vanished by the late 1980s. Implementation funds for teacher evaluation were cut as the legislature realized it was on the verge of dealing with some serious economic problems.

The impact of the Education Enhancement Act of 1986 on teacher evaluation practices in Connecticut schools is difficult to determine. By the summer of 1989 all school districts submitted teacher evaluation programs to the Department of Education which complied with the new Guidelines for Teacher Evaluation Programs. Many of these programs included provisions for more enlightened, productive approaches to the teacher evaluation process. Unfortunately these programs were developed when ample resources were available to schools and the focus of educators' efforts was on innovation. As Connecticut experienced its worst economic recession in history during the early 1990s, the atmosphere in the public schools changed dramatically. In many school districts, attention shifted to the need to survive with the limited resources available. Teacher evaluation was not afforded priority status under these conditions.

The mid- to late 1990s will be an interesting period for education as Connecticut recovers from its recession. While all school districts have gone through some difficult times in recent years, this experience has left some districts in better shape than others. When teachers' salaries were raised as a result of the Education Enhancement Act, the responsibility for maintaining these higher salaries was turned over gradually to cities and towns. As this financial burden was assumed by local communities, taxes were often increased. In communities with higher concentrations of senior citizens on fixed incomes and/or families impacted by the massive layoffs of the recession, substantial tax increases were not accepted quietly by the public. The public went to the source of the tax increases, the teacher unions. In many situations this issue pulled teacher and community leaders together to resolve their differences productively. Often both the community and teachers union made the concessions necessary to maintain a quality educational program. Sometimes the inability of teacher and community leaders to resolve their differences over school funding issues resulted in resentment and distrust. Although it was not widely prevalent, this problem of trust between teachers and the community had to be addressed in a serious and timely manner since it diminished the quality of all aspects of schooling, including the teacher evaluation and professional growth process.

In looking to the future, it is clear that Connecticut school districts as well as others across the nation will be expected to accomplish more than in the past without a proportionate increased in resources. Whether schools are successful or not in the future will be a function of their ability to better integrate the various aspects of schooling, that is, to approach school reform systemically. In Connecticut, teacher evaluation has been integrated with professional development and school improvement as part of the state's systemic reform initiative.

The Systemic Reform Initiative of 1993

Two critical aspects of Connecticut's systemic reform initiative are (a) the Department of Education's definition of comprehensive professional development, and (b) the manner in which the Department of Education will assist school systems to develop programs consistent with this definition. From the department's perspective,

> Comprehensive professional development is an ongoing process for determining and addressing what educators need to know and be able to do individually and collectively to ensure that each student performs at high levels. Effective comprehensive professional development includes teacher performance evaluation and results in:
>
> • a way of thinking by educators as to what they believe, what is important for students to learn, and what they need to know and be able to do to ensure that each student performs at high levels;
>
> • a way of working where educators feel comfortable and confident working collaboratively with other educators, parents, and business and community members to ensure that each student performs at high levels;

• **a way of monitoring** where educators assume the responsibility for evaluating their performance individually and collectively based on student need and performance; and

• **a way of focusing** by educators on their actions to ensure that they are leading to the achievement of desired student outcomes (Connecticut State Department of Education 1993, p.1).

Consistent with this definition, the Department of Education has developed a series of "Principles of Good Practice" to guide school districts in the development and implementation of their comprehensive professional development plans.

The major outcome resulting from the development and implementation of a comprehensive professional development plan, including teacher evaluation, is that:

Educators, working with each other, parents, the community and supporting agencies, create a learning environment that enables each student to perform at high levels (Connecticut State Department of Education 1993, p. 3).

With respect to how the Department of Education will assist school districts to develop their comprehensive professional development programs, it is noted that,

The guidelines [for comprehensive professional development programs] do not focus on monitoring activities. Rather, we [the Department] have renewed our commitment to serve and assist you and your school communities as you work to incorporate the very best practices into all levels of your efforts to ensure that each of your students performs at high levels (Connecticut State Department of Education 1993, p. i).

In summary, Connecticut's systemic reform initiative has integrated the processes of professional development, teacher evaluation, and school improvement with a common focus on student learning. The term "comprehensive" has been used to convey this need for integration. Rather than setting guidelines with which school districts must comply as in the past, the Department of Education has shared some "Principles of Good Practice" to guide school systems in the development of their comprehensive professional development plans. Rather than monitor such school district efforts, the department has made a commitment to provide assistance and support. December 15, 1994, has been set by the commissioner as the deadline for the completion of comprehensive professional development plans, with implementation beginning during the 1994–95 school year (Connecticut General Statute Section 10–220a(b)(2)). While school districts are required to develop and to implement these plans according to this schedule, they are not required to submit these plans to the Department of Education for approval as in the past. Sclan (1994, p. 22) notes that . . .

> The evaluation efforts of the Connecticut Department of Education appear to be in the forefront of state-level reform regarding teacher professionalization. In their new evaluation plan, they address the central need to confirm teachers' differentiated roles as *professionals*. Connecticut legislatively links teacher evaluation with professional development, which inevitably strengthens teacher professionalism and school performance.

II. What Have We Learned About Teacher Evaluation

Teacher Evaluation in Organizational Context

In much of the literature on teacher evaluation the assumption is made that the key to more productive teacher evaluation is to involve teachers and administrators in the development of the process, provide them with the appropriate in-service support to implement the process, and in time (i.e., 3–5 years) you will see positive results with respect to improvements in the quality of teaching and learning in schools. After almost twenty years experience with teacher evaluation in Connecticut, we see that this does not happen. One explanation for the lack of results has been that the process developed was flawed in some way—"we need to build a better mouse trap." While in some cases there may be some truth to this explanation, we need to look further. There are too many school systems in Connecticut that have implemented sound, professional approaches to the development of effective teacher evaluation programs and provided appropriate in-service support for the implementation of these programs, but now have little evidence to show that these programs are improving the quality of teaching and learning in schools. These teacher evaluation programs look good on paper, but they are just not productive.

Our contention is that effective teacher evaluation programs are productive to the extent that they are consistent with and integrated into the organizational context of the school system and its schools. There are certain beliefs about the teaching-learning process in schools which the leadership of the school system holds to be true. These beliefs help shape the organizational context of the system. There are certain beliefs about the teaching-learning process which teachers, supervisors, and administrators at the school building level hold to be true. These beliefs help shape the organizational context of the school building. To the extent that these system and building level beliefs are consistent with the assumptions underlying more effective teacher evaluation practices, there is a higher probability that the teacher evaluation process will be more productive.

Building a Professional Organizational Context

T. J. Sergiovanni (1988) takes the position that schools exist for two purposes, (a) to foster student learning, and (b) to promote meaningful professional growth among staff. Staff are the human resources of the school organization. Student learning potential is realized to the extent that the school system invests continually in the development of its human resources. This position is very compatible with the professional growth orientation taken in Connecticut's new Guidelines for the Development of Comprehensive Professional Development Plans. Now, let us say that the Yahoo Board of Education does not support this position. On the contrary, it believes that teachers are being paid darn well, and thus, they should be responsible for and pay for their own professional development. The board sees to it that the 180 school days are focused on the teachers doing what they are paid to do, teach kids. Those mandatory in-service days that are required are organized around programs that meet what the board and central office administrators perceive as the critical staff development needs of teachers in order for the school system to comply with new state mandates. It is difficult, if not impossible, to implement more effective teacher evaluation practices in such an organizational context.

Sergiovanni's (1985) metaphor of "mindscapes" and "landscapes" is an interesting way of looking at the actions of the Yahoo Board of Education. This board had a certain belief (mindscape) about professional development (i.e., it is the teacher's responsibility) and was consistent in putting that belief into practice (landscape) by not supporting teachers' professional development. While one may not accept the position on professional development taken by the Yahoo Board of Education, it is clear that its beliefs guided its actions; there was consistency between its mindscape and landscape. Let us turn to another setting, the Soundville Public Schools. By contrast, the Soundville Board of Education has always believed in the need to support teacher professional development. It has used this mindscape to create a landscape where resources are provided to support teachers taking courses and attending conferences, provided such activities have benefit for the school system. Numerous teacher initiated staff and professional development programs have been planned at the team/department, building, and school system levels. While not all such activities are conducted during released time, the equivalent of fourteen half days have been allocated for staff and professional development activities.

The intent here is to show that the organizational context of the *school system* does impact the ability to implement more professional and effective growth-oriented approaches to teacher evaluation. The organizational context of the *school* also determines the extent to which such practices can be implemented. Weick's (1976) work on school organizations as loosely coupled systems indicated that staff in individual schools have considerable control over their destiny. For this reason we can find schools, both "beacons of success" and "pockets of pestilence," that are anomalies given the other characteristics of the school systems in which they reside. More successful schools are healthy school organizations (Miles 1965) where teachers function as professionals in a climate of respect and trust (Darling-Hammond, Wise, and Pease 1983). Healthy school organizations are those where (a) goals are reasonably clear and well accepted by staff, (b) there is good communication, (c) staff are empowered to make decisions, and (d) staff derive a sense of fulfillment from their work. The probability of implementing productive, growth-oriented teacher evaluation practices in healthy school contexts where teachers function as professionals is excellent, especially as compared to those schools organized along more traditional, bureaucratic lines of authority where teachers are viewed more as workers than professionals.

In many schools, bureaucracy is not something we impose on teachers, but rather, a culture to which teachers and administrators have become accustomed. In more bureaucratic, hierarchical school systems, principals and teachers are told what to do and not encouraged to think as professionals. This can become a comfortable arrangement in school settings where the problems are serious, the resources are limited, and learning distractions are plentiful. Principals and teachers in such school settings do not have to be accountable. They can just blame the system.

Even in successful schools where principals and teachers function as professionals, effective teacher evaluation practices may not be having an appreciable impact on student learning. The reason for this is largely due to the fact that teacher evaluation is implemented in isolation rather than in combination with other school improvement initiatives. Teachers may all be growing professionally in these settings, but in so many different ways that the impact of such growth on the quality of learning in the school is difficult to determine. Also, effective teacher evaluation programs that are implemented in isolation are eventually placed on the "back burner" when the next school initiative comes along. As one teacher commented, "We gave teacher evaluation a lot of attention a few years ago when the new process came in, but now we are into math manipulatives as part of our school-wide improvement plan."

Integrating Teacher Evaluation, Staff Development, and
School Improvement

It is critical for teacher evaluation to be implemented in a more integrated manner, namely in combination with school improvement and staff development (Iwanicki 1990). We have given considerable thought to this integration through our work with schools and have concluded that school improvement is critical to the productivity of both staff development and teacher evaluation. In systems where a continuous school improvement or total quality improvement process is in place, teacher evaluation and staff development can be used productively to support that improvement so it has an appreciable impact on student learning.

For example, one school set the following improvement goal: *Students will meet world class standards in mathematics in three years.* Given this goal, some implications were drawn for teaching and learning as noted below.

- More problem solving activities will be included in the teaching of mathematics.
- Students will be involved more actively in the instructional process through the use of manipulatives and group projects.
- Students will exhibit an increase in problem-solving ability on district and state performance measures.

This goal and its associated implications set a focus for staff development and teacher evaluation. As classroom observations were conducted, aspects of teaching problem solving were a focus (albeit not the sole focus) of the conversations that transpired in both the pre- and post-observation conferences. Also, this goal and its associated implications created a broad range of possibilities that teachers considered in developing objectives that served as the basis of their professional growth plans. Some professional growth plans were even developed collaboratively by teams of teachers. As the superintendent commented, "When the process is done this way there is less threat and teachers understand how it will make a difference for kids." The commitment to and active involvement of the superintendent in this integrated approach to teacher evaluation is critical to its effective implementation (McLaughlin and Pfeifer 1988).

State agency leadership also is critical to meaningful and productive school improvement. Departments of education need to provide direction to the school improvement process by setting expectations for learning, assessment, and teaching. Curriculum frameworks need to be developed to provide school districts with a better understanding of what students need to know and be able to do. Performance standards need to be developed to inform school districts of (a) what is expected of students with respect to these frameworks, and (b) how these expectations will be assessed. Teaching standards need to be developed to convey to teachers what they need to know and be able to do in light of the new curriculum frameworks and performance standards.

This section on Teacher Evaluation in Organizational Context is important for two reasons. First, often this issue is not addressed in discussions of effective teacher evaluation practices. Second, this is the most critical aspect of effective teacher evaluation. Our experiences have led us to conclude that teacher evaluation will not be productive (i.e., have an appreciable impact on student learning) unless it is implemented in a school setting characterized by a relatively high degree of professionalism and preferably, it is implemented as part of an ongoing school improvement process. Effective teacher evaluation is not as much an issue of appropriate instrumentation as it is one of appropriate organization.

In summary, the issues discussed in this section have at least two major implications for strengthening teacher evaluation practices in schools as follows:

1. Teacher evaluation practices cannot be strengthened unless healthy school environments are created where principals and teachers work as professionals in a climate of respect and trust.
2. The impact of teacher evaluation on student learning is enhanced when implemented as part of a continuous school improvement process that is also supported by quality professional development.

Philosophy and Purposes for Teacher Evaluation

The philosophy and purposes are the foundation of the teacher evaluation process. The philosophy includes the goal(s) of teacher evaluation (i.e., to improve the quality of teaching and learning in schools) as well as the basic beliefs about schools, teaching, learning, and evaluation that guide the process. The purposes state how teacher evaluation will be used in schools. The purposes that tend to appear most often in the teacher evaluation programs developed by Connecticut school systems are the following:

1. **Accountability**—to insure the public that only effective teachers continue in the classroom.
2. **School Improvement**—to promote continuous school improvement and the enhancement of student learning.
3. **Professional Growth**—to foster the professional growth of new and continuing teachers.
4. **Selection**—to ensure that the most qualified teachers are hired.

Too often, school districts develop a statement of philosophy and purposes and then focus their efforts on developing a teacher evaluation process without looking back at this statement. Such school districts get caught up in the procedures, rather than the substance of teacher evaluation. The substance of the evaluation process lies in its philosophy and purposes. A teacher evaluation process is effective to the extent that it is successful in achieving its goal(s) and purposes. If the goal of teacher evaluation is to improve the student learning experience, then the process is effective to the extent that it is making this happen.

The effectiveness of teacher evaluation programs should be assessed by reviewing teacher evaluation reports rather than procedures. If the evaluation reports provide evidence that the program is successful in achieving its goal(s) and purposes, then it is a good program. To the extent that a purpose is not being achieved, then the evaluation procedures need to be strengthened in that area.

Evaluation Criteria

One of the principles of good practice in developing and carrying out a Comprehensive Professional Development Plan is to "clearly state in writing the responsibilities of all educators" (Connecticut State Department of Education 1993, p.4). But how should these responsibilities or criteria be determined? While the research on effective teaching is useful when defining the duties of the effective teacher, it is really the profession, and the teachers themselves that make this determination. These sources were tapped when Connecticut developed the Connecticut Competency Instrument (CCI) for the certification assessment of beginning teachers. In developing the CCI, reviews of the literature were conducted, criteria of effective teaching were derived from these reviews, and criteria were refined by teams of teachers. As a result of this process, teachers accepted the criteria that were developed as valid indicators of their performance.

Although the CCI was developed for the assessment of beginning teachers, it was also adapted for the evaluation of experienced teachers (Iwanicki 1988). Teachers readily accepted this adaptation, the Indicators and Defining Attributes of Effective Teaching, for at least two reasons, (a) the indicators and defining attributes made sense to them, and (b) teachers felt that it was reasonable to expect experienced teachers to demonstrate the same teaching behaviors as were being required for beginning teachers. As the initial version of these indicators and defining attributes was applied to the evaluation of teaching, it became clear that it was appropriate for evaluating competency, but it was not appropriate for challenging teachers to develop higher levels of proficiency.

Thus, in 1993 the Indicators and Defining Attributes of Effective Teaching were revised to make them more appropriate for challenging ex-

perienced teachers to develop higher levels of proficiency. They were revised by soliciting feedback from teachers and administrators who were
already using the indicators and defining attributes in the teacher evaluation process. In revising these indicators and defining attributes, it was
also important to examine the literature on teaching effectiveness for the
experienced teacher. E. A. Covino (1991) conducted an extensive review
of the literature on the experienced teacher that led to the validation of a
set of proficiencies for experienced teachers in Connecticut. The feedback
from teachers and administrators as well as the findings of the Covino
study were compiled by indicator and defining attribute and used to develop an expanded version of the Indicators and Defining Attributes of
Effective Teaching for experienced teachers (Iwanicki 1993). Given the
manner in which these indicators and defining attributes were developed,
they are clearly what Scriven (1987) would call duty-based descriptors of
effective teaching.

The Indicators of Effective Teaching for experienced teachers are
listed in Exhibit 4-1. Each of these indicators was elaborated upon further to included a rationale, defining attributes, and key aspects. The rationale includes the justification for the indicator in light of the literature
on effective teaching and teacher professionalism. The defining attributes
are the criteria used to evaluate teaching with respect to a particular indicator. The key aspects are what the evaluator will focus on when evaluating teaching with respect to a particular defining attribute. These key
aspects have been compiled into a guide which teachers can use to conduct a self-assessment of their performance in light of the indicators and
defining attributes of effective teaching.

The Indicators and Defining Attributes of Effective Teaching were
developed as a point of departure for teacher evaluation steering committees as they worked to refine their criteria for the evaluation of classroom teachers. In practice, they were adopted by many committees
without much modification because they were perceived as a good frame
of reference for guiding teachers and evaluators in their conversations
about how teaching and learning could be enhanced in the classroom. It
is important to note that these Indicators and Defining Attributes were
developed to guide conversations about teaching, rather than to rate
teachers. The current literature on teacher evaluation (McGreal 1990;
Good and Mulryan 1990) does not advocate using teacher ratings in the
evaluation process except for self-evaluation. When teacher ratings are
used in the evaluation process, evaluation conferences focus less on teaching and more on the rating. The evaluation conference degenerates into a
forum for negotiating the rating rather than for discussing how teaching
can be strengthened or enhanced.

EXHIBIT 4-1.   The Indicators of Effective Teaching

Planning

I. The teacher effectively plans instruction.

Management of the Classroom Environment

II. The teacher promotes a positive learning environment.

III. The teacher maintains appropriate standards of behavior.

IV. The teacher engages the students in meeting the objectives of the lesson.

V. The teacher effectively manages routines and transitions.

Instruction

VI. The teacher creates a structure for learning.

VII. The teacher develops the lesson effectively, using appropriate instructional techniques.

VIII. The teacher presents appropriate content.

IX. The teacher uses appropriate questioning techniques.

X. The teacher communicates clearly, using precise language and acceptable oral expressions.

Assessment

XI. The teacher monitors student learning and adjusts teaching when appropriate.

Professional Responsibility

XII. The teacher performs noninstructional duties.

XIII. The teacher assumes responsibility for meaningful professional growth.

XIV. The teacher assumes leadership for school improvement and professional growth.

Identifying the Critical Indicators of Effective Teaching

One reaction to the Indicators and Defining Attributes of Effective Teaching has been that they may be good for guiding the induction of new teachers or for dealing with the problems associated with marginal or incompetent teachers, but they do not really capture the essence of what distinguishes between those teachers who are more versus those teachers who are less successful in facilitating meaningful student learning. Until we capture the essence of the indicators of effective teaching, we will be limited in our efforts to enhance the quality of teaching and learning in schools.

To obtain some insights into this issue, the Indicators were cross-referenced with the Core Propositions of the National Board for Professional Teaching Standards (NBPTS 1989, p. 4) as presented below.

1. Teachers are committed to students and their learning.
2. Teachers know the subjects they teach and how to teach those subjects to students.
3. Teachers are responsible for managing and monitoring student learning.
4. Teachers think systematically about their practice and learn from their experience.
5. Teachers are members of learning communities.

These core propositions have been developed to guide the assessment of experienced teachers to determine whether they meet high and rigorous standards for the teaching profession. Thus, if there is overlap between an indicator and a core proposition, then there is a good probability that the indicator addresses a critical aspect of what successful experienced teachers need to know and be able to do to facilitate meaningful student learning. The NBPTS Core Propositions are cross-referenced with the indicators in Table 4-1. From Table 4-1, it is evident that there is considerable commonality between the core propositions and the general categories used to group the indicators in Exhibit 4-1:

• Core Propositions 1 and 4 have much in common with Planning
• Core Proposition 3 has much in common with Management of the Classroom Environment and Assessment
• Proposition 2 has much in common with Instruction
• Proposition 5 has much in common with Professional Responsibilites

Furthermore, the indicators listed below overlap considerably with the core propositions. Thus, if an argument were to be made for a subset of "critical indicators" that address what successful experienced teachers need to know and be able to do to facilitate meaningful student learning, then these five indicators would certainly be included.

    I. The teacher effectively plans instruction
   II. The teacher promotes a positive environment for learning

TABLE 4-1.   Relationship Between the Indicators of Effective Teaching and the National Board for Professional Teaching Standards Core Propositions

	NBPTS Core Propositions				
Indicators	1	2	3	4	5
Planning					
I	✓			✓	
Classroom Management					
II	✓		✓		
III			✓		
IV			✓		
V			✓		
Instruction					
VI					
VII	✓	✓			
VIII		✓			
IX		✓			
X		✓			
Assessment					
XI			✓		
Professional Responsibilities					
XII					✓
XIII				✓	✓
XIV					✓

VII. The teacher develops the lesson effectively using appropriate instructional techniques

XI. The teacher monitors student learning and adjusts teaching when appropriate

XIII. The teacher assumes responsibility and leadership for meaningful school improvement and professional growth

Moving Beyond the Indicators of Effective Teaching

It has become evident that all of the Indicators of Effective Teaching are important for teachers at the early stages of their careers. As just discussed, some of these indicators continue to be critical even at the later stages of a teacher's development. The problem with the indicators of effective teaching is that they are generic indicators. As shown in Figure 4-1, the generic indicators are necessary, but not sufficient descriptors of effective teaching. They need to be complemented by grade/content specific teaching standards, especially at the later stages of a teacher's development.

FIGURE 4-1.   Relative Emphasis on Generic Indicators of Effective Teaching and Grade/Content Specific Teaching Standards at Various Stages of Experience and Teacher Development

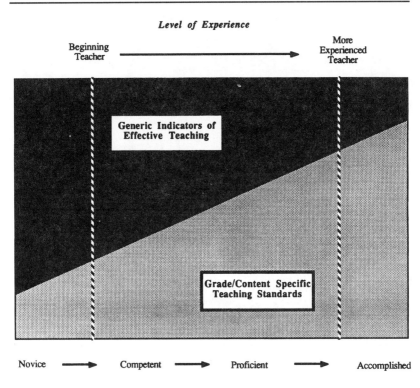

Continuum of Teacher Development

When you ask good, experienced teachers what they are doing to strengthen their teaching, they usually describe something which is central to the subject or grade level they are teaching: "I'm integrating a unit on bioethics into my biology course," or "I'm trying to develop better ways to help second graders understand part-whole relationships." As we look to develop better approaches to teacher evaluation in the future, grade/content specific teaching standards need to be crafted to address this complementary dimension of teaching. The grade specific standards should be based on the developmental and style needs of students. The content specific standards should be based on the discipline being taught. For example, the National Council of Teachers of Mathematics Standards for Teaching Mathematics (1991) would be an excellent point of departure in developing grade/content specific standards for the teaching of mathematics.

Evaluation Procedures

One way to develop procedures for teacher evaluation is to begin with the goal of teacher evaluation, to decide what needs to be done from a personnel standpoint to reach that goal, and then to develop a teacher evaluation process that supports such personnel decisions/practices. If the goal of teacher evaluation is to enhance the quality of teaching and learning in schools, then we need to (a) hire the best and brightest teachers, (b) induct these new teachers into the profession properly, (c) foster the professional growth and school improvement initiatives of newer and more experienced teachers, and (d) take appropriate action in those situations where effective teaching is not occurring in the classroom.

Role of Evaluation in Teacher Selection

One of the more important evaluation decisions a school system makes is the decision to hire a particular teacher. Since very few teachers are denied tenure and only a scant number are dismissed for performance reasons, being hired almost insures a teacher a job for as long as he/she wishes to teach in that school system. Thus, it is essential for the school system to hire the best qualified candidates. Many school systems in Connecticut have well developed selection procedures that insure that the best qualified candidates are hired. In such systems, teachers are hired on the basis of demonstrated teaching ability, not only on paper credentials. Hiring teachers through paper screening is still common in too many school systems. It is important for LEAs to employ coherent teacher selection procedures that insure this first and most important evaluation decision is made properly.

Role of Evaluation in Teacher Induction

Hiring the best and brightest teachers enhances the quality of education in a school system to the extent that such teachers are inducted into that system properly. We can set high expectations for these new teachers and provide them with the necessary support to meet these expectations or we can leave them virtually alone to be assimilated by the normative culture of their professional peer group. The literature indicates that it is best not to leave induction up to the informal interactions of the professional peer group, but rather, to structure the process to achieve the outcomes desired. Schools having problems with the induction of new teachers should consider implementing Peer Assistance and Review (PAR) programs.

In PAR programs, the induction and evaluation of beginning teachers is handled by trained specialists, PAR consultants. Usually these are classroom teachers who have been selected to participate in the program on a full-time basis for up to three years. At the end of this period such teachers return to their classrooms. PAR consultants are responsible for seeing that PAR guidelines are followed in the induction and evaluation of new teachers. Throughout the PAR program support for beginning teachers and those new to the school system is provided by peers. The decision as to whether a teacher meets system expectations and should be granted a subsequent one-year or continuing contract is made by a PAR committee that reviews the report and recommendations of the PAR consultant. The PAR committee is usually comprised of an equal number of teachers and administrators.

A problem with PAR programs can be the cost, since full-time staff are assigned to the program and outside assistance is needed periodically to train PAR consultants. The advantages based on the experiences of districts using such programs (e.g., Des Moines, IA; Columbus, OH) is that new teachers are inducted into the profession properly and only qualified teachers are rehired and granted tenure. The percentage of new teachers who do not continue in the school district has been sufficient (about 6 percent) to convince some boards of education that PAR programs are worth the investment.

Role of Evaluation When There Is Concern about a Teacher's Effectiveness

A second advantage of PAR programs is that they are also used when there is concern about an experienced teacher's effectiveness. If there is reason to believe that an experienced teacher is not effective, that teacher can be referred to PAR. That teacher's performance is reviewed and the PAR Committee decides whether such performance justifies placing the teacher in the PAR program. If a teacher is placed in PAR, the PAR Committee would decide in time whether remediation efforts were sufficiently successful for the teacher to exit the PAR program or it would recommend dismissal. In school systems where PAR programs have been implemented, they have been sufficiently successful in removing ineffective teachers to justify their cost.

One of the criticisms of teacher evaluation is that the process has no "teeth"—almost everyone is granted tenure and virtually no one is fired. This is due largely to the fact that building administrators often do not have the time and the training to make difficult evaluation decisions, those that impact a teacher's employment status. Through PAR programs this time and expertise is available to the school system.

Role of Evaluation for Professional Growth and School Improvement

Most of the experience in Connecticut has been in using teacher evaluation for professional growth and school improvement. A large number of school districts evaluate their staff using a variation of the Teacher Evaluation and Professional Growth Cycle (Iwanicki 1990; 1993). The key features of this three-year cycle are described in Exhibit 4-2. In applying this cycle, three factors are considered when evaluating experienced teachers (a) performance in the classroom based on observations, (b) professional growth based on mutually determined objectives, and (c) self-evaluation. Back in the 1970s and early 1980s, efforts were made to evaluate teachers with respect to these three factors on a yearly basis. The results were not gratifying. Teachers tended to develop shorter term, bland objectives tied to the recommendations which resulted from classroom observations. Self-evaluations were conducted in a cursory manner. When teachers were confronted with such concerns, they commented, "If you want us to address these aspects of evaluation in a meaningful manner, then give us the time to do so." The Teacher Evaluation and Professional Growth Cycle was developed to spread out these three critical aspects of teacher evaluation so they could be addressed thoughtfully.

Administrators also experienced difficulty in managing a teacher evaluation program which focused on these three critical aspects of teaching each year. Time constraints prevented them from observing all classrooms and developing meaningful professional growth plans for all teachers. The Teacher Evaluation and Professional Growth Cycle was developed so administrators could work closely with roughly one-third of their staff each year in the analysis of their classroom performance as well as in the development of their professional growth plans. Thus, an administrator responsible for the evaluation of thirty professional staff would work closely with about ten teachers. This 1:10 evaluator to teacher ratio is realistic, since experience has shown that an administrator can effectively evaluate between ten and fifteen staff each year.

The Teacher Evaluation and Professional Growth Cycle is a good point of departure for strengthening teacher evaluation practices. For example, in the Appraisal phase a series of classroom observations are conducted to analyze teaching and learning in the classroom. Rather than spread out these observations over the school year, it might be better to conduct this analysis of teaching and learning in reference to a two to

EXHIBIT 4-2.   An Overview of the Teacher Evaluation and Professional
Growth Cycle

Year 1—Appraisal

Focus: To conduct a thorough appraisal of teacher performance in light of the indicators of effective teaching

Events: (a) Fall conference to discuss and initiate the appraisal process
      (b) Minimum of three classroom observations, each with follow-up conferences resulting in a written Classroom Observation Report
      (c) Spring evaluation conference to discuss the teacher's Appraisal Report and to develop a Professional Growth Plan for the next two years. This plan is based on objectives which can focus on
          1. Strengthening performance with respect to the indicators of effective teaching
          2. Professional growth initiatives
          3. School improvement targets

Orientation: This is a collegial but accountability oriented process where the evaluator assumes leadership for evaluating teaching. The teacher and the valuator use this information as they work collaboratively to develop a two-year Professional Growth Plan to strengthen or enhance the teacher's performance.

Year 2—Support

Focus: To support the teacher as work begins on the objectives which serve as the basis of his/her Professional Growth Plan and to monitor progress in this regard

Events: (a) Fall conference with supervisor to review objectives and to decide how the teacher's progress will be supported and monitored
      (b) At least two conferences to support and to monitor the teacher's progress toward objectives
      (c) Formal classroom observations and informal class visits as necessary
      (d) Spring conference to complete the teacher's Spring Progress Report on Objectives

Orientation: This is a collegial partnership, where the supervisor supports and guides the teacher's efforts to achieve the objectives which serve as the basis of his/her Professional Growth Plan.

Year 3—Continued Professional Growth

Focus: To provide the teacher with the opportunity to
      (a) pursue what needs to be done to achieve the objectives which serve as the basis of his/her Professional Growth Plan
      (b) conduct a self-evaluation and to reflect on where he/she is going professionally

Events: (a) Fall conference with supervisor to review what the teacher needs to do to achieve his/her objectives, to discuss what strategies the teacher might use to conduct a self-evaluation, and to reflect upon his/her performance
(b) Interim evaluation conferences as necessary
(c) Formal classroom observations and informal class visits as necessary
(d) In spring the teacher completes the Final Evaluation Report, which is forwarded to the evaluator. This report includes a self-assessment of
  1. the extent to which the teacher's objectives have been achieved and
  2. those indicators of effective teaching which will provide the focus for his/her future professional development

Orientation: This is a reflective process, where the teacher assumes a more direct role in evaluating his/her performance and in setting a direction for future professional development.

---

three week unit of instruction selected by the teacher, preferably a unit that the teacher has difficulty teaching. The teacher and evaluator would meet before the unit commenced.

- to review and discuss the teacher's instructional plan, including the objectives of the unit
- to make suggestions for strengthening that plan
- to consider others who might participate in the evaluation process (i.e., peers, supervisors, curriculum consultants)
- to identify the performance measures which will be used to monitor student progress
- to schedule classroom observations for those key lessons where feedback to the teacher would be most helpful

Throughout the evaluation of this unit, the analysis of teaching would be based largely on what students have accomplished.

The cognitive perspective that teaching is thinking is essential as we try to focus teacher evaluation more on student learning. Teaching is

- thinking about what students need to know and be able to do,
- thinking about what the teacher can do to foster such learning,
- thinking about how successful the teacher has been in achieving the desired outcomes, and
- thinking about how the teacher should teach that lesson or unit of instruction the next time

If teaching is thinking, teacher evaluation becomes a conversation about teaching between the teacher and whoever else is participating in the evaluation process (i.e., administrator, supervisor, and/or peer). This conversation focuses on not only what students need to know and do but also what the teacher *can do* to strengthen or enhance the level of learning in the classroom. Three basic questions can serve as a point of departure in this conversation:

1. Did the teacher focus on worthwhile objectives?
2. How successful were students in achieving these objectives?
3. Did the teacher treat the students with dignity and respect?

If a teacher is successful in fostering worthwhile objectives with all students and maintains an atmosphere of dignity and respect, then that teacher is doing a good job. The focus of the evaluation conversation would be on reinforcing those aspects of teaching which contributed to the success of that lesson. To the extent that the answers to any of the questions above are other than "yes," then the dialogue focuses on aspects of teaching which need to be strengthened. The key feature of this approach is that the recommendations for strengthening, enhancing, or reinforcing teaching are based on an analysis of what students are learning. Too often the evaluation process begins with an analysis of teaching in light of best practices. While the recommendations which result have direct implications for enhancing teaching practice, they may have little impact on what students are actually learning in the classroom. As one teacher noted, "They have taught me to dance like Madeline [Hunter], but my kids are not learning better."

A traditional hierarchy of formal authority tends to built into the Teacher Evaluation and Professional Growth Cycle—the evaluator, supervisor, and teacher. It is time for this formal authority structure to become more functional. Those with the most expertise need to take leadership in the teacher evaluation process at the appropriate times. This means that evaluation needs to be a more collaborative process where teachers assume a more active role in their evaluation and in the evaluation of their peers. While traditionally administrators and supervisors have assumed the leadership in conducting observation conferences, teachers now need to assume more responsibility. If teaching is thinking, who is in a better position to analyze teaching that the teacher him- or herself with input from an informed peer, administrator, or supervisor who is skilled in facilitating reflection?

Also, there is a need to build a stronger peer collaboration component into the Support and Continued Professional Growth phases of the

Teacher Evaluation and Professional Growth Cycle. The Connecticut State Department of Education's experience with the Professional Educator Development (PED) Program is a good example of the powerful contribution that peers can make to the professional growth and development of their colleagues (see *Teacher: A New Definition and Model for Development and Evaluation* [Regan, Anctil, Dubea, Hoffman, and Vaillancourt 1992]). As efforts to extend such collaboration among peers continue, it would be helpful to include mechanisms for feedback on teaching from students and parents.

Conclusion

Using the term popularized by futurist Joel Barker (1992), a concerted effort has been made to change the "paradigm" of teacher evaluation in Connecticut schools over the past twenty years. Rather than being a "got ya" process for weeding out incompetent teachers, teacher evaluation becomes a means for professional growth and development as well as for improving student learning on a continuous basis. It is important to note that the various Connecticut teacher evaluation initiatives were never driven by a prescriptive state model. Under the Teacher Evaluation Act of 1974 and the Education Enhancement Act of 1986, local school districts were given the latitude to customize the teacher evaluation process to their local needs as long as the process complied with the state guidelines. The role of the State Department of Education was to support the development of effective teacher evaluation programs, to monitor the implementation of these programs, and to assure the State Legislature that such programs complied with state guidelines. Under the Systemic Reform Initiative of 1993, school districts have been given even more freedom to develop more productive approaches for teacher evaluation, where evaluation is integrated with professional development and school improvement in a systemic manner. The Department of Education's role is no longer to monitor and approve, but rather, to support and assist LEAs in the development of comprehensive professional development plans which include teacher evaluation.

Since few states have devoted the attention Connecticut has to teacher evaluation over the past twenty years, many educators and policymakers have asked how teacher evaluation has impacted the quality of education in school classrooms. We believe it has improved the teaching-learning process in many schools. Effective teacher evaluation programs provide staff the opportunity to think about what they are doing in the classroom in light of more promising alternatives. Such reflection leads to professional growth, better teaching, and improved student learning.

While this does not happen in all classrooms, it is difficult to determine the exact proportion of classrooms where it does happen. Based on our experiences with limited opportunity samples, we would estimate that teacher evaluation is having an impact on the professional growth of teachers in 60–70 percent of the classrooms in 60–70 percent of the school districts. Teacher evaluation is having little to no impact on teachers' professional development in settings where teachers and/or administrators believe this is not the purpose of the process. Regardless of what their school districts' teacher evaluation handbooks may state, some teachers and/or administrators still believe the purpose of teacher evaluation is to make employment decisions. As Albert Einstein commented, "The world we have created is a product of our ways of thinking. It cannot be changed until we change those patterns of thinking." Our continuing challenge is to change the patterns of thinking of those who refuse to accept the new paradigm for teacher evaluation in Connecticut. In "the land of steady habits," this may take a few more years.

Notes

1. This act was included later in Section 10–151b of the Connecticut General Statutes, Evaluation by Superintendents of Certain Educational Personnel. In Connecticut new legislation is passed as a public act and later incorporated appropriately into the general statutes.

2. This act was included later in Sections 10–155ee and 10–155ff of the Connecticut General Statutes.

References

Barker, J. (1992). *The Business of Paradigms.* (video). Burnsville, MN: Chart House International Learning Corporation.

Capitol Region Education Council. (1976). *In-service Training for the Evaluation of Teaching.* (Title IV Proposal). Bloomfield, CT: Author.

Carrano, A. S. (1978). *Teacher Evaluation: A Guidebook for Connecticut School Districts.* Hartford, CT: Connecticut State Department of Education.

Commission on Career Incentives and Teacher Evaluation. (1986a). Letter to superintendents. Hartford, CT: Education Committee of the Connecticut General Assembly.

Commission on Career Incentives and Teacher Evaluation. (1986b). *Commonly Asked Questions Regarding the Career Incentive and Teacher Evaluation*

Grant Program. Hartford, CT: Education Committee of the Connecticut General Assembly.

Connecticut State Department of Education. (1977). *Teacher Evaluation in Connecticut: Questions and Answers.* Hartford, CT: Author.

Connecticut State Department of Education. (1990). Education Enhancement Act Sourcebook. Hartford, CT: Author.

Connecticut State Department of Education. (1993). *Guidelines for Comprehensive Professional Development Plans Including Teacher Evaluation.* Hartford, CT: Author.

Covino, E. A. (1991). *Effective Teaching Behaviors of Experiences Connecticut Teachers: A Validation.* Ph.D. diss., The University of Connecticut (UMI# 9129921).

Darling-Hammond, L., Wise, A. E., and Pease, S. R. (1983). Teacher Evaluation in the Organizational Context: A Review of the Literature. *Review of Educational Research* 53 (3): 285–328.

Good, T. L., and Mulryan, C. (1990). Teacher Ratings: A Call for Teacher Control and Self-evaluation. In Millman, J., and Darling-Hammond, L., eds. *The New Handbook of Evaluation: Assessing Elementary and Secondary School Teachers,* (pp. 191–215. Newbury Park, CA: Sage Publications, Inc.

Governor's Commission on Equity and Excellence in Education. (1985). *The Report of the Governor's Commission on Equity and Excellence in Education: Teachers for Today and Tomorrow.* Hartford, CT: Author.

Iwanicki, E. F. (1976). Activity Analysis in Evaluation Design. *Planning and Changing,* 6 (3–4): 239–244.

———. (1988). *Indicators and Defining Attributes of Effective Teaching.* Storrs, CT: The Connecticut Institute for Personnel Evaluation, Department of Educational Leadership, The University of Connecticut.

———. (1990). Teacher Evaluation for School Improvement. In Millman, J., and Darling-Hammond, L., eds. *The New Handbook of Evaluation: Assessing Elementary and Secondary School Teachers,* (pp. 158–171). Newbury Park, CA: Sage Publications, Inc.

———. (1993). *Teacher Evaluation and Professional Growth in More Productive Schools.* Storrs, CT: The Connecticut Institute for Personnel Evaluation, Department of Educational Leadership, The University of Connecticut.

Joint Committee on Standards for Educational Evaluation. (1988). *The Personnel Evaluation Standards.* Newbury Park, CA: Sage Publications.

Juran Institute. (1993). *Quality Improvement Pocket Guide.* Wilton, CT: Author.

Martin, J. M. (1992). *The Other Side of the Equation: Impact of the Teacher Standards Provisions of the Education Enhancement Act*. Hartford CT: Connecticut State Department of Education.

McGreal, T. L. (1990). The Use of Ratings in Teacher Evaluation: Concerns and Recommendation. *Journal of Personnel Evaluation in Education* 4:41–58.

McLaughlin, M. W., and Pfeifer, R. S. (1988). *Teacher Evaluation: Improvement, Accountability, and Effective Learning*. New York: Teachers College Press.

McNally, H. J. (1973). What Makes a Good Evaluation Program. *The National Elementary Principal* 52:24–29.

Miles, M. B. (1965). Planned Change and Organizational Health: Figure and Ground. In *Change Processes in Public Schools*. (pp. 11–34). Eugene, OR: Center for the Advanced Study of Educational Administration, University of Oregon.

National Board of Professional Teaching Standards. (1989). *Toward High and Rigorous Standards for the Teaching Profession: Initial Policies and Perspectives of the National Board for Professional Teaching Standards*. Washington, D.C.: Author.

National Council of Teachers of Mathematics. (1991). *Professional Standards for Teaching Mathematics*. Reston, VA: Author.

Regan, H. B., Anctil, M., Dubea, C., Hoffman, J. M., and Vaillancourt, R. (1992). *Teacher: A New Definition and Model for Development and Evaluation*. Philadelphia, PA: Research for Better Schools.

Sclan, E. M. (1994). *Performance Evaluation for Experienced Teachers: An Overview of State Policies* (draft). Paper presented at the annual conference of the Center for Research in Educational Accountability and Teacher Evaluation, Gatlinburg, TN.

Scriven, M. (1987). Landscapes, Mindscapes, and Reflective Practice in Supervision. *Journal of Curriculum and Supervision* 1 (1):5–17.

Sergiovanni, T. J., and Starratt, R. J. (1988). *Supervision: Human Perspectives*. New York: McGraw-Hill Book Co.

Weick, K. (1976). Educational Organizations as Loosely Coupled Systems. *Administrative Science Quarterly* 21 (2):1–19.

5

Lessons Learned From Louisiana's Teacher Evaluation Experience

Beatrice Baldwin

Efforts by the state of Louisiana to exercise leadership in the area of teacher evaluation essentially began in 1988 with the passage of legislation that instituted a politically motivated program of teacher accountability. From that point in time to the present, the policies governing teacher evaluation have been alternately praised, attacked, reviewed, revised, suspended, reformed, and lauded.

Judging from the events surrounding teacher evaluation programs in other states, Louisiana's story is not necessarily unique in most regards. Prompted by a general population and by businesses that viewed public education as a failure, numerous states have initiated new teacher evaluation programs. Louisiana's experience, however, does provide unusually powerful and poignant lessons for examining how state policyshapers and policymakers should approach the formulation of teacher evaluation programs.

Political Beginnings

"Panel Suggests Higher Salaries for Teachers"[1]

The first mention of what was to be the most controversial education program in Louisiana's history came in the form of a recommendation from an advisory panel appointed by newly elected Governor Buddy Roemer. The education package proposed by the "transition team" included higher salaries for teacher, state-wide teacher evaluation, and "report cards" for schools.

Prior to 1988, teacher accountability had been a local responsibility in Louisiana. The state granted lifetime teaching certification with no requirements for continuing education. Legislation dating back to 1977 directed local school districts to evaluate non-tenured and tenured teachers. The school districts were required to follow some general guidelines concerning the documentation of evaluations and the number of professional personnel receiving satisfactory and non-satisfactory evaluations.

The criteria for teacher evaluation and the competencies to be observed in the classroom were left to the discretion of each of the sixty-six districts. Standardized reporting to the Louisiana Department of Education was required by the 1977 legislation, and the department's only responsibility was data gathering and monitoring.

Roemer's campaign promises had emphasized that the state must " . . . find out who can teach and pay them, find out who can't and show them how."[2] Touted as "the education governor," Roemer advocated boosting teacher salaries. In return for the extra money, public schoolteachers were to give up lifetime teaching certificates and submit to state-administered evaluations every five years in order to reearn their right to teach.

Business and industry representatives on the Governor's transition team supported the notion of teacher accountability. Although high visibility leaders in the business community and representatives from organizations such as the Louisiana Association of Business and Industry (LABI) and the Public Affairs Research Council (PAR) unequivocally endorsed the concept of renewable certification for all teachers, the transition team's official report indicated that teachers presently holding lifetime certification could *voluntarily* convert to five-year certification to participate in pay raises.

"BESE Bucks Roemer on School Reforms"[3]

The first few months of 1988 seemed to unfold smoothly for the Roemer administration as the Governor worked to plan his reform agenda. In April, the state Board of Elementary and Secondary Education (BESE) and the Governor worked together to select the state's first appointed state superintendent of education. Major discussions took place during the hiring process as the eleven board members and Roemer debated the issue of whether the superintendent should be a Louisianian. State legislator Cecil Picard was a top candidate for the post. Picard had been a teacher and a principal in Louisiana before coming to state government, and, although he did not possess a doctorate, several BESE members deemed his qualifications to be top-notch. However, the post was ultimately offered to Wilmer Cody, a Harvard-trained educator who had gained experience as a district superintendent in Alabama, North Carolina, and Maryland. Cody was brought in at an annual salary of $100,000.

The Board got its first look at Roemer's plan for education reform in early May. The major tenets of the reform agenda focused on increasing teacher pay, eliminating lifetime certification for new teachers, instituting teacher evaluation for recertification, eliminating state teacher salary compensation for those classroom teachers who were deemed unsatisfactory, and creating school report cards. But Roemer and BESE had their first falling out in late May as the Board voted 10–1 not to approve Roemer's plan for financing the reforms. Many educators had voiced concerns to the board that Roemer was trying to do too much, too fast. The Board's decision not to throw support behind the Governor effectively left the fate of reform to the state legislature.

"Senate OKs Bill to Give Teachers More Pay"[4]

Roemer's reform plan, designated the Children First Act, became reality in the summer of 1988. Roemer's bill was approved by both the House and the Senate without any major changes. A total of $250 million dollars was budgeted for teacher pay raises for 1988 to 1991. The bill's accountability provisions were of some concern to education groups. Rather than allow experienced teachers to voluntarily give up lifetime certification in exchange for the extra pay, the bill required that all teachers be evaluated for recertification purposes and established provisions for local school boards to hold tenure hearings and dismiss teachers after the state had revoked certification for unsatisfactory evaluations. The bill provided for remediation for teachers deemed unsatisfactory, but did not specifically address how remediation was to take place. In addition, teachers who earned superior ratings would be given opportunities to participate in "master teacher" activities for more pay.

"Teachers Ready to Help Roemer with Reform"[5]

At the fall conventions of the state's two largest teacher groups, the Louisiana Association of Educators (LAE) and the Louisiana Federation of Teachers (LFT), Governor Roemer was given a friendly reception. Although teacher leaders expressed some reservations about the decertification aspect of the evaluation system, the groups were represented on the Governor's commission to develop recommendations for evaluation, and overall they seemed pleased that educational issues were receiving so much attention. "We were impressed with his commitment to education, remarked LFT President Fred Skelton. "Even in these tough times, he made it a top priority."[6]

"Teachers To Size Up System"[7]

Teacher evaluation received very little attention during its design phase. The assessment systems, referred to as the Louisiana Teacher Evaluation Program (LaTEP) and its companion program for intern teachers, the Louisiana Teaching Internship Program (LTIP), were not scheduled for implementation until the 1990–1991 school year. At that time, approximately one-fifth of the state's teachers—about 9,000—were to be assessed.

Chad Ellett, a professor in the College of Education at Louisiana State University (LSU), was hired by the state department of education to develop and direct the evaluation project. Dr. Ellett's background included extensive expertise in teacher assessment systems—Ellett had developed the teacher evaluation system that had been used in Georgia for nearly ten years, and he had also created the local evaluation plan for Dade County, Florida.

Initial instrument development and validation activities received very little attention from teachers or the media. At the 1989 meeting of the Louisiana Federation of Teachers, informational workshops on the evaluation processes were conducted, and the Louisiana Association of Educators also sponsored seminars on LaTEP and LTIP. Both associations were cautious about either endorsing or condemning the evaluations. "Evaluation can be nothing more than a political witch hunt or can be a legitimate effort to determine a teacher's ability in the classroom,"[8] said a LAE spokesperson.

Ellett assured educators that any fears about teacher evaluation were groundless. He related that personnel in each of the sixty-six school districts were being trained to inform teachers about how the evaluation system was going to work. In addition, he insisted that the system being designed had safeguards against bias. A team of assessors were to evaluate each teacher once per semester, and assessors were to get standardized training to conduct evaluations "with fairness and equity."

The Rising Tide of Revolution

"Educators Say Review Is too Costly[9]

As the details of the teacher evaluation program continued to be publicized, educators began criticizing numerous aspects of the program. Parish affiliate organizations of LAE and LFT released information on the time and the costs associated with training. Principals and master teachers were required to spend seven days in assessor training, and the local districts were forced to pick up the tab for hiring teacher substitutes, over $35,000 per year for East Baton Rouge Parish Schools alone. Many educators also had criticisms about the evaluation procedures including the use of peer teachers as evaluators and the Comprehensive Unit Plan (CUP), a special lesson plan format that required teachers to document far more than what had been previously required.

Chad Ellett responded by saying that the program was still in the pilot stage and that the program was misunderstood. He acknowledged that the program had some problems. For instance, it had not been determined whether two or three trained assessors would judge the performance of experienced classroom teachers. Louisiana Department of Education staff were still working with Ellett's development team to finalize the evaluation instrument, the STAR (System for Teaching and Learning Assessment and Review). The STAR initially contained 140 rating criteria, including how well teachers prepared their lessons, managed their classrooms, delivered instruction, established a classroom climate, and interacted with students.

Although Roemer received a "B–" grade from over 3,000 teachers participating in an LFT poll in March, many educators were so worried about the still-unresolved details of the plan that by mid-April 1990 they had convinced state representative J. R. Smith (D-Leesville) to file legislation that would postpone it for a year. "There's so much fear of the unknown that they'd almost rather stay with what we've got than jump into the unknown,"[10] LFT President Fred Skelton said.

"Most of the education community is for evaluation. It's just that the State Department of Education is not prepared to implement the program," commented Representative Smith. "Without approval and support from the education community, it's doomed to fail."[11] Other legislators, worried that business interests would try to force through legislation on a voucher system, were less inclined to postpone the program regardless of the objections. House Education Committee Chairman Jimmy Long (D-Natchitoches) maintained that the evaluation system must proceed as a show of good faith to taxpayers. "We made a commitment," Long said, "to the people of the state that we're going to implement the Children First Act." Long insisted that most of the hitches could be worked out before the plan was to go into effect in the fall. "The worst that can happen is we make some mistakes. And we can correct those,"[12] he said.

"Principals Complain to Roemer"[13]

As preparations for the 1990 legislative session began, Governor Roemer minimized the challenges to program implementation. "I think there are some legitimate items to be discussed and worked through in teacher evaluation" Roemer said. "But my commitment—I think shared by the people of this state—is to start that program now."[14] By April 19, public school teachers and principals had been promised two days' training—and two extra days' pay—to make up for the exploding communication gap. A group of principals then met with Roemer to air their gripes about the program. "We're about to do something that we don't even understand," said Jerry Boudreaux, principal of Zachary High School in Baton Rouge. "And if we're that nervous, imagine how the classroom teachers must feel."[15]

Mindful of the growing public interest and concern, Roemer frequently fielded questions from the news media on the subject of teacher evaluations. He repeated that he was firmly committed to beginning the evaluations in the fall. "I'm not going to put the teachers down," Roemer stated. "They're concerned that they might not be evaluated fairly. We've met with teachers, principals and superintendents all over the state about the evaluation process. If there are any problems with it, we'll iron them out. But we are going to proceed with teacher evaluations. I will not delay the evaluation for one year as some are suggesting."[16]

By May, Roemer had conceded at least privately that there were serious problems. The Governor's Office and Superintendent of Education Wilmer Cody entered into negotiations with representatives of LAE and LFT in an effort to resolve implementation difficulties. "If these two groups are going to work constructively to get this done, we will give them a chance to make all the recommendations they want," he said. "But if the groups want a 7 percent teacher pay raise without evaluation, we will push the program through without them. The taxpayers would go bananas if there was a pay raise without requiring teacher evaluation."[17]

On May 29, the Senate Education Committee approved SB452 by Senator Armand J. Brinkhaus (D-Sunset) to eliminate the renewable teaching certificates and reinstate lifetime teaching certificates. Senator John Saunders (D-Ville Platte) called the legislation "a litmus test" for senators' support for school teachers. According to Saunders, the evaluation system was a "totally arbitrary process," a "sadistic" program concocted by big-money interests to "torture" school teachers. Teacher groups supported the Brinkhaus bill, claiming that promises had been broken, including guarantees by Roemer and Cody that all the details of how the evaluations would work would be completed by the end of May so that educators could review them before the legislative session ended. The evaluation program had enough legislative supporters, however, to make it through the session intact.

"LFT Files 3rd Lawsuit to Kill New Teacher Evaluation Program"[18]

As the school year began, numerous details of the evaluation program had still to be resolved. Cutoff scores for the "superior," "satisfactory," and "nonsatisfactory" ratings that were to result from the STAR had yet to be determined. In addition, teachers were still being notified in September that they had been selected to be evaluated, despite a May 15 BESE-established deadline for notification.

President Fred Skelton said LFT's injunction requests were attempts to stop the evaluation program from being implemented "until they correct the violations of their own guidelines and until they adopt the passing and the superior scores so the teachers will know what they have to do to pass the evaluation."[19] LFT and LAE subsequently filed suits challenging the constitutionality of the 1988 Children First Act. The teacher groups maintained that, in requiring teachers to give up already earned lifetime certification, the act conflicted with teachers' constitutional rights. Although state District Judge Robert Downing agreed to allow the teacher evaluation program to begin October 1, Downing scheduled a hearing for November 1 to discuss the lawsuits. Additionally, Downing issued a gag order prohibiting representatives of LAE and LFT and the state from speaking publicly about the case before the hearing. "We'll proceed as we had planned," state Education Superintendent Cody said.

BESE Turns Down Attempts to Alter Evaluation Program"[20]

As the controversy increased, the state Board of Elementary and Secondary Education refused attempts to make changes to the teacher evaluation program. LFT and LAE had urged the board members to reconsider a decision to keep secret the individual evaluation sheets of the three assessors and to release only the composite score. Additionally, the teacher groups requested that the board clarify what they called an "unfair and confusing" grievance procedure. Despite a spirited, sometimes bitter public debate, eight members of the eleven-member board were unified in wanting to maintain the status quo.

"Roemer Defends Record Against School Employee Unions' Criticism"[21]

In mid-November, Governor Buddy Roemer went on the defensive by suggesting that the LFT and the LAE had initiated lawsuits only because they were fighting for membership. LAE had publicly given Roemer failing grades for his performance in office and had announced that they would begin searching for "a real education governor" to elect during the 1991 campaign. "The teachers and students of Louisiana are searching for a real education governor—a governor who truly puts children first, not only in words, but in deeds as well,"[22] said LAE President Linda B. Day. Meanwhile, the LFT held a convention meeting in which teachers lambasted the evaluation program. "This program is not going to go away, in our estimation, unless the governor goes away,"[23] LFT Executive Director Bob Crowley told the members.

Although the teacher groups had had little influence on the governor's race which had brought Buddy Roemer to office, they became increasingly vocal in their intentions to unseat the Governor. "I would hope that teachers have learned their lesson," Day said when she later announced that the association's political action committee would begin gearing up for the election. "LAE-PAC is raising funds for an election war chest," LAE said in a prepared press conference statement. "We will work to ensure that those who hold high political office are true friends of education.[24]

The tension between the governor and the teacher groups turned into an all-out feud at the end of November 1990 at the LAE convention in Baton Rouge. At the convention, Roemer said the complaints about teacher evaluation put forward by LAE and LFT did not reflect the opinions of their memberships, a claim angrily denounced by both groups. Roemer spoke at the convention, and then, rather than field questions from teachers, abruptly left the meeting.

"Cody Sends 'Report Cards' on Schools to Parents"[25]

Another component of Roemer's education agenda came under fire in the last days of 1990. The Children First Act of 1988, in addition to creating the teacher evaluation program, authorized the state's first school "report cards." The Louisiana Department of Education shipped 37,000 pounds of the report cards to the state's 1,456 schools. The reports—enough for the parents of every child in public school—contained information on teacher certification, student attendance, standardized test scores, and the number of student suspensions and expulsions in addition to other indicators. Within days of the report cards' release, controversy over accuracy of the data on the report cards created additional credibility problems for Roemer and the state education department. Roemer opponents used the inaccuracy of the report cards as further evidence of the Governor's ineptness in setting an appropriate course for Louisiana public education.

"La. Evaluation Guidelines Flunk 35 Percent of Tested Teachers"[26]

Nearly three full months after the evaluation program had begun, Louisiana's teachers still did not know what cutoff scores would be used to determine "superior," "satisfactory," and "nonsatisfactory" performances. In mid-December, the Board of Elementary and Secondary Education received score-setting recommendations from advisory panels, only to delay making a decision because they felt they did not have adequate information. Under the recommended scoring system, experienced teachers would receive a "satisfactory" rating if they passed at least 75 percent of the ninty-one indicators in the evaluation and eleven of fifteen major component areas.

Then, in an unexpected move, the Board adopted cutoff scores that were more stringent than those recommended. The approved cutoff scores would have "failed" almost 35 percent of the 4,500 teachers rated during the first semester of 1991. The teachers receiving the nonsatisfactory ratings consequently would have been subject to losing their certification. Teacher groups immediately went on the attack. "We do not believe that a teaching certificate should be taken from a teacher because of her score on an ill-advised, flawed, disjointed, subjective, and unproven teacher evaluation instrument and evaluation process,"[27] LAE representative Lawrence Narcisse said.

State Education Superintendent Wilmer Cody tried to soften the blow, reminding teachers and the public that the evaluations conducted in the fall were only the first of what could have been three sets of evaluations for some nonsatisfactory teachers. He claimed that by the time the full evaluation process was complete, up to 83 percent of those teachers rated likely would receive passing ratings, and that the percentage would reach up to 92 percent if evaluations were extended to fall 1991.

"Roemer's New Education Adviser Says She Hopes to Map Future"[28]

Roemer named a new education adviser to the Governor's office, hoping that his appointment of a classroom teacher would help mitigate continued attacks on his education reforms. Roemer's first education adviser had resigned and the deputy chief of staff for administration had served as the interim adviser. Describing herself as "very dedicated to quality education," Claudia Fowler, a Baton Rouge teacher, believed she would be able to provide insight into the teacher evaluation program because she had been evaluated herself. She stated in her first press conference that teacher evaluation was the "No. 1 issue on teachers' minds these days" and that she understood teachers' doubts and fears about the new program. "I think, as with any new program, there are some things that will need to be looked at and talked about, but I think basically the program is a good one,"[29] Fowler said.

"LSU's Chad Ellett Defends His Teacher Evaluation Plan and Credentials"[30]

At the beginning of the new year, outraged educators found a new target for their frustrations—Louisiana State University professor Chad Ellett. "I'm so full of bullet holes and tomato stains that I don't even try to defend myself anymore,"[31] Ellett said. Teachers questioned Ellett's credentials because of his limited background in schools; Ellett's only classroom experience was as a student teacher. Ellett replied that his teaching experience was irrelevant due to his seventeen years of research experience with teacher evaluation programs.

Teacher groups saw Ellett's lack of experience as further evidence that the evaluation system was the product of ivory tower thinking. Continued reasurrances by the governor, the state department of education, and Ellett's design team only served to increase the credibility gap. Teachers heard the promises, but felt that very little action was being taken to address their concerns.

French Class Was Greek to Evaluators[32]

Fighting against what they believed were the injustices inherent in the system, teachers and other educators put a personal face on the evaluation experience by releasing to the media accounts of evaluation "horror stories." One story recounted the experience of a high school French teacher who claimed she missed a superior rating on her evaluation because the assessors did not understand French, yet tried to evaluate her in a class where less than 20 percent of the words spoken were English. In another tale, a special education teacher lost points on her state evaluation for failing to teach critical thinking skills to a class of children with Down's syndrome.

And in yet another school, a special education teacher claimed she was docked for using sign language to communicate with her class of behavioral disordered students. A high-school chemistry teacher who had been honored as Louisiana Teacher of the Year as an instructor of advanced chemistry and biology failed her evaluation when two elementary school trained assessors rated her as not meeting the standards for content and accuracy in the field of chemistry.

"Teachers Air Problems with Evaluations"[33]

Several hundred teachers met with legislators and public officials at a high school in Baton Rouge on January 7, 1991, and aired some of their problems with LaTEP. The event was highly publicized and emotionally charged. The teachers' complaints centered around their claims that the STAR makes no differentiation between elementary teaching, high-school teaching, or special education teaching. They faulted the instrument's lack of flexibility, claiming that it did not take different teaching styles into account, nor did it adjust the standards for teachers in different classroom situations. Teachers also criticized the continual policy changes. One teacher told the legislators that her evaluators refused to tell her in post-evaluation conferences what she had done wrong during her evaluation, but the policy was changed by the state two days after her conference. "The reason there are so many changes in midstream . . . is we don't know what we're doing,"[34] remarked a legislator.

At the meeting, legislators also indicted the evaluation process. "I was against this garbage in the first place," one Senator said, a remark that was responded to by cheering from the teachers. "While Georgia was repealing this instrument, we were implementing it. Seems like we're ten years behind everybody else."[35] Other legislators echoed these sentiments, and some were quick to remind teachers that during the last legislative session they had been in favor of delaying full implementation of the evaluation process.

State education officials attempted to put a positive spin on some of the most adverse publicity. State Superintendent Wilmer Cody was reported as saying that he did not believe Louisiana would overhaul the teacher evaluation program or the "report cards" on public schools. "I think 'fine-tuning' is the best word," Cody said. "I see no need to change the basic framework for the evaluation . . . I'm real pleased with what the staff has accomplished and really pleased with the cooperation of school districts across the state in those two efforts. We still have some improvements to make, but the basic programs are in place."[36]

"Defending Teacher Evaluation Suits May Cost La. $200,000"[37]

Teacher groups got more ammunition for their fight against teacher evaluation when the Board of Elementary and Secondary Education was asked to authorize $200,000 to defend the state against lawsuits. In addition, the board was told that additional funds beyond the $200,000 may be needed for appeals.

LAE and LFT had filed a joint motion asking the court to rule without trial that the state cannot revoke the lifetime certificates of teachers failing to pass the teacher evaluation program. Attorneys for the two groups argued that because "no facts are disputed," the court should issue a favorable ruling to them "in light of the fact that the Louisiana Supreme Court ruled in 1983 that it is unconstitutional for the state to revoke the teaching certificate of a teacher employed by a local school board."[38] Roemer's legal counsel replied, "The only thing clear to me in this case is that the teacher unions will do anything, say anything and go to any length to sabotage teacher evaluation in the state of Louisiana. The issue is what's best for our children, not what's best for the teacher unions."[39]

LFT and LAE officials also revealed other plans to derail teacher evaluation including asking the state legislature to abolish the teacher evaluation program. They announced that state Senator Armand Brinkhaus

(D-Sunset) had agreed to introduce legislation to discontinue the evaluation portion of Roemer's 1988 Children First Act. "We're not asking that the laws that call for the evaluation of teachers be repealed," LFT President Fred Skelton said. "We want to make it clear that we don't want to get out of evaluation as a professional responsibility, but this program is just unacceptable. We probably ought to go back to the drawing board. One of the things we have learned on this thing is haste makes waste."[40]

Skelton said that his organization had met with LAE to discuss other types of collective protest, "up to and including a statewide strike." LFT members were circulating anti-teacher evaluation petitions among public school teachers, and LAE was polling its 23,000 members to determine how far they were willing to go to force a repeal. Skelton said in a statement about the LFT petitions, "The problem is an evaluation program that seeks to make robots of our teachers, that has no educational value, and indeed punishes teachers who bring creativity and compassion into their classrooms."[41] LAE representatives remarked that classroom teachers " . . . are demoralized and are threatening to leave by the droves. Learning has taken a backseat to a state-sponsored dog-and-pony show."

"Teacher Evaluation Changes Planned"[42]

"I don't think there is any question in anybody's mind that we need to make some changes to improve the process," state Superintendent Wilmer Cody said. Cody's remarks preceded a series of proactive strategies to quell criticism on all fronts. State Department of Education staff members conducted meetings with leaders of the Louisiana Association of Educators, the Louisiana Federation of Teachers, the Associated Professional Educators of Louisiana, the Louisiana Association of Principals and the Louisiana Association of School Superintendents. In addition, Cody and Governor Roemer's press secretary began a month-long tour to meet with teachers across the state concerning problems with the program. Roemer's press secretary had also been commandeered to write news releases for the education department.

While state officials said the meetings were a positive step towards making needed changes, teacher representatives scathingly condemned Cody's plan, calling it "just a stalling tactic." "I think it is an unnecessary delay because we've made these concerns known to Dr. Cody . . . and BESE over the last several months,"[43] said Michael Deshotels, associate executive director for the LAE.

"EWE Calls Himself 'Solution to the Revolution'"[44]

Former Governor Edwin Edwards declared himself a candidate for an unprecedented fourth term as governor. Humiliated in the 1987 primary election, Edwards had stepped out of the race rather than lose to Roemer. Edwards said he would campaign against the incumbent Roemer by reminding voters of Roemer's record. "Now, as he runs for re-election as an incumbent governor, we can replay his silly television ad, repeat his irresponsible statements and compare his performance to his promise," remarked the flamboyant Edwards. "He said 'Read my lips,' but meant 'kiss my hips.'"[45]

Edwards lost no time in attacking Roemer's education agenda. He said that Roemer had " . . . politicized the appointment of college presidents, imported a $100,000 per year out-of-stater to run our schools, made no significant changes in our educational system, turned his back on the colleges and universities . . . and has frustrated, alienated and insulted the dedicated men and women who teach our children."[46] Edwards declared that the teacher evaluation program should be scrapped "and we ought to start over."

On the same day that Edwards announced his plans to unseat Roemer, District Court Judge Robert Downing ruled that the state did not have the constitutional authority to revoke the teaching certificates of teachers who failed the teacher evaluation program. Governor Roemer immediately issued a statement saying Downing's decision would be appealed to Louisiana's Supreme Court. Downing explained that a 1982 Louisiana Supreme Court decision set a precedent. In that decision, decertification was considered tantamount to dismissal and, therefore, in violation of the 1974 state constitution which prohibits the state from hiring and firing employees of local school boards.

"Panel Blasts Education Chief for Evaluation Flaws"[47]

The demise of Louisiana's state-wide teacher evaluation program seemed virtually certain when a joint legislative subcommittee publicly berated state Superintendent Wilmer Cody for numerous design and implementation problems. Members of the Joint Subcommittee on Elementary and Secondary Education spent almost an hour rebuking Cody for assuring the previous legislative session that problems would be corrected. Some state education officials referred to the committee's treatment of Cody as the "St. Valentine's Day Massacre."

Legislators appeared willing to place all of the blame on Cody, and indirectly, Governor Roemer. "Someone has dropped the ball," state Representative Francis Thompson (D-Delhi) said, "and certainly it's not the Legislature because all we did was give you an opportunity to develop an (evaluation) instrument."[48] "Albert Einstein could not have taught in Louisiana with the way the law is set up right now,"[49] commented state Representative Bernard Carrier (D-Denham Springs).

Cody maintained that while there had been problems, they were not "major problems." Some legislators appeared unwilling to denounce teacher evaluation entirely. "We're getting so much feedback on it I think it is going to get slowed down," said state Representative Billy W. Montgomery (D-Haughton). "If we don't do something between now and April 15, there are going to be some bills that are going to be hard to deal with."[50]

In early June, hoping to stem the increasing call for suspension of teacher evaluation, Governor Roemer suggested changes to the program during a House committee meeting. Roemer recommended cutting back on the number of teachers to be evaluated during the 1991–92 school year (from 8,000 to less than 6,000) and reducing the number of criteria used to judge a teacher's classroom performance (from 91 to 86). "My idea is to have an alternative to a suspension that is real, that keeps evaluation alive, but gives assurances both to teachers and the Legislature that it'll be done properly . . ."[51] Roemer said.

Under proposed House legislation, the program would have been suspended, and educational experts recommended by the Southern Regional Education Board would come to Louisiana to review the program. The experts would report by October 1 to the state Board of Elementary and Secondary Education and legislative education committees with recommendations for changes in the current evaluation system. By January 15, 1992, BESE was to have acted on the recommended changes, with the revised program being tested in the spring and full implementation during the 1992–1993 school year.

Legislators claimed that the difference between their plan and Roemer's was primarily a matter of semantics. "He (Roemer) just can't spit out, 'Suspension,'" Senator Cecil Picard (D-Maurice) said. "I prefer to use 'pause' or 'timeout.'"[52] Picard noted that the proposed suspension technically was for only one semester because teachers who participated in the pilot test in the spring of 1992 and pass would be credited for a satisfactory evaluation. Roemer replied that he feared that if the program shut down, it would never be restarted. "Louisiana has two or three times in its history in the last twenty years been on the cutting edge of reform," Roemer remarked. "And, each time they've tried it, they've backed down—and suspension to me sounds like backing down."[53]

"La. High Court Reaffirms State's Authority to Act on Evaluations"[54]

Roemer's education agenda supporters got a boost when the Louisiana Supreme Court concluded that the state had the authority to revoke the certificates of teachers who failed the evaluation program. Unfortunately, the court's support had come too late. The day before, the House

Education Committee had approved a Senate plan to suspend the system for a year.

Roemer was delighted with the high court's decision to overturn the lower court ruling. "There are now no excuses for the Legislature not to move forward with the teacher evaluation program," Roemer said. "For the benefit of the children there are no excuses. Let's go."[55]

In the Supreme Court case, attorneys for LAE and LFT had argued that the state constitution prohibits the state from hiring and firing employees of local school boards, and that decertification was the same as dismissal. The state convinced the court that local districts still have the authority to hire and fire teachers. While teachers who still fail the evaluation after receiving remedial help would not be paid by the state, school boards can continue to employ them if they wish.

"Teacher Exams Suspended"[56]

State legislators suspended the evaluation program for a year to provide time to make changes, by giving final approval to Senator Cecil Picard's plans. The House voted 82–20 to suspend the program and 100–3 to make changes prior to restart in 1992. Under state law, Roemer could not veto the suspension resolution, but could have vetoed the bill which called for revamping the program. Roemer termed the House measures " . . . incredible, unnecessary, dysfunctional, scary."[57]

"Suspension is not the way to go. I think teachers ought to be held accountable . . . ," Roemer said. Roemer reported that he would carefully review the bill that set out the changes to be made in the program and a time schedule for reinstatement before making a decision about a veto. "If the bill helps us live through a bad resolution, then I will sign it."[58]

In early July, Roemer reluctantly signed the bill. "If I didn't sign the bill, there'd be no money for teacher evaluation, you couldn't do a pilot test and we couldn't do anything."[59] The Legislature allocated $1.5 million to revise and test the program during the one-year suspension, but state officials maintained that the amount was not enough. Assistant Education Superintendent Barbara Dunbar indicated that lawmakers should have set aside at least $7 million for the Department of Education.

"Keep, Improve Evaluation Plan, Panel Leader Urges"[60]

A twelve-member Teacher Evaluation Advisory Commission was charged with making recommendations to the state Board of Elementary and Secondary Education on how to revise and test teacher evaluation before restarting it during the 1992–93 school year. Six of the twelve members were representatives of LAE and LFT. The committee also included the chairs of the House and Senate education committees, one representative each from the Louisiana School Boards Association, the Louisiana Association of School Executives and the Louisiana Association of Principals, and a representative of the state's colleges of education.

The chair of the panel, Billy Archement of the Louisiana School Boards Association, said that the goal of the group was to merely make suggestions, while the job of the BESE was to make the actual decisions. Because of the heavy teacher representation in the group, some in the Department of Education dubbed the panel the "Committee from Hell," and while LFT President Fred Skelton indicated that the teacher organizations' only interests were in helping to ensure that problems would be corrected, it was quickly evident that the teacher groups would band together to try to take control of the panel.

The Advisory Commission's first task was to nominate up to five out-of-state consultants who were to review the program. Commission members were quick to vote acceptance of two consultants suggested by the Southern Regional Education Board. The teacher representatives then proposed that the remaining three members of the study group be chosen by the teacher organizations. Further progress on selecting the consultants was stalled by disagreement. Teacher representatives were concerned that the other suggested consultants on the list possessed the same perspectives toward teacher evaluation as LSU's Chad Ellett. Ultimately, the BESE broke the stalemate by naming a third consultant.

Moving Towards Professional Development

"Evaluation Review Urges Local Control"[61]

In a twenty-page report presented to the Board of Elementary and Secondary Education, the consultant review team recommended a multiple approach to teacher evaluation—initial evaluation by the state for certification, followed by local evaluation for experienced teachers. Initial reactions by teachers to the recommendations were positive. "It's a fairer approach to resolving the issues," said Linda Day, president of the Louisiana Association of Educators.[62]

The report, written by consultants Dr. Ed Iwanicki of the University of Connecticut, Southwest Texas State University Assistant Education Dean Dr. Susan Barnes and Dr. Betty Frye, chief of teacher education for the Florida Department of Education, suggested that teachers who met criteria set at the state level would receive a renewable teaching certificate. This certificate could be renewed every five years based on evidence collected through the local teacher evaluations using state criteria.

The consultant team had interviewed more than 100 people who were involved in the original program and came to the general conclusion that the program as developed was not meeting its goal of improving teaching and learning. Iwanicki said, "We are not proposing something that is totally new, but . . . putting it together in a more systematic, cohesive manner."[63]

Beginning teachers would be provided support during their first year by the teacher's principal, a master teacher from the teacher's district, and a college faculty member. Each intern would be assessed for purposes of certification by a state assessment team. Interns meeting state standards on assessments would get a renewable five-year teaching certificate. Teaching certificates would then be renewed every five years based on local evaluations. The experienced teachers being evaluated locally would have to meet two standards—that they are proficiently teaching in the classroom and that they are participating in a program of professional development. If the teacher could not meet the standards, the teacher would be removed from the classroom.

Furthermore, the consultant team recommended that the state take more time and not begin the new evaluation systems until the 1993–94 school year. Iwanicki emphasized that the program could not be adequately tested and refined by the fall of 1992. Thus, it was likely that the Board of Elementary and Secondary Education would have to ask the state Legislature to delay restarting the program until the 1993–94 school year.

After reviewing the consultants' report, the Teacher Evaluation Advisory Commission supported postponing the program until 1993–94 school term. However, the commission recommended that the state not revoke the certificates of teachers who could not pass the evaluation.

"It's Edwards and Duke—Gov. Roemer Squeezed Out of Runoff"[64]

Roemer bowed out of the governor's race after late night primary returns showed him running third to former Governor Edwin Edwards, who twice had been tried in federal court on corruption charges, and state Representative David Duke, a former head of the Ku Klux Klan. Education groups had vigorously campaigned against Roemer, and their votes and funds figured heavily in Roemer's defeat.

Edwards had openly courted teachers during the campaign, stating that he would send state Superintendent of Education Wilmer Cody " . . . back to Massachusetts with his illegitimate offspring, LTIP and LaTEP." While Edwards said he supported the concept of teacher evaluation, he contended classroom teachers should have input in creating the evaluation. "I really think we ought to scrap that whole system and go back to basics," Edwards said. "Get with supervisors, principals, legislators, interested private citizens and educators, and work out an evaluation system that has not already failed in Florida, failed in Georgia and has failed here."[65] In addition, Edwards let it be known that he opposed revoking lifetime certification.

During the campaign, Edwards maintained that he was "totally committed" to teacher evaluation. "I commit again to the teachers and to the students and to the parents of this state that we are going to work together to develop an evaluation system that will be fair and equitable and identify the teachers that need corrective attention to work with them to make them better teachers."[66]

BESE Edges toward Second Evaluation Delay[67]

As plans for teacher evaluation moved into 1992, support for delaying evaluation another year seemed to be coalescing. A majority of BESE members had indicated that they would be open to recommending a delay of teacher evaluation until 1993–94, based on the consultant team's report and the recommendation of the Teacher Evaluation Advisory Commission. BESE members were very cognizant of the fact that the delay would require legislative approval as the original resolution had only specified delay until 1992–93, but appeared to be willing to ask for such a measure.

In the remaining days of the Roemer administration, some teacher evaluation supporters insisted that a further delay would essentially kill the program. "Teacher evaluation sure looks like it's heading down the slippery slope of compromise, of temporization and delay,"[68] Roemer said. However, in December, even members of Roemer's administration admitted that the program's restart would have to be set back a year. Speaking to the Joint Legislative Committee on Education, Roemer's education adviser Claudia Fowler said evaluation could not effectively be continued until it had the support of the public and, more importantly, of educators. "If it's going to take some extra time to do it well, let's take some extra time."[69]

Within days after the election, Governor-elect Edwin Edwards had appointed members of a transition team to make recommendations for education. Over 100 suggestions were made by the group, including more equitable funding for local school districts and a more reasonable state-wide teacher evaluation program. Edwards noted the task force accepted the findings of the consultant team that Roemer's teacher evaluation program was implemented too quickly.

Teacher Exam Overhaul Urged—Two-Year Delay Recommended[70]

Ready to get to the issues of how to redesign and restart the evaluation program, the BESE hired three in-state consultants to develop an overall management plan and budget. Sequestered for ten working days, the consultants reviewed the report of the various advisory groups and worked with members of the state department to outline the necessary steps for overhauling the program.

Based on the reports, the in-state consultants recommended that a series of panels meet to complete four tasks: identify and validate the essential teaching skills to be measured in Louisiana's state evaluation system; examine how local evaluation procedures should be standardized and strengthened; identify and recommend resources for professional development; and develop a reasonable instrument for measuring classroom performance skills. The consultants set up a timeline for the panel meetings, developed recommendations for sampling and testing the state system, and projected costs for the redesign activities. In establishing the timeline, the consultants suggested that the program should not be resumed until the 1994–95 school year. The group believed the state should not rush into restarting the program and should allow time for it to be properly designed and tested.

The BESE supported the management plan and delaying the start of evaluations until the fall of 1994. They approved a plan to ask the 1992 Legislature to agree to the extra delay. The Board also approved in concept the idea that the state evaluation program should have professional development as its focus. As the pros and cons of delaying the state evaluation system were debated, officials in the Governor's office were working with legislators to amend a 1977 accountability law which would improve state oversight and regulation of local teacher evaluation programs while the state program was being overhauled.

"Teacher Evaluation Set For '94"[71]

During the 1992 legislative session, a coalition consisting of the teacher groups, other education associations, the Governor's office, the state Department of Education, and the Public Affairs Research Council convinced lawmakers to strengthen state oversight of local teacher evaluation and to delay implementation of the state assessment program until the fall of 1994. Governor Edwards personally came to the Senate Education Committee, saying "Teachers were demoralized by what they felt was an unfair, insulting process, and they wanted someone to listen to their concerns. Parents were frustrated because they wanted assurances that their children were getting quality education, and they wanted the schools held accountable for education. From parish to parish, from one city to another, I could almost feel the anger and distrust among the public, the disappointment in our school systems, and the defeatist attitude of our educators. I wanted to look you in the eye and tell you that we will have a real evaluation program in our schools."[72]

The legislature went along with the requests for change, including the delay. The BESE-approved management plan required the state Department of Education to form the four panels, the second of which would review the local evaluation plans for the state's sixty-six public school districts and develop uniform guidelines and procedures for the local school districts to follow. Each system was to be allowed some flexibility within the guidelines in consideration of each system's unique characteristics. The legislation also mandated that the districts keep the local evaluations as a permanent part of a teacher's record, so that every system hiring a teacher could request that teacher's evaluation results from his or her previous employer.

BESE Panel OKs "Foundation" for Teacher Evaluation[73]

After the in-state consultants' management plan was approved by the BESE, a panel of educators consisting of teachers, principals, superintendents, and college faculty met to determine what teaching proficiencies Louisiana educators would be expected to possess and demonstrate in a classroom. Called the "Louisiana Components of Effective Teaching," the list of skills was used as the framework for designing the state assessment as well as revamping local evaluation systems. According to the Components, teachers would be judged on their ability to perform teaching skills such as preparing objectives for instruction, maintaining an environment conducive to learning, maximizing the amount of time available for instruction, delivering instruction effectively, and presenting appropriate content. The content of the Components was very similar in many ways to the content of the STAR used in LaTEP and LTIP; although the statements were broader in scope and much fewer in number—twenty-three attributes compared to ninety-one STAR indicators. The Components also had an additional dimension that was not a part of the STAR, the specification of a "non-performance" domain that recognized professional development was an expected behavior of every education professional. The Components of Effective Teaching were later confirmed as being appropriate by a state-wide survey of over 7,000 educators including principals, teachers, and superintendents.

The BESE approved the Components as well as the second panel's recommendations on strengthening local evaluation. A timeline for reviewing and standardizing local evaluation systems was established. Local Steering Committees were to critique their systems and submit self-assessment reports by February 1993 to the state department of education. Revisions to local systems were to be planned in accordance with state guidelines, and the specifics were to be documented by June 1993 with the new local systems in full implementation by the fall of 1993. Panel Three completed a report on the resources available and the resources necessary for successful professional development in Louisiana.

Panel Four, the panel responsible for designing an instrument to be used in the state assessment, experienced difficulties in completing their task in the summer of 1993. Based on their knowledge of evaluation systems in other states, their awareness of how local evaluation was being strengthened in Louisiana, and their fear that such an instrument might lead to another LaTEP/LTIP experience, the majority of panel members rejected the idea of periodic state assessment for experienced teachers.

Concentrating instead on the initial assessment of interns for certification, the panel outlined an evaluation procedure that included preobservation conferences, classroom observations, and postobservation conferences by a principal, a master teacher, and a college faculty member or alternative third assessor. The individual assessments culminated in a four-way professional development conference and a written professional development plan. At that point, the Department of Education made the critical decision to limit the consideration of state assessment to intern teachers only and to defer planning assessments for experienced teachers. An additional panel completed the design of training and orientation materials in late 1992.

"State Seeks Districts to Test Revised Teacher Evaluation Program"[74]

Based on the timelines outlined in the management plan, the state Department of Education planned a "preliminary field test" for the intern assessment during the spring of 1993. The department asked thirteen school districts to test the instruments and training materials with a small sample of interns so that any major problems could be resolved prior to a larger scale pilot test in 1993–94.

Training sessions for assessors were conducted in several regions of the state and data collected and shared with yet another advisory group. Modifications were made to the instruments and procedures, and a pilot test for approximately 400 interns planned.

"Teacher Exam a Far Cry from Roemer Plan"[75]

The 1993–94 school year has seen the completion of the pilot test for the state assessment program for interns and the first full year of implementation for the revised local evaluation programs. In addition, the design of a complementary evaluation program for principals has begun. Numerous activities have yet to be completed. Standard setting for the assessment program, which will determine the criterion level for beginning teacher certification, will be addressed in early summer 1994. Because the 1992 legislation which delayed state evaluation was based on assessing beginning and experienced teachers, a new statute will have to be drafted and approved during a special legislative session in June 1994.

Analysis of pilot test data indicates that the vast majority of interns and assessors are satisfied with the state assessment program. Also, teachers throughout the state seem to be happier with the concept of professional development than with the concept of decertification. Mari Ann Fowler, director of research and development for the state department of education, said the biggest hurdle has been convincing teachers the evaluation program is not the one that Roemer tried to push. " . . . the strongest barrier we've had in trying to implement this program is the resistance to teacher evaluation because of the fear of what had happened in the past,"[76] Fowler said.

Fowler adds that Louisiana's approach to developing a new teacher evaluation program has attracted attention. For instance, the Southern Regional Education Board (SREB) has asked to review the program "because we are doing what the studies are showing works in terms of evaluation and assessment," Fowler commented. "We tried to remove the punitive part (of evaluation). We're focused more on the positive." Governor Edwin Edwards maintains that the new program acknowledges that "we're dealing with adult professionals," helping teachers grow and "making them more professional."[77]

Not everyone, however, believes that Louisiana is on the right track. "I have not seen exactly where they are (with the revision of teacher evaluation), but I have talked to four or five knowledgeable educators . . . and they say it is a total disaster," Buddy Roemer said recently. "They say it is non-substantive . . . It does not promote or advance the art of teaching. It is not a conduit to better pay or better public scrutiny. It does none of the things that we began five years ago trying to do."[78]

Lessons Learned

Louisiana's effort to establish a meaningful program of teacher evaluation has gone through three distinctive stages: implementation of a political agenda, revolution, and, finally, a movement toward professional development. The experiences in this state from 1988 to the present time point to several fundamental lessons which could be applied to other states and systems as they seek to develop professional accountability policies and procedures:

Lesson No. 1: If professional development is to be the ultimate objective of a teacher evaluation program, then the professional development component must be clearly articulated and evident.

As LaTEP and LTIP were being implemented, the developers of the system, the state department of education, and even the Governor continually stressed that the purpose of teacher evaluation was to improve teaching in the classroom. Teachers refused to believe these claims, however. To them, LaTEP/LTIP consisted of an inflexible observation, an unreasonable checklist, and the possibility of losing certification.

Lesson No. 2: The development of a teacher evaluation program must involve collaboration, consensus, and compromise.

To be effective, evaluation cannot be something that one group of professionals *do* to another group of professionals without their full consent and cooperation. Collaboration from all sectors is necessary from the initial stages of development through implementation.

Lesson No. 3: State leaders should not make the assumption that public opinion will propel an objectionable program into implementation.

While the majority of Louisianans believed that the public education system needed improvements, many came to wonder if the Roemer administration had the right plan.

Lesson No. 4: All critical questions must be answered prior to implementation.

For instance, the teacher evaluation program had been in full swing for several months before the scoring criteria for passing the evaluation had been established. Program developers have a professional obligation (and probably an ethical one as well) to disclose all policies and procedures to the people most affected by the program.

Lesson No. 5: "No one is an expert in his own backyard."

The old adage is true—local experts often seem less credible than outside experts, particularly during a controversy. Many concepts are more palatable when voiced by external consultants who appear to have more qualifications and more cosmopolitan viewpoints, whether they actually do or not. A related lesson deals with the number of experts employed to develop a teacher evaluation program. Pointing fingers is more difficult when a team of advisers is involved rather than a single, identifiable person. Louisiana's revamped evaluation program has relied on the cumulative expertise of over a dozen in-state and out-of-state consultants.

Lesson No. 6: Good communication is essential.

Communication between the governing bodies, teachers, state department personnel, and the professional associations must be continuous throughout the entire development process. Public relations are of paramount importance as well. The power of the press is substantial when issues of public policy and public interest are at stake.

Lesson No. 7: You can't change the rules in the middle of the game.

Veteran teachers who had met all the requirements for Louisiana certification years earlier and who were practicing their profession suddenly found their licensure at risk with LaTEP. They felt that the "contract" they had entered into with the state had been breached. Even though, in the final analysis, over 95 percent of teachers would have been able to pass the evaluation, they felt betrayed and insulted, their livelihood and security threatened. Many have speculated that teacher evaluation would have met with far less resistance if renewable certification had been phased in for beginning teachers only.

Notes

1. *Baton Rouge Morning Advocate,* 21 March 1988, p. 1B, 8B. All subheadings are actual newspaper headlines, taken from the indicated newspaper on the date shown. The quotations cited are taken from the newspaper accounts as well.

2. Ibid., p. 1B.

3. *New Orleans Times-Picayune,* 27 May 1988, pp. A1, A4.

4. *New Orleans Times-Picayune,* 30 June 1988, pp. A1, A4.

5. *New Orleans Times-Picayune,* 23 November 1988, pp. B1, B2.

6. Ibid., p. B2.

7. *New Orleans Times-Picayune,* 20 November 1989, pp. B1, B3.

8. Ibid., p. B1.

9. *Baton Rouge State Times,* 10 January 1990, p. B2.

10. *Baton Rouge Morning Advocate,* 28 March 1990, p. B2.

11. *Baton Rouge Morning Advocate,* 12 April 1990, p. B2.

12. Ibid.

13. *Baton Rouge Morning Advocate,* 20 April 1990, p. A13.

14. *Baton Rouge Sunday Advocate,* 15 April 1990, p. A1.

15. *Baton Rouge Morning Advocate,* 20 April 1990, p. A13.

16. *Baton Rouge Morning Advocate*, 4 May 1990, p. B7.

17. *Baton Rouge Sunday Advocate*, 27 May 1990, p. A1.

18. *Baton Rouge State Times*, 6 September 1990, p. E7.

19. Ibid.

20. *Baton Rouge State Times*, 26 October 1990, p. B2.

21. *Baton Rouge State Times*, 19 November 1990, p. B2.

22. Ibid.

23. Ibid.

24. Ibid.

25. *Baton Rouge State Times*, 1 December 1990, p. A1.

26. *Baton Rouge State Times*, 14 December 1990, p. D3.

27. *Baton Rouge Morning Advocate*, 14 December 1990, p. A1.

28. *Baton Rouge State Times*, 28 December 1990, p. C6.

29. *Baton Rouge Morning Advocate*, 14 December 1990, p. A1.

30. *Baton Rouge State Times*, 2 January 1991, p. A4.

31. Ibid.

32. *Baton Rouge State Times*, 3 January 1991, p. A4.

33. *Baton Rouge Morning Advocate*, 8 January 1991, p. B1.

34. Ibid.

35. Ibid.

36. Ibid.

37. *Baton Rouge State Times*, 23 January 1991, p. B1.

38. *Baton Rouge State Times*, 29 January 1991, p. A10.

39. Ibid.

40. Ibid.

41. *Baton Rouge State Times*, 30 January 1991, p. B1.

42. *Baton Rouge Morning Advocate*, 7 February 1991, p. B1.

43. *Baton Rouge State Times*, 7 February 1991, p. E6.

44. *Saturday State Times/Morning Advocate*, 9 February 1991, p. B1.

45. Ibid.

46. Ibid.

47. *Baton Rouge Morning Advocate*, 15 February 1991, p. A1.

48. Ibid.

49. Ibid.

50. Ibid.

51. Ibid.

52. Ibid.

53. Ibid.

54. *Baton Rouge State Times*, 14 June 1991, p. B1.

55. Ibid.

56. *Baton Rouge Morning Advocate*, 25 June 1991, p. A1.

57. Ibid.

58. Ibid.

59. Ibid.

60. *Baton Rouge State Times*, 13 August 1991, p. B1.

61. *Baton Rouge State Times*, 26 September 1991, p. B1.

62. Ibid.

63. Ibid.

64. *Baton Rouge Sunday Advocate*, 20 October 1991, p. A1.

65. Ibid.

66. Ibid.

67. *Baton Rouge Morning Advocate*, 9 January 1992, p. A1.

68. Ibid.

69. Ibid.

70. *Baton Rouge Morning Advocate*, 13 February 1992, p. A1.

71. *Baton Rouge Morning Advocate*, 19 June 1992, p. A12.

72. *Baton Rouge Morning Advocate*, 8 May 1992, p. A1.

73. *Baton Rouge Morning Advocate*, 22 July 1992, pp. B1–B2.

74. *Baton Rouge Morning Advocate*, 21 January 1993, p. B2.

75. *Baton Rouge Morning Advocate*, 2 August 1993, p. A4.

76. Ibid.

77. *Baton Rouge Morning Advocate*, 23 November 1993, p. A14.

78. *Baton Rouge Morning Advocate*, 2 August 1993, p. A4.

6

Compromise and Persistence: The Evolution of Teacher Evaluation Policy in Washington State[1]

*Daniel L. Duke, Doris Lyon, Patty Raichle,
Ann Randall, and Jim Russell*

For a decade, from 1984 to 1994, policymakers and educators in Washington State worked to develop and implement new policies governing teacher evaluation and professional growth. The process was characterized by compromise and persistence. The Washington State story is an account of the convergence of conflicting political and professional agendas, represented on one hand by pressure from business leaders and legislators for greater teacher accountability and performance pay and on the other hand by educators' dissatisfaction with conventional evaluation practice and concern for the continuing growth of competent teachers. Accounts of policy development often conclude with the adoption of the new policy. We, too, could have chosen to end our case study in November of 1990 with the filing of Washington Administrative Code (WAC) 392.192, the regulations that called for changes in teacher evaluation practices designed to streamline teacher evaluation and promote greater professional development. Had we done so, the story would have concluded with successful negotiations between accountability proponents and professional development advocates concerning policy language that encompassed both formative and summative evaluation.

In the aftermath of compromise, however, came the challenge of implementing WAC 392.192. The circumstances surrounding policy implementation frequently differ from those under which policies originally are developed. Such was the case in Washington State. By the time school districts were expected to initiate planning for revised teacher evaluation systems, the political and economic climate had changed, confronting educators with a new set of issues. In addition, the rallying cries of the proaccountability and the proprofessional development forces were not silenced by policy compromise. Each group continued to advance its original position, the former using the creation of the Governor's Commission on Educational Reform and Finance to revive calls for performance pay, the latter introducing legislation to lengthen the period of formative evaluation for competent teachers and thereby extend the time for professional development. Based on the example of Washington State, policy compromise should not necessarily be regarded as the end of policy development. Agreements, whether arrived at in the political arena or at the bargaining table, simply may mark stages in an evolutionary process of policy development and reformulation.

The case study begins with a description of the bifurcated context in which policy development in Washington initially took place. The origins of WAC 392.192 can be traced to two separate contexts, one characterized by ferment, the other by frustration. At the state level, legislators and business leaders became caught up in the educational reform movement of the early 1980s, a movement that sought to increase the economic competitiveness of the United States by increasing educational accountability and applying business practices to the operation of school systems. Meanwhile, on the local level some school systems were growing frustrated with conventional teacher evaluation practices. One district in particular, South Kitsap, a moderately sized district close to Seattle, struggled to find a way of improving relations between teachers and their evaluators. Eventually South Kitsap would play a key role in the policy development process.

The next part of the case study covers the formation and deliberations of a state task force to develop guidelines for the reform of teacher evaluation. This group provided an opportunity for proaccountability and proprofessional development groups to clarify and debate their positions. They eventually reached an accord which led to the adoption of new regulations governing teacher evaluation.

Part four deals with the implementation of these regulations—WAC 392.192. The regulations required that new teacher evaluation systems be adopted in all Washington school districts by the fall of 1991. The extent to which this requirement was met and the reasons why one particular approach to teacher evaluation—the South Kitsap model—seemed to prevail are covered in this part of the chapter.

As indicated earlier, compromise and agreement do not necessarily signify the end of policy development. As WAC 392.192 was being implemented, proaccountability and proprofessional development forces persisted in advancing their positions. Parts five and six describe these efforts. The chapter closes with some reflections on the policy development process in Washington and its implications for other states.

Ferment in Olympia

In 1983, the National Commission on Excellence in Education issued *A Nation At Risk*, thereby initiating a wave of school reform. Subsequently came a spate of reports, including the Carnegie Forum on Education and the Economy's *A Nation Prepared: Teachers for the 21st Century* and the Holmes Group's *Tomorrow's Teachers*. Both of these documents suggested that the teaching profession needed greater role differentiation based on credentials and performance as well as more attractive incentives for highly capable teachers. While the education profession studied these reports, two other groups began to engage in discussions of educational reform. The business community, acting through national and regional organizations such as the Business Roundtable, pressed school systems to adopt certain private sector practices like career ladders and merit pay. Governors and state legislators, sensing widespread public disaffection with schools, sought new approaches to educational accountability.

Such was the national context as Washington State began to consider issues of teacher performance and evaluation in 1984. During the 1984 legislative session, the House Education Committee drafted and passed out of committee an ill-fated bill that would have altered the mandate that Washington teachers undergo an annual sixty-minute observation and evaluation. The proposed legislation, which failed on the floor of the House, would have required a sixty-minute evaluation *every other year.* The 1985 legislative session saw two more bills related to teacher evaluation. Although introduced independently, HB 849 and HB 925 increasingly became linked in the minds of legislators. These bills framed the issues surrounding teacher evaluation that legislators and educators would debate for the next three years.

HB 849 was introduced by Representative Art Wang, a Democrat from Tacoma, Washington, and member of the House Education Committee. According to Wang, the bill was inspired by his wife, a Tacoma public school teacher who had grown dissatisfied with the existing teacher evaluation system. She felt the system was "a joke," since it failed to assist good teachers, weed out bad teachers, or provide constructive feedback. Representative Wang visited schools in Tacoma and talked to principals, who voiced their concern over the extraordinary amount of time involved in teacher observation and evaluation. Little time was left, they claimed, to work with truly deficient staff members.

The intent of Wang's bill is best captured in his testimony during a February 19, 1985, public hearing on the bill:

> There seems to be a little bit of a dichotomy in how evaluation is used and perceived—whether it's used as a constructive technique to assist people in improving the quality of their work or whether it's used as a means of, in effect, punishing bad performance as opposed to rewarding good performance. The bill does not really resolve the dichotomy, but it does put more emphasis on the constructive use of evaluation. . . . Frankly, I think it's a necessary and separate first step for any sort of career ladder proposal. This bill attempts to put evaluation on a more consistent level and at the same time provide for more innovative techniques. The bill calls for pilot proposals that would include such things as peer review, input from parents and students, and instructional assistance teams from inside or outside the building.[2]

In an effort to ensure consistent evaluations, HB 849 required that (1) all teacher evaluators receive training in evaluation techniques, and (2) the Office of Superintendent of Public Instruction "develop and test standards for conducting evaluations." The bill further stipulated that the Superintendent of Public Instruction develop or purchase model evaluation programs which could be tested in local districts. The Superintendent of Public Instruction was directed to select, by July 1, 1988, one to five model evaluation programs that could be used by local districts.[3] While this particular provision of the bill appeared to allow a measure of discretion in local teacher evaluation, Wang's intent was far from promoting flexibility, as his remarks during the Education Committee's deliberations on the bill indicated. At the February 27, 1985, meeting of the committee, Wang said,

> The concept is that we want to move toward a state mandated evaluation program. The minimum standards will be adopted in 1986 and the full models will be adopted in 1988. This will reduce the flexibility of districts. We need to take advantage of centralized knowledge about evaluation. The decision in each school district would only be over which of the five models they could choose.[4]

In an effort to reward good teachers and free administrators to work with deficient teachers, the bill permitted districts to "provide for a short evaluation procedure for teachers who have had four years of satisfactory evaluations."[5] This provision came to be known as the "short form." Furthermore, a complete summative evaluation was required only once every three years for these teachers. The desire to move away from full annual evaluations of competent teachers actually had been around for several years. A representative of Tacoma Public Schools reminded legislators, in fact, that a system similar to that called for in HB 849 had been proposed in 1982.[6]

Most of the public testimony on HB 849 supported the proposed legislation. The Association of Washington School Principals (AWSP) testified in favor of the shortened evaluation procedure, claiming that "it would allocate time in a demanding schedule for additional instruction and supervision."[7] Furthermore AWSP endorsed the concept of a differentiated evaluation model. As one speaker noted, "The present process involves a great deal of principals' and teachers' time even though the staff members may be most competent and not need it. . . . I rewrite reports for good teachers trying to find new ways each year to say they're good teachers."[8] The Washington Education Association (WEA) also lent its support to the bill, as did the Office of Superintendent of Public Instruction (OSPI). The Washington School Administrators Association (WSAA) cautioned, however, that any move to initiate a career ladder system could undermine part of the intent of HB 849. One speaker doubted that administrators would have time to focus on deficient teachers if they had to manage career ladder assessments.[9]

At the same time the bill was being considered, members of the Business Roundtable were lobbying for merit pay. They realized, however, that no state-wide performance standards existed to enable school administrators to differentiate among teachers in a legally defensible way. Their hope was that HB 849 would lead to teacher evaluation systems driven by common performance standards.

The companion legislation to HB 849, HB 925 was proposed and sponsored by Representative Georgette Valle, a Democrat from Seattle and a member of the House Education Committee. Valle's bill sought to "make evaluation a meaningful component of teacher development and to encourage staff development by creating incentives."[10] The bill also mandated that (1) principals should be evaluated on their ability to perform evaluations; (2) principals who were deficient in evaluation skills should receive training; (3) The Superintendent of Public Instruction should randomly check evaluations of teachers; (4) a twelve-member panel should be created to study the state's evaluation system and compare it to other states; (5) the provisional period (before tenure) for teachers should be extended from one to two years; and (6) a mentor teacher program should be established for provisional teachers. The section of the bill that created the most discussion among sponsors of HB 925 and supporters of HB 849 was the provision that,

> the Superintendent of Public Instruction shall establish a pilot program in ten districts enabling a career ladder. The career ladder shall be implemented in 1985–86 and 1986–87 and shall be designed within existing revenue limits. A report on the program shall be made to the legislature by January 15, 1987.[11]

In the deliberations on HB 925 that followed the public hearing, members of the House Education Committee appeared to associate the bill's career ladder provision with the evaluation system called for in HB 849. Whether this commingling of provisions from separate bills was intentional or the result of confusion could not be ascertained. During the February 25, 1985, session, Representative Wang pointed out that his bill, HB 849, was "a significant step in the direction of standardized, stringent criteria for evaluation that can be used in conjunction with the career ladder we're discussing."[12] Representative Todd added, "Our staff has told us that the current evaluation system will not work with the career ladder proposal. This bill [HB 925] revises evaluation so that it will be useful with career ladders."[13]

Seven years after the introduction of the two bills, when asked what conditions in the mid-1980s created the momentum to change teacher evaluation, Wang recalled, "The impetus at the time was the focus on career ladders and master teachers. . . . Was there any such thing as meaningful and fair evaluations which could be used for the purposes of determining compensation—ultimately determining compensation and determining promotions?"[14] Greater accountability was the order of the day. If concern for the ongoing professional growth of teachers figured in the thinking of legislators at the time, Wang was unaware of it.

HB 925 ultimately failed to pass the legislature during the 1985 session, but HB 849, with all of its unanticipated links to failed HB 925, did pass in 1985 and became Revised Code of Washington (RCW) 28.A.67.065 and 28.A.67.115–225. Charged with the task of developing the procedural evaluation standards and model evaluation programs called for in HB 849, the Office of State Superintendent of Public Instruction approached the legislature during the 1986 session with an amendment that delineated the process by which it would develop standards and identify model programs. The amendment extended the timeline for field testing and adoption for one year and created an advisory task force composed of school administrators, teachers, parents, students, and business leaders to oversee the process.[15] Because of the overly ambitious timeline and difficulty procuring funding for field testing, deadlines were extended twice more, in 1988, and again in 1989.

In early 1986, OSPI invited nine organizations to appoint representatives to an Advisory Task Force on Evaluation (ATFE). The Washington Education Association, the major teacher organization in the state, was assigned three seats on the task force. The Washington Federation of Teachers, the Washington State School Directors Association, the Washington School Administrators Association, the Association of Washington School Principals, the Washington Parent Teacher Association, the Washington Business Roundtable and Citizens Education Northwest, each were allotted one representative. Over the next three years, the appointees to ATFE and the staff assigned by the respective organizations to assist them deliberated the future of teacher evaluation in Washington State and whether it should be linked to some form of performance pay. An account of the task force's work follows the next part of the chapter.

Frustration at the District Level

In October of 1985, Jim Russell, a staff member from the Washington Education Association and the Olympic UniServ Council, and Jack Nelson, President of the South Kitsap Education Association, met for lunch to discuss a possible grievance regarding the alleged failure of the South Kitsap School District to follow the evaluation procedures specified in the local collective bargaining agreement. Their discussion moved from the specific grievance to concern that the entire evaluation system was not working well. The school district and the education association were not getting what they wanted—a system to raise the quality of instruction and improve student performance. Russell introduced the concept of formative evaluation, which he had read about and discussed during a recent meeting at the National Education Association.[16] He suggested that a teacher-initiated growth system made more sense, since research indicated the vast majority of teachers were competent and met minimum standards for continued employment. To focus an entire evaluation system on a relatively small number of teachers who were not meeting minimum standards hardly seemed an effective use of limited administrative resources. Furthermore, existing teacher evaluation practices rarely contributed to improved teacher performance or greater student learning.

The lunch ended with Russell agreeing to share the material he had reviewed at NEA headquarters and Nelson promising to meet with the district's personnel director, Colin Hergert, to explore the idea of a new approach to teacher evaluation. Neither man knew at the time that their discussion would lead, over the next five years, to the development, adoption, and implementation of a pathbreaking professional growth system for the South Kitsap School District. Moreover, these efforts, because of their timing, would directly affect the formulation of state teacher evaluation policy, eventually influencing each school district in Washington.

Nelson's initial discussions with Hergert were very promising. As the district's personnel director, Hergert had taken the brunt of several teacher association grievances regarding teacher evaluation. Additionally, the topic of teacher evaluation regularly came up at the bargaining table, prompting Hergert to think there must be a better way to evaluate teachers. Both Nelson and Hergert discussed the issue with their respective bargaining teams, and during contract negotiations in the summer of 1985 the two sides agreed to assemble a joint committee to study different evaluation models and design a new teacher evaluation system.

The committee was composed of some of South Kitsap's most respected and knowledgeable teachers and administrators. Interviewed eight years later, John Long, the joint committee chair and, at that time, an elementary principal, recalled:

> We put some pretty influential people together—people from the association that were identified leaders. They were key movers. All were past presidents of the association and bargainers. The people that represented the administration were influential leaders among their peers—both building principals and district administrators . . . it was a group of people that did not have to iron out those idiosyncrasies that exist when you put a group of people together for the first time. The people knew each other from their leadership positions.[17]

Not only was the group composed of influential leaders, but, as Long also pointed out:

> We had the good fortune of finding cooperative people with a single aim, a single vision and a tremendous commitment that was reinforced by the district's superintendent.[18]

The superintendent, Dr. Dwayne Gower, gave the committee few directions for its work, other than the charge that it was to develop something new that promoted both accountability and professional growth. In a memo to the community, Gower wrote:

> The specific charge of this committee will be to recommend to the superintendent an evaluation system that will accurately and fairly assess the skills and performance of each staff member. That the system should provide direction to both staff members and administrators for instructional growth and development.

The system must provide a clear and distinct procedure for communicating success, needs for improvement, or consequences of unsuccessful performance.

The committee will be provided with the resources and time to thoroughly study the topic. It is recommended that they follow these steps:

1. Develop a statement of purpose.
2. Build an information base.
3. Study current trends in the state.
4. Accept a set of foundations to use in designing the system.
5. Design the steps, procedures, and forms to implement those foundations.
6. Recommend the system to the superintendent.[19]

The superintendent supported the group's work with funding that allowed the committee to meet frequently over the next two years. As one committee member reflected,

I think that the key element of long-term success and impact was the ability of the task force to establish trust to enable us to problem solve and communicate to the various audiences with a great deal of immediate effectiveness. I also believe that it was vital that the district leadership and association leadership committed time and resources to assure success.

The agenda for the first two or three committee meetings consisted exclusively of team-building activities—a strategy that eventually paid great dividends. As committee member Ann Randall remembered:

Our first meetings allowed the group to set ground rules for how we were going to work with each other and it also gave an opportunity for everyone—teachers, principals, and district administrators to share our feelings about the existing evaluation system. I remember how surprised I was to find out that principals were as frustrated with the constraints as we were. They knew that for veteran teachers it was just a dog and pony show. That was a real revelation for teachers on the committee. Those early discussions also let us get on the table right away issues that we called rhinoceros heads—the issues that kept reappearing throughout the committee's work. There were never hidden agendas that blind-sided the group later because we all knew the rhinoceros heads early on in the process.[20]

The first year of the committee's work also included gathering information, reading and sharing articles, bringing in outside experts, and attending conferences. The idea of a two-part evaluation system with summative and formative components began to gel when the committee received assistance from the Northwest Regional Educational Laboratory, which recently had sponsored some research on teacher evaluation and professional growth.

The committee took two years to develop language describing the new evaluation system. Throughout the two years all teachers and administrators in the district were kept apprised of the committee work through a newsletter. During the summer of 1987, a description of the new evaluation system was added to the collective bargaining agreement—five pages of unorthodox contract language that described in "user friendly" language how teachers in South Kitsap would be evaluated. New teachers would begin with annual summative evaluations based on class observations, conferences with principals, and specific performance standards. Once tenured, teachers would spend two of every three years in formative evaluation, working on professional development goals and conferring with a supervisor. During the third year, teachers returned to the summative evaluation system. A "safety valve" was provided in the event a teacher in formative evaluation started to experience serious problems.

In 1988, the district agreed to provide every teacher in the district with $625 in professional development funds to support their formative evaluation efforts. Funds could be used for substitutes, materials, or payment for extra hours. Financial support for teachers' professional growth activities gave even more credibility to the new system. Teachers signed up for university coursework and in-service classes in significantly greater numbers than before, compelling South Kitsap to expand its staff development offerings. The results so impressed the district and association that in 1990 the two sides agreed to nearly double the amount available for professional growth.

Because the stakes were so high in this complete overhaul of teacher evaluation, the committee made two important decisions prior to implementing the new model. It decided to contract with the Northwest Regional Educational Laboratory (NWREL) to conduct an assessment of teacher and principal attitudes regarding evaluation at the outset of implementation and again three years later. The committee also decided to continue to meet in order to oversee the implementation of the new evaluation system.

Research on the new system's effectiveness has been ongoing. In 1990, the second NWREL assessment was administered, and the results indicated a statistically significant shift in attitude regarding evaluation and professional growth in South Kitsap. For the next two years, Allen Hughes, a district administrator and member of the joint committee, conducted his doctoral dissertation research on the new evaluation process and provided additional insights into the new system. Hughes' work emphasized the need for ongoing training for principals and teachers.[21]

A Convergence of Concerns

While South Kitsap was designing its new evaluation system in the fall of 1986, the Advisory Task Force on Evaluation began meeting. The initial meetings were contentious, as the intent of HB 849 was debated at length. Conflict mainly involved representatives of the WEA and the Business Roundtable. Neal Supplee, a Boeing executive and representative of the Roundtable, supported the idea of performance pay. He recalled that, when he joined the task force, performance pay, though not mentioned specifically in the new legislation, was "in the mind of some of the legislators."[22] These individuals believed that teachers should be differentiated by achievement and that the best should be rewarded accordingly.

The WEA, represented by Gail Mathison, a teacher from South Kitsap, and Jim Russell, were opposed to differentiating pay based on performance. Committed to formative evaluation and professional growth, they felt that any link between teacher evaluation and merit pay would undermine teacher development. Their involvement in the planning of South Kitsap's growth-oriented teacher evaluation system soon became a key focus for task force discussion. Jan Stout, a task force member representing Citizen's Action Northwest, recalled:

> Had it not been for the vision and inspiration that South Kitsap brought because of . . . the progress they had made in defining a new system, I don't think we would have every come out with a product of any kind.[23]

By the spring of 1987, the ATFE had reached agreement that the new evaluation "standards" should have a formative thrust. Performance pay advocates either were converted to the WEA's growth-oriented perspective or they conceded that the timing for their recommendations was wrong. For one thing, state resources to support performance pay were unavailable. The WEA representatives also succeeded in convincing other members of the ATFE that formative teacher evaluation should be separate from summative evaluation. Once accepted, the belief that districts needed separate evaluation systems for separate purposes became the foundation of the task force's recommendations. The accountability or summative system was designated for employment decisions such as promotion and dismissal, while the formative system was reserved for professional growth.[24]

Task force members representing school administrators expressed the opinion that teachers on formative systems should not be allowed to include results from growth experiences in their personnel files. Such material could be used, they argued, to weaken the summative system. Administrators reasoned that marginal teachers might pack their files with positive evaluations from their formative system activities, thereby making it more difficult for principals to demonstrate the need for remediation if teachers did not fare well in summative evaluation. The WEA representatives on the ATFE argued that they did not want the opposite situation to arise—where files could be filled with negative information on teachers participating in professional growth activities. The very possibility that such data could be gathered, they reasoned, might discourage teachers from experimenting and undertaking ambitious goals. These two opposing viewpoints finally were resolved by the adoption of the principle of a "data curtain." As a result, neither positive nor negative material could be placed in teachers' personnel files during the formative evaluation period. The "data curtain" originally had been tried by South Kitsap and found to be a valuable component of the new teacher evaluation system.

By the spring of 1987, OSPI officials realized that the task force would be unable to meet the legislative timetable. An extension was granted by the legislature, but no funding was provided for field testing model teacher-evaluation programs.[25] Using its own budget, OSPI was able to offer $1,500 to each participating school system. Thirty-eight school districts submitted proposals for pilot projects. Eleven districts, rather than the five originally specified in the statute, were selected to conduct field tests. The eleven school districts included South Kitsap, Warden, North Thurston, Wenatchee, Prosser, Arlington, Kent, Snohomish, Camas, Riverview, and Adna. Six of the districts implemented locally developed models, while five of the districts used imported models such as the Florida Performance Measurement System. Several of the locally developed models were based on a multitrack teacher evaluation system designed by Daniel Duke and Richard Stiggins.[26] This system, which was similar to South Kitsap's, provided separate evaluation processes for the purposes of teacher accountability, remediation, and professional growth. Each track involved different procedures and consequences. If evaluation on the accountability track revealed performance problems, teachers could be placed on a remedial track. Failure to correct deficiencies on the remedial track might result in dismissal. Teachers on the professional growth track were evaluated on their progress toward individual goals, but failure to achieve these goals did not occasion any negative consequences. The system assumed that only teachers who had been judged competent would be eligible for the professional development track, thereby obviating the need for sanctions.

Once the pilot tests began, OSPI lobbied to extend the time period for field testing. The task force held the view that a field test of one year would not produce sufficient data to permit endorsement of one "recommended" model. Not only was an extension denied, but no funds were appropriated to support additional field testing. Without adequate time or funds from the legislature, the original charge to test competing models of teacher evaluation no longer made much sense. Task force members began to consider altering the intent of the enabling statute and heading in another direction. With the Business Roundtable and the WEA working together, at least for the moment, the task force opted to de-emphasize accountability and focus squarely on professional growth. As Neal Supplee of the Business Roundtable recalled:

> I think that we stretched the RCW [Revised Code of Washington] sufficiently far that everyone kept their heads down and didn't want to wave the flag very much. . . . We took that hummer and stretched every way come Christmas. I felt fine about it and of course my job wasn't on the line for it. I think Ted [OSPI coordinator] was holding his breath and had its fingers crossed that it would be okay. Not that what we did was not good, but our authority to do so was restrained.[27]

In 1989, OSPI submitted a report to the legislature with the following recommendation: "One to five evaluation models will be developed only if the OSPI Advisory Task Force on Evaluation and the eleven school districts agree on one or more models to be used."[28] The agency received approval for their recommendation, which was regarded as a signal to the task force that they could proceed to develop new procedural standards for teacher evaluation, ones that focused on professional development. No mention of performance pay would be made. Since agreement on a single model of teacher evaluation could not be reached, school districts would be allowed to design their own systems.

By early spring of 1990, the task force had completed its work on a revision of WAC 392.192. Besides minor changes in sections .001 through .020, material addressing the minimum procedural standards required by the legislature were added. Sections .060 through .100 contained the professional growth component. In the summer of 1990, the regulations governing the implementation of the WAC were adopted by the State Board of Education. The new growth component required each district to establish a committee of teachers and administrators to develop a professional growth program (PGP) by September of 1990. Implementation of these locally developed plans was scheduled for September of 1991.

Implementing Professional Growth Programs

Early in 1993, the Washington Education Association conducted a survey of local association presidents to determine the extent to which OSPI's new regulations governing teacher evaluation and professional growth had been implemented. Of 208 respondents, representing 70 percent of all presidents surveyed, one-third (69) reported that a new teacher evaluation system including a professional growth program had been implemented.[29] Almost 11 percent[29] (22) of the presidents indicated that a new teacher evaluation system would be implemented by the end of the 1992–93 school years. An additional 26 percent (54) stated that their districts currently were in the process of developing new systems. Slightly more than 30 percent of the respondents (63) revealed that no steps had been taken to comply with the new regulations. Table 6-1 indicates that parts of the implementation process had been completed by those districts that were developing new teacher evaluation systems.

The WEA survey also gathered information regarding the characteristics of the new teacher evaluation systems that had been implemented or, at the very least, bargained. As Table 6-2 suggests, the new systems tended to share several common features. As it turned out, these common features also were found in the original South Kitsap model. Why this model might have been emulated by so many school districts will be addressed shortly.

Seventy-five percent of the 108 districts that had implemented, or approved for implementation, new teacher evaluation systems opted for a multitrack arrangement in which teachers who were not involved in accountability-based evaluation and who met basic performance standards could participate in a professional growth program. Participation in the latter was voluntary in 91 percent of the districts with professional growth programs. A majority of districts (58 percent) did not require teachers either to set a specific number or type of goal. Teachers negotiated goals with their principals in over half of the eighty-eight districts, but principals were given the authority to reject or alter teachers' goals in less than 40 percent of the districts.

From the perspective of policy compliance, it is interesting to note the instances where state regulations seem to have been disregarded. The sixty-three districts that were reported to have taken no steps to develop or implement a new teacher evaluation system appear to be in violation of state law, since it is doubtful that they already had systems in place that would satisfy the new guidelines. As of the spring of 1994, OSPI had taken no initiative to identify or reprimand school districts that were out of compliance with WAC 392–192.

While the guidelines called for joint planning by teachers and administrators, 9 percent of the association presidents reported that such broadbased involvement had not occurred. Guidelines also required training for teachers prior to implementing new evaluation systems, but more

TABLE 6-1. Stage of Implementation of New Teacher Evaluation System

Has your district developed a new teacher evaluation process in response to the 1990 revisions in OSPI's evaluation regulations that require a professional growth option for certificated staff?

All 208 Respondents

Percent	Frequency	
30.3	63	A. No steps have been taken to develop a new teacher evaluation system that includes a professional growth option.
26.0	54	B. We are currently in the process of developing a new teacher evaluation system that includes a professional growth option.
10.6	22	C. A new teacher evaluation system that includes a professional growth option will be implemented within the 1992–93 school year.
33.2	69	D. A new teacher evaluation system that includes a professional growth option has already been implemented.

If the answer to the above question was "B" or "C," please mark the step that has been reached in your district at the time of this survey.

54 Respondents for Question 1-B		22 Respondents for Question 1-C		
Percent	Frequency	Percent	Frequency	
13.0	7	0.0	0	A. A joint committee has been formed.
33.3	18	0.0	0	B. A joint committee is meeting to develop a new teacher evaluation system.
27.8	15	18.2	4	C. A joint committee has agreed upon a new teacher evaluation model with a professional growth option.
5.6	3	72.7	16	D. The new model, with a professional growth option, has been bargained into the contract.
20.4	11	4.5	1	Missing data

TABLE 6-2. Characteristics of New Teacher Evaluation System

replied D to question 1 (teacher evaluation system implemented with professional growth option) or C, D, and E to question 3 (joint committee as agreed on new teacher evalutation model or new evaluation model has been bargained).

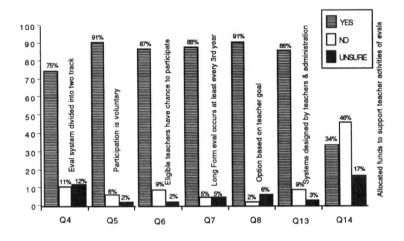

TABLE 6-3. Characteristics of Professional Growth Component

Characteristics of the new teacher evaluation systems for the 88 people who replied YES on question 8 (professional growth option of new teacher evaluation system based on teacher goals).

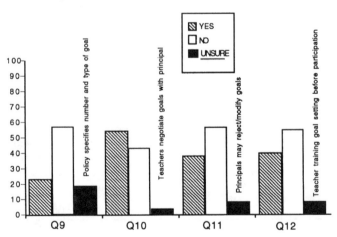

than half of the districts with goal-based professional growth programs reported that no such training had taken place. Indeed, local resources to assure successful implementation of the new teacher evaluation policies seemed relatively scarce. Only 34 percent of the 108 districts with a new system either in place or set to be implemented indicated that funds had been allocated specifically for teachers' professional growth activities.

If the survey of association presidents is accurate, many of the new teacher evaluation systems contained characteristics found in the South Kitsap system, which had been implemented in 1986. Like most of the districts with new teacher evaluation plans, South Kitsap developed a multitrack system in which teachers not undergoing a triennial ("long form") summative evaluation could choose to set goals and develop a professional growth plan. Teachers negotiated these goals with their principals. Unlike many districts, however, South Kitsap's policies earmarked funds to support teachers on professional growth plans and specified the number and types of goals teachers were expected to set.

Of all the possible explanations for why the South Kitsap model seemed so similar to the teacher evaluation systems developed elsewhere, coincidence appears the least likely. As one of the first districts to develop a new teacher evaluation system and as one of the eleven pilot districts supported by OSPI, South Kitsap was in a position from the outset to share its policies and experiences with other districts. The fact that the National Education Association singled out South Kitsap's system for special national recognition only increased the likelihood of emulation. Members of the South Kitsap evaluation committee who had helped to formulate the new teacher evaluation system were invited by a number of school districts to meet with planning groups and explain their new system. Copies of South Kitsap's teacher evaluation policies were shared widely. Consultants from the Northwest Regional Educational Laboratory who had provided South Kitsap with technical assistance also worked with other districts in Washington, thereby providing another mechanism for proliferating the South Kitsap model. When OSPI issued the regulations governing revisions in teacher evaluation, the Washington Education Association created a special cadre of trainers to assist school districts faced with implementing WAC 392.192.[30] The head of the cadre had been a member of the South Kitsap Evaluation Committee. She used the policies and experiences from South Kitsap to illustrate what was entailed in developing local teacher evaluation systems.

The popularity of the South Kitsap model also might be explained by the compressed time frame for local policy development and implementation. While a handful of districts anticipated the regulations and began planning early, most waited until WAC 392.192 was issued in the summer of 1990. The target date for implementation was the fall of 1991. Given this brief period of time, many districts were inclined either to adapt or adopt South Kitsap's model rather than start from scratch.

In 1993, feelings about the new system were shared by association presidents in thirty-four districts that had at least a year's experience with a new teacher evaluation system involving a professional growth program. About two in five (41 percent) said they were very satisfied, while another 47 percent indicated they were somewhat satisfied. Only 11.7 percent—four individuals—responded that they were somewhat or very dissatisfied with the new system.

Recent Developments—GCERF

The context in which policy is formulated and implemented often in unstable. Such has been the case with teacher evaluation policy in Washington State. In 1991, before most districts had had a chance to respond to the new procedural standards, a state-wide strike by school employees compelled Governor Booth Gardner to create the Governor's Council on Educational Reform and Funding (GCERF). The twenty-one member panel, consisting of education, business, and government leaders, was charged with developing a plan for Washington's education system that would "significantly improve the performance of all students as evidenced by a well-developed system of assessment and accountability."

By the end of 1991, GCERF had established subcommittees to address various segments of the council's charge. One such group was the Professional Development Subcommittee, and it invited people from education and business to assist subcommittee members in their work. Among these recruits were several members of WEA's Formative Teacher Evaluation Cadre and individuals who had been involved in South Kitsap's efforts to establish a new evaluation system. Neal Supplee, the Business Roundtable representative to the ATFE, also worked with the subcommittee as one of several representatives from the private sector.

The Professional Development Subcommittee initially met on January 21, 1992, to "establish characteristics of effective educators and their relevant professional development requirements; tie effective teacher characteristics to teacher salaries; and test ideas with educators, students, and communities statewide." To WEA representatives, however, these duties did not seem to be consistent with those originally put forth by the Governor's Council. They wondered how the issue of merit pay managed to resurface after presumably being laid to rest during the meetings of the ATFE. The subcommittee finally agreed to set aside the matter of compensation and whether or not it should be tied to professional development. Instead, they focused on evaluation processes and growth opportunities for teachers in student-based outcome systems. The prior work of the ATFE and school districts' experiences with the implementation of PGP's convinced the subcommittee that teacher evaluation should not be linked to student evaluation. The final recommendations of the subcommittee laid the groundwork for HB1209's professional development and planning grants, which became available to schools in June of 1994.

In a last-ditch effort to keep the merit pay issue alive, GCERF constituted a new subcommittee, the Compensation Subcommittee, made up of people from the Professional Development and Funding Subcommittees of the Council. This subcommittee was instructed to address teacher compensation. While a series of contentious meetings was held on the subject, no agreement could be reached, and the subject was dropped.

In the final report of the GCERF, the references to professional accountability tended to be vague. For example:

> Accountability is a major theme of the Council's proposals. *Accountability across the board drives a performance-based system.* It is at the heart of the learning goals established by the Council and the outcomes by which they will be measured. It permeates the Council's recommendations for new standards and assessments, and the requirements for school site plans responsive to local needs.[31]

Comments in the report's appendix suggested that several groups were concerned about the lack of specificity. Four Republican members of GCERF, for example, were bothered that "continuing-contract problems that prevent school districts from relieving incompetent teachers of their positions" had not been resolved.[32] They also called on educators, parents, business, and community people to address the question sidestepped by the Council—"How can incentives, rewards, and sanctions be implemented effectively to improve teacher and student performance?"[33] For its part, WEA registered concern over the unclear consequences for lack of successful teaching performance and the absence of specific recommendations regarding how performance would be measured. The WEA's spokespersons concluded, "This lack of clarity produces a risky, threatening environment for school employees."[34]

Recent Developments—House Bills 1812 and 2277

Supporters of merit pay were not the only ones who kept the policy pot boiling. During the 1993 legislative session, the WEA attempted to amend the new teacher evaluation regulations. These regulations allowed teachers to remain in professional growth plans for two years before cycling back into a summative evaluation system. The WEA's experience working with school districts on formative evaluation models indicated that two years might not be enough time for ambitious professional growth projects. Teachers who were in their second or third cycle of the new formative evaluation process were setting multiyear goals. Additionally, a curious phenomena that WEA members dubbed the "summative slump" had been noted among teachers involved in formative evaluation. After two years of self-directed professional growth, returning to the summative evaluation track resulted in feelings of lost momentum.

WEA drafted and promoted House Bill 1812, a bill that would extend the formative evaluation phase from two to four years and eliminate the requirement that teachers on growth plans still had to undergo an annual thirty minute short-form observation. The bill, which easily passed the entire House and the Senate Education Committee, fell victim to a political trade-off on the floor of the Senate, where it was defeated, moved for reconsideration, and defeated again.

Reintroduced by WEA in 1994 as House Bill 2277, the legislation went through several drafts as representatives from the WEA and organizations representing various school administrators hammered out their differences. By this point, however, the latter groups were on record as supporting the concepts of growth-oriented teacher evaluation and separate tracks for separate purposes. These organizations, in fact, were instrumental in lobbying certain legislators who were concerned that the new bill might be too "soft."

For its part, the WEA had come to recognize the need for more structure and acknowledgement of teachers' responsibilities in the legislation. A spirit of compromise prevailed long enough in 1994 for all groups to agree on a version of House Bill 2277. The passage of the bill means that statutory constraints such as mandatory short-form evaluations during the professional development cycle and the two-year cycle limit have been eliminated. In addition, the ability of principals to move a teacher from formative to summative evaluation has been strengthened.

As this book goes to press, some school districts in Washington are revising their formative evaluation policies in light of House Bill 2277. They are opting to allow teachers who maintain instructional competence to remain on the formative evaluation track for the rest of their careers or to lengthen the duration of the formative cycle beyond two years. The WEA and the administrators' organizations have agreed for the first time to cooperate in the delivery of local training related to the implementation of the new policy.

Lessons from Washington State

Opportunism and luck may have as much to do with policy formulation as intentionality and politics, if the story of Washington's new teacher evaluation policy is indicative. The proposals originally put forward in 1985, for example, focused more on accountability and merit pay than professional development. When the Advisory Task Force on Evaluation was convened to develop implementation guidelines for HB 849, the WEA was able to seize the opportunity and make its case for formative evaluation. The ability of the WEA to appropriate the ATFE's agenda was, in part, a function of fortuitous timing. If WEA representatives to the ATFE had not had South Kitsap to use as an example of new thinking about teacher evaluation—thinking which constituted proof that teachers and administrators could work together, it is doubtful if growth-oriented evaluation guidelines would have been adopted. Washington may have wound up with a summative evaluation process similar to the Florida Performance Measurement System.

Opportunism and luck may have provided the chance to alter the course of policymaking, but persistence, hard work, and compromise were needed to accomplish the feat. While some organizations' representatives changed over the course of the ATFE's deliberations, WEA members remained the same, thereby providing the continuity and leadership so critical to sustaining a policy initiative. When disagreements arose, as they did over the issue of documentation for formative evaluation, ATFE members also displayed a remarkable willingness to compromise. Had members failed to agree on the "data curtain" concept, the ATFE might not have succeeded in developing guidelines for differentiated teacher evaluation.

Despite the importance of compromise, the Washington State story demonstrates that momentary agreement should not necessarily be regarded as a fundamental change of direction by the sides involved. Though willing to moderate their positions in the interests of reaching agreement on the ATFE, proaccountability and proprofessional-development groups continued to look for opportunities to press their separate platforms. The Governor's Council on Educational Reform and Funding offered an occasion for proaccountability forces, such as the Business Roundtable, to raise anew the issue of merit pay. The WEA, for its part, refused to abandon the quest for longer periods of formative evaluation for competent, experienced teachers. Compromise at one point in the process of policy formulation may belie, therefore, the continuing commitments of interest groups to move in original directions. In light of such persistence, it may be more accurate to think of policies like Washington State's teacher evaluation policy as "under continuing development" rather than "developed." Just because a policy is agreed upon and implemented does not mean efforts to modify or alter it cease.

Another lesson from Washington State concerns educational accountability. The fact that the WEA was able to convert an accountability-oriented policy agenda to one dedicated primarily to professional development is testimony, not only to the perceived importance of ongoing growth for experienced teachers, but also the weakness of current conceptions of accountability. These conceptions, based on questionable assumptions about incentive-based control, minimal performance standards, and the evaluation of individual performance, are frequently associated with wasted time, increased paperwork, and conflict between teachers and administrators. Little evidence exists that such notions of accountability have captured the imagination of teachers, administrators, or the general public. The time may have come to rethink accountability for professional educators. Accountability that emphasizes collective achievement, collaboration, and continuing professional development ultimately may hold the key to meaningful school improvement.

Notes

1. The preparation of this case study was supported by the Washington Education Association. The views expressed by the authors however, are entirely their own. The research team, consisting of the editor and four staff members from the Washington Education Association, collected background information and met to analyze it over an eighteen month period. Interviews were conducted with legislators, task force members, state education department officials, and other individuals who played a role in shaping the new professional development regulations in Washington State. Tapes of legislative hearings also were reviewed.

2. Representative Art Wang, taped proceedings, Public Hearing on HB 849, February 19, 1985. Washington State Archives.

3. HB 849, 1985 Legislative Session.

4. Representative Art Wang, taped proceedings, House Education Committee, February 27, 1985, Washington State Archives.

5. HB 849, 1985 Legislative Session.

6. Reuben Kvamme, Tacoma Public Schools, taped proceedings, Public Hearing on HB 849, February 19, 1985.

7. Richard Timm, Association of Washington School Principals, taped proceedings, Public Hearing on HB 849, February 19, 1985.

8. Richard Green, Association of Washington School Principals, taped proceedings. Public Hearing, February 19, 1985.

9. Howard Coble, Association of Washington School Principals, taped proceedings, Public Hearing, February 19, 1985.

10. HB 925, 1985 Legislative Session.

11. HB 925, 1985 Legislative Session.

12. Representative Art Wang, taped proceedings, House Education Committee, February 25, 1985.

13. Representative Mike Todd, taped proceedings, House Education Committee, February 25, 1985.

14. Interview by Ann Randall with Representative Art Wang, 2 December 1992.

15. SHB 1831. Bulletin No. 2–86 ES, OSPI, April 15, 1986, p. 5.

16. In September of 1985, the National Education Association (NEA) invited eight field representatives to Washington, D.C. to critique a research paper and manual on teacher evaluation. The manual was to be sent to all state affiliates and UniServ Directors. Jim Russell from the Washington Education Association and Olympic Uniserv Council was one of the eight staff members to attend and critique the newly developed evaluation manual. The NEA, in 1985, believed that accountability and performance evaluation were two of the most explosive political issues that state legislatures would confront out of the growing education reform movement. *The School Personnel Evaluation Manual* was an effort to assist state affiliates with research and policy positions the NEA supported.

17. Interview by Daniel Duke with John Long, conducted 2 December 1992, Port Orchard, Washington.

18. Interview by Daniel Duke with John Long, conducted 2 December 1992, Port Orchard, Washington.

19. Dr. Dwayne Gower, superintendent's memorandum, September 27, 1985.

20. Interview by Daniel Duke with Ann Randall, teacher member of the Joint Committee, 14 December 1993, Poulsbo, Washington.

21. Allen Hughes, *Teacher Evaluation: an Analysis of Implementation of a Professional Growth Model*. Ph.D. diss., Washington State University, 1992.

22. Interview by Ann Randall with Neil Supplee, ATFE representative from Washington Business Roundtable, 7 December 1992, Seattle, Washington.

23. Interview by Ann Randall with Jan Stout, ATFE representative from Citizen's Action Northwest, 2 December 1992, Seattle, Washington.

24. Ted Andrews, the chair of ATFE and an OSPI official, harbored doubts at the time that the provisions for the formative system met the intent of the law concerning teacher evaluation. The policy eventually approved by the legislature never specified the relationship between evaluation and professional develop-

ment. Section 392–192–010 of the WAC simply defined professional development programs as "a form of personnel evaluation in which the emphasis is on growth and improvement rather than on decisions related to probation, nonrenewal, and discharge."

25. The chair of the ATFE, Ted Andrews, admitted being baffled by the legislature's eleventh-hour decision not to fund the pilot projects. His guess was that some legislators who had hoped for a merit pay scheme were sufficiently disappointed with the task force's sidestepping of the issue that they refused to support additional resources for teacher evaluation.

26. Richard J. Stiggins and Daniel L. Duke, *The Case for Commitment to Teacher Growth: Research on Teacher Evaluation* (Albany, N.Y.: State University of New York Press, 1988).

27. Interview by Ann Randall with Neil Supplee, 7 December 1992, Seattle, Washington.

28. OSPI Report to Legislature on the Development of Teacher Evaluation Models, January 1989.

29. Results are based on survey returns as of 22 June 1993.

30. The WEA cadre was the only group in the state that developed specific training materials to use with districts interested in revising their teacher evaluation systems. The WEA also provided grants to enable locals to make the training available. For reasons that remain unclear, associations of administrators and personnel directors in Washington State decided to provide limited technical assistance for their members. In addition, OSPI, since the pilot phase, has not been active in helping to implement the professional growth program.

31. *Putting Children First* (Governor's Council on Educational Reform and Funding, December 1992), p. 16.

32. Ibid., p. 49.

33. Ibid., p. 50.

34. Ibid., p. 54.

References

Stiggins, R. J. and Duke, D. L. (1988). *The Case for Commitment to Teacher Growth: Research on Teacher Evaluation.* Albany: State University of New York Press.

7

Teacher Appraisal in England and Wales

Agnes McMahon

Introduction

A quiet revolution is taking place in the nearly 25,000 primary and secondary schools in England and Wales. By July 1995, if current progress is sustained, all teachers and headteachers in maintained (i.e. government funded) primary, secondary, and special schools in England and Wales (approx. 450,000) will have been appraised as participants in a national scheme for school teacher appraisal (evaluation). Formal responsibility for implementing the appraisal scheme rests with the employers who are the officers in the 117 local education authorities (LEAs) in England and Wales. This is a major innovation in the education system and one which, to date, is being implemented without any significant opposition. The scheme was introduced by the British Government in September 1991; it is legally binding and is being phased in over a four year period. Prior to this, there was no requirement that teacher performance be evaluated and, though individual teachers would periodically have been involved in an inspection of their school by local or national inspectors, many teachers never received specific feedback about their work. The autonomy of the teacher in the classroom, virtually unchallenged hitherto, is now being questioned.

Dan Duke, in the introductory chapter to this book, has argued that policy evolves gradually over a period of time and that a study of teacher evaluation policy ". . . requires historical perspective along with a sense of context." He suggests that policymaking is essentially about making choices. An examination of the policy for teacher appraisal in England and Wales would certainly support these views. The policy has been evolving for almost twenty years, sometimes center stage but on other occasions relegated to the "back burner." During this period the context has changed significantly and there have been and still are conflicting interpretations about the main focus and purposes of the policy. Indeed its very existence is due in no small measure to a process of bargaining and compromise between the key interest groups, the department for education, the local authority employers, and the teacher unions. The purpose of this chapter is to explore the origins of the policy and to trace how it has developed and is still being modified as it is being implemented. In particular, a number of significant points, where choices between policy options were made, will be highlighted.

Changing Direction

What were the origins of the policy for teacher appraisal? There appears to be no single motivating factor, rather the policy seems to have emerged out of a dissatisfaction with the performance of schools and teachers which developed throughout the late 1970s and 1980s and which coincided with a desire to strengthen arrangements for the professional development of teachers. In the 1970s, there was no National Curriculum, no national system of testing and assessment and teachers had considerable professional autonomy which was protected by strong teacher unions; by the 1990s this situation had changed in every respect. Maclure (1988) has argued that in the postwar period, lasting until the mid-1970s, there was a generally held assumption that education was "a self-justifying good" and that this belief was lost in the 1980s. He argued that the rhetoric changed in the 1980s and that it ". . . moved away from a concern with 'the whole person' and 'education for life' to a more sceptical insistence that education must be useful in some directly marketable way . . . " It is certainly the case that since the 1970s there has been a growing concern expressed by policymakers that teachers and schools should become more accountable. Whereas in the early 1970s, policymakers regarded the provision of further professional development and training as a key strategy for raising the quality of the teacher force, the introduction of performance related pay or dismissal might be regarded as a 1990s way of dealing with the same issue. An influential report on Teacher Education and Training (DES 1972), which had been commissioned by Margaret Thatcher as Secretary of State for Education, included the comment that: "Many teachers at present are outstandingly effective and successful, have a clear understanding of their professional aims, and enjoy a high degree of satisfaction in their work. Others are less fortunate. It is no accident that teachers in the former category tend to be those who have had the benefit of inservice opportunities to extend their personal education and professional skills." The report recommended that in-service education for teachers should be properly coordinated and that provision should be increased, even to the extent of giving teachers the opportunity to take three months study leave once every seven years. The Government responded positively to this report but, in practice, the recommendation about study leave was never enacted. As the 1970s progressed the position changed; the impact of the 1973 oil crisis on the economic climate led to cuts in education budgets (Bolam 1981); groups on the political right were outspoken in their criticism of various aspects of education (e.g. Cox and Boyson 1977) and similar views were evident on the left. In particular, concerns were expressed about standards of achievement in schools, the content of the school curriculum, and about how to increase parental participation in school matters. In fact, it was a Labor Prime Minister, James Callaghan, who made a critical speech in 1976 which sparked a "great debate" about education and signaled the start of a period in which the government would adopt a more interventionist stance toward education (Becher and Maclure 1978, p. 10).

The first reference to teacher appraisal was contained in the 1977 Green Paper, published when a Labor Government was in power. The paper spoke of the need to establish procedures for the assessment of teacher performance and emphasized the accountability purposes of such a move, although the need to work with the teacher unions was explicitly recognized:

> The establishment of standard procedures for the assessment of teachers' performance, for advice and, where necessary, warning to teachers whose performance is consistently unsatisfactory, and for all the other steps required by employment protection legislation, or judged necessary as part of a fair procedure for considering dismissal of staff, are all matters which unquestionably call for the most extensive consultation with the teachers associations. (DES 1977, para. 6.38)

A determined effort to introduce teacher appraisal was made in the 1980s. In 1979, a Conservative Government was elected and the Conservative Party have remained in power ever since. Keith Joseph, who was secretary of state for education from 1981 to 1986, had a profound influence on educational policy during this period and was one of the main architects of the teacher appraisal scheme. He was determined to upgrade the quality of the teacher force and saw appraisal as a strategy which could help to achieve this, not least by making a link between teacher performance and salary. His commitment to the introduction of teacher appraisal was first publicised in the White Paper *Teaching Quality* (DES 1983), a statement of government policy which suggested that a system of appraisal was necessary for effective school management and explicitly linked teacher salary to performance.

> The government sees important connections between the structure of the salary scales on which teachers are paid and policies for promoting commitment and high standards of professional performance amongst teachers. . . . In the Government's view the salary structure should be designed to offer relatively greater awards to the best classroom teachers as well as to encourage good teachers to seek wider responsibilities in senior posts. (para 90)
>
> . . . .
>
> . . . employers can manage their teacher force effectively only if they have accurate knowledge of each teacher's performance. The Government believes that for this purpose formal assessment of teacher performance is necessary and should be based on classroom visiting by the head or head of department, and an appraisal of both pupils' work and of the teacher's contribution to the life of the school . . . those responsible for managing the school teacher force have a clear responsibility to establish, in consultation with their teachers, a policy for staff deployment and training based on a systematic assessment of every teacher's performance and related to their policy for the school curriculum. (para 92)

These ideas were further developed two years later in the White Paper *Better Schools* (DES 1985):

> The Government holds to the view . . . that the regular and formal appraisal of the performance of all teachers is necessary if LEAs are to have the reliable, comprehensive and up-to-date information necessary for the systematic and effective provision of professional support and development and the deployment of staff to best advantage. Only if this information relates to performance in post can LEA management make decisions affecting the career development of its teachers fairly and consistently. Taken together, these decisions should result in improved deployment and distribution of the talent within the teaching force, with all teachers being helped to respond to changing demands and to realise their full professional potential by developing their strengths and improving upon their weaknesses; with the most promising and effective being identified for timely promotion; with those encountering professional difficulties being promptly identified for appropriate counselling, guidance and support; and, where such assistance does not restore performance to a satisfactory level, with the teachers concerned being considered for early retirement or dismissal. (para 180)

The managerial purposes of appraisal were clearly emphasized as were the potential benefits for teacher professional development. There was no recognition that it might be difficult to implement a scheme that was intended to meet demands for accountability as well as professional development. The White Paper stated that appraisal was necessary if the arrangements for in-service education were to be improved and again made a link between appraisal and salaries:

> The appraisal of teacher performance has been widely seen as the key instrument for managing this relationship (between pay, responsibilities and performance), with teachers' professional and career development assisted and salary progression largely determined by reference to periodic assessment of performance. (para 181)

The Government used these policy papers to send clear messages to the education profession that it wanted to introduce teacher appraisal, thereby making teachers more accountable and strengthening the management of the teacher force. However, given that day-to-day control of the schools was effectively in the hands of the local education authorities (LEAs), it was not in a position to put these ideas to the test. In 1984, the government, through the DES, attempted to fund a project on teacher management and appraisal in a number of LEAs as a means of developing suitable procedures for appraisal. Negotiations were conducted with the LEA employers and the teacher unions, initially to little effect because the teachers were strongly opposed to any proposal to link appraisal to salary, promotion, and dismissal. Finally, a team from Suffolk LEA led by the Chief Education Officer, Duncan Graham, who had a long-standing interest in the issue, were funded by the DES to conduct an investigative study into teacher appraisal. The team reported on appraisal in North America, Germany, and in industry and examined the arguments in favor of merit pay, concluding that " . . . the necessary conditions for the success (of merit pay) do not currently exist in England and Wales" (Suffolk LEA 1985). They subsequently received a second grant to investigate further issues including classroom observation and headteacher appraisal (Suffolk LEA 1987).

Throughout this period, the teacher associations, particularly the National Union of Teachers (NUT), the largest union, were playing an active part in the debate, mainly from a desire to improve arrangements for the professional and career development of teachers rather than a concern to strengthen the hand of management. In 1981, the NUT published a document on appointment, promotion, and career development for teachers which argued that every teacher would benefit from regular periods of discussion and evaluation about their current work and career with a senior member of staff. However, the model for these review discussions was very different from the one envisaged by the DES. It was to start with the job description, be based on a system of self-appraisal, and would conclude with a "jointly composed written statement, identifying the teachers' training needs and making suitable recommendations, which will include objectives and activities for the coming year" (NUT 1981). The review was envisaged as a reciprocal process between one teacher and another at the next level of responsibility. The question of whether appraisal should be linked to salary was not discussed in this document, but in 1983, in its response to the White paper (DES 1983), the NUT said that any such scheme would be " . . . *divisive and further undermine the morale of the teaching profession.*"

Discussions about appraisal between the DES, the employers, and the teachers' associations continued through 1985 but made little progress; the debate seemed to have reached an impasse. The Secretary of State was keen to introduce a system of appraisal which was managerial in emphasis and which linked salary to performance; the teacher and headteacher associations were opposed to this and would not cooperate, despite favoring review for professional development. At this critical point, Keith Joseph chose to abandon the notion of merit pay and thereby enabled some progress to be made. In November 1985, at a national conference organized by the DES, he reiterated his belief in appraisal but acknowledged the problematic nature of merit pay: "A sensitively worked out scheme, carefully introduced and embodying adequate safeguards for the individual, would, I am confident, help all teachers realise their full professional potential by providing them with better job satisfaction, more appropriate in-service training, and better planned career development. . . . I understand the concern that has been expressed to me about the possibility that annual appraisal procedures might be directly linked to merit pay or annual increments, or be used in other ways by headteachers to give instant rewards or penalties. That is quite definitely not the sort of arrangement that I have in mind" (Joseph 1985). He also noted that if appraisal was to be introduced, teachers would need training and time to allocate to the process.

This speech signaled a substantial move in Joseph's thinking and brought the DES position much closer to that of the teacher associations. It was a significant choice point where what had been seen as a major goal of the policy, namely, to introduce performance related pay, was apparently abandoned. It is unclear why Keith Joseph changed his mind on this occasion. One possible explanation is that he was persuaded by the teacher unions that linking appraisal to salary would be harmful. Alternatively, he may have recognized that, unless concessions were made, the unions were sufficiently powerful to block any action and he was determined to have schools test systems for appraisal. It could be interpreted as a political decision to modify or conceal the aims of the policy so as to make progress.

Agreement about the Principles for Teacher Appraisal

The Government's determination to introduce appraisal was apparent in the 1986 Education Act which included a clause to enable the introduction of regulations to make appraisal a legal requirement, although this clause was not activated until 1991. In the meantime, 1986 was marked by acrimonious disputes between the DES and the teacher unions about salary and conditions of service which culminated in teachers losing their salary bargaining rights. During the dispute the Advisory Conciliation and Arbitration Service (ACAS) was called in to assist the negotiations between the teacher associations, the LEA employers, and the British Government about teachers' conditions of service. The negotiations as a whole were unsuccessful, but one important outcome was that a Working Party, chaired by ACAS and including representatives of all three groups, did reach agreement about the principles that should underpin an appraisal scheme (ACAS, June 1986). Counted among the Working Party membership were individuals who already had some knowledge of appraisal, including Duncan Graham and his deputy in Suffolk LEA, Tom Cornthwaite, who represented one of the employers' associations, and the NUT representative, Peter Griffin, who was to play a key role at a later stage. The agreed principles for appraisal emphasized teacher professional development, made no reference to pay, and explicitly stated that disciplinary procedures would be separate—" . . . what the Working Party has in mind is a positive process, intended to raise the quality of education in schools by providing teachers with better job satisfaction, more appropriate in-service training and better planned career development based upon more informed decisions." The Working Party also recommended that appraisal should be piloted before any attempt was made to introduce it on a national basis.

The ACAS principles established the foundation for the introduction of teacher appraisal. The principles were subsequently endorsed at the "Coventry Agreement" and the path was clear to initiate some pilot work. The DES invited interested LEAs to take part in a project in the autumn of 1986, and by the end of November 1986, six LEAs (Croydon, Cumbria, Newcastle, Salford, Somerset, and Suffolk) had been selected by the DES to work in a consortium to pilot approaches for teacher and headteacher appraisal. It was the Government's intention that the pilot project would start in January 1987 and that some policy recommendations would be available by autumn 1987. A strategy for managing a pilot appraisal project had also been approved during the ACAS working group's negotiation. The central recommendation was that the project should have a steering group:

> *We agree that the project should be directed and monitored by a National Steering Group (with representatives of the unions and officers of the Department and LEAs) responsible for reporting and disseminating the results of the project and for ensuring that the methods developed will be replicable throughout the country.* (ACAS 1986)

A National Steering Group (NSG) was duly established and, as agreed, it contained representatives from the teacher unions, the LEA employers and the DES. Several of the representatives had previously served on the ACAS Working Party and initially the ACAS chairman, Bill Kendal, chaired the NSG. The first meeting of the NSG was held on November 5, 1986, but by this time the context had changed.

On May 21, 1986, Keith Joseph had been replaced as secretary of state for education by Kenneth Baker. Relations between the DES and the teacher unions were then at a low ebb, something Joseph recognized in advising Baker before his departure, "Don't make the same mistake I did of attacking the teachers" (Baker 1993).

Throughout 1986, the Government and the teacher unions had been locked in a dispute about teachers' pay and conditions. Baker was determined to resolve this as speedily as possible; he adopted a dual strategy which was spelled out in March 1987 when a new Bill that he had introduced on Teachers' Pay and Conditions was enacted. This gave teachers a significant pay increase but also removed their salary bargaining rights and instead set up an Interim Advisory Committee to make recommendations about teachers' pay. This action simultaneously weakened the power of the teacher unions while earning the support of many teachers for the salary increase and removing public sympathy for teachers taking strike action. The teacher unions were strongly opposed to the new conditions of service, and in the spring term 1987 two of the largest ones, NUT and NASUWT, balloted their members and gained approval for strike action in opposition to the Government's action on pay and conditions. A number of short strikes followed before the action was finally called off on May 14, 1987. Although this dispute was not directly about teacher appraisal, it did have an important negative impact on the pilot scheme. On March 9, 1987, the representatives of the NASUWT and NUT walked out of the fifth meeting of the National Steering Group for the appraisal project in protest at the Government's policy; the NUT did not return until January 1988 and the NASUWT only rejoined the Steering Group in June 1989 when the final report on appraisal was being drawn up.

Trialing Appraisal Models

Nevertheless, the pilot work on school teacher appraisal in the six LEAs progressed throughout this rather difficult period. Following a process of competitive tendering, two groups of consultants were appointed in April 1987 to assist in the project. A team from the Cambridge Institute of Education became the National Evaluators while a team from the School of Education at the University of Bristol acted as National Coordinators of the work. The pilot authorities and the coordinators reported regularly to the NSG. However, without the cooperation of two of the largest teacher unions it was not possible to pilot appraisal in the schools. During this period of noncooperation the LEA appraisal coordinators concentrated on raising teachers' awareness of appraisal issues and upon preliminary training. They subsequently argued that this groundwork had aided the implementation of appraisal by allowing teachers to raise their concerns and clarify their understanding of the process, but an alternative view was that this led to " . . . both suspicion of and preciousness about the whole business" (Morris 1991). The one exception to this pattern was in Cumbria, where teachers supported a prior local agreement with their LEA on appraisal and defied their unions by participating in pilot work. The DES maintained its commitment to the project; agreeing to extend the time scale and provide additional funding when it became clear that it would not be possible to produce any guidance by the autumn of 1987. In September 1987, the chair of the NSG resigned for personal reasons and was replaced by Duncan Graham, an appointment undoubtedly favored by Kenneth Baker who later said, in his autobiography, that he "liked his down to earth, very Scottish approach" and the fact that " . . . he was not in thrall to the prejudices to academics" (Baker 1993).

Nevertheless, had the NUT not decided to rejoin the Steering Committee and support trialing appraisal in schools, the pilot project would almost certainly have ground to a halt. Credit for winning the argument with the union's executive group must go to Peter Griffin and colleagues, including some from Cumbria, who were convinced that appraisal could be of positive benefit for the teaching profession. This was another criti-

cal choice point, one at which the NUT executives opted to cooperate
rather than continue their opposition to the appraisal project.

Over the next eighteen months, procedures for teacher and headteacher appraisal were trialed in schools and LEAs and were actively discussed by members of the National Steering Group. The debate about
what should be the components of an appraisal scheme was one in which
all three constituents, the DES, the LEA employers, and the teacher associations participated vigorously. Three factors helped to enhance the quality of the debate. First, the National Coordinators organized a series of
workshop conferences on different aspects of the appraisal process (e.g.
classroom observation, headteacher appraisal) which, though primarily
intended for members of the LEA appraisal coordination teams, were also
attended by NSG members who were thus able to hear at first hand how
appraisal was being implemented, what problems had arisen, and how
these were being overcome. Second, the National Evaluators wrote regular reports on the project for the NSG, which provided formative feedback about the schemes. Third, the National Coordinators wrote a series
of position papers for the Steering Committee that contained recommendations about the appraisal procedures. These papers went through an extensive consultation process with all the main parties at national and local
level and were then discussed at NSG meetings until consensus was
reached. This process could be described as one of negotiation and bargaining and, although it was extremely time-consuming, it provided a
sound basis for the NSG's final report *School Teacher Appraisal: A National Framework* (DES 1989a), which was presented to Ministers in August 1989. Given the hostility that had existed between some of the major
parties, the fact that this report contained clear recommendations, accepted by all the teacher associations and the employers and sanctioned
by the DES officials, was a major achievement. The Government had a
clear consensus on which to move forward with appraisal based on a professional development model.

Throughout this period attempts had been made by both the NSG
and the DES to keep the wider educational community informed about
the progress of the pilot work on appraisal. In May 1988 representatives
of all the LEAs in England and Wales were invited to participate in a conference to discuss the interim findings emerging from the project and all
LEAs also received copies of a regular newsletter about appraisal issues
which was produced by the National Coordinators. In turn, the DES gave
clear signals that the Government intended to introduce a national
teacher appraisal scheme in September 1989. In August 1988, the DES
sent a letter to all LEAs which included the statement that "DES Circular
5/88 . . . record(s) the Government's intention that appraisal of school

teachers' performance should be progressively applied throughout maintained schools once the results of the pilot projects are available" (DES 12/8/88). This letter included some practical guidance for LEAs on how to plan for the introduction of appraisal and made it clear that some of the funds made available for teacher in-service training in 1989/90 could be spent on training teachers in preparation for appraisal. It seemed at that stage as if a national scheme would be underway in September 1989.

Delay in the Implementation of Appraisal

No action to introduce appraisal was taken in the autumn of 1989, however, and much of the momentum that had been built up was lost. Why this hesitation? It was due to a combination of circumstances. First, the context had again changed significantly because of the passing of the 1988 Education Reform Act. This major piece of legislation had a profound impact on the teacher's role and the organization and management of schools. It introduced a National Curriculum and a national scheme for assessment and testing; required that LEAs devolve budgets, including staffing costs, to schools; increased competition between schools through schemes for open enrollment of pupils; and enhanced the powers of school governing bodies. Many of these innovations were unpopular with teachers and, even though they were to be phased in over a number of years, schools were overwhelmed with the quantity and magnitude of the changes that they had to implement. This was accompanied by further changes at Ministerial level; Kenneth Baker was appointed chairman of the Tory party in July 1989 and was replaced as Secretary of State for Education by John McGregor. Second, the national inspectorate, known then as Her Majesty's Inspectors (HMI), produced a report on appraisal which concluded that the teachers were preoccupied with other innovations arising from the 1988 Education Act and were unprepared for the implementation of appraisal. HMI also warned that supporting implementation likely would require the equivalent of 1,800 additional teachers, this at a time when there was a teacher shortage (HMI, 1989). Third, ministers might have been unhappy with the strong professional development emphasis in the NSG's report and were reluctant to accept the estimated price tag of £40 million a year for implementation; a substantial sum but only 0.5 percent of the annual salary bill for teachers in England and Wales. In October 1989, John McGregor announced that, though he welcomed the NSG report, he would not be making regulations on appraisal in the autumn " . . . because he recognised that schools were already engaged on a full programme of reforms following the Education Reform Act 1988, and that some schools did not currently have the capacity to introduce a further innovation as significant as appraisal" (DES 1989b). He stated that he intended to make regulations at some future date and, in the meantime, would consult widely on the NSG's recommendations. During this consultative process, seven regional conferences were organized by the National Coordinators on behalf of the DES, which also invited written comment from interested parties. Industrialists, as well as all sectors of the education service, were asked for their views on the NSG's proposals. The outcome of this exercise was to confirm broad support for the recommendations. Despite this, John McGregor announced in September 1990 that, though he recognized the value of appraisal and hoped it would be introduced on a voluntary basis, he did not intend to make it mandatory. Two main reasons were cited in support of this decision: first, schools were already under pressure to implement the National Curriculum and appraisal should be introduced " . . . at a pace which is realistic and manageable for schools," and second, that appraisal was " . . . essentially a management issue" and decisions about the management of schools and teachers should be taken locally (McGregor 1990).

School teacher appraisal looked set to be an innovation that would fade away, a good idea that would never be implemented. LEAs were no longer undertaking any preparatory work for appraisal, the DES had allowed them to spend the money in their in-service budgets, originally allocated for appraisal, on other aspects of management training; the teacher unions and the employers were occupied with other priorities. Faced with seeming Government indifference, teachers were not going to fight for the introduction of appraisal. However, within a few months the position had changed once more, again following a change in personnel at the DES. In November 1990, John McGregor was replaced by Kenneth Clarke and within a month the policy on appraisal had been reversed. The new Secretary of State announced that appraisal would be mandatory and said that "*Regular appraisal will help to develop the professionalism of teachers, and so improve the education of their pupils*" and added that he wanted " . . . *to see an appraisal system which is simple but effective*" (DES 1990a). The reasons for this change in direction are unclear, though one contributory factor was probably the realization that, unless appraisal was mandatory, LEAs would not treat it as a priority. Regulations on appraisal were finally published in July, 1991, to take effect as of September 1991.

The National Appraisal Scheme

The details of the national scheme are contained in two documents, copies of which were distributed to every school in England and Wales. The first is the Government Regulations (DES 1991a) that set out those aspects of the scheme which are legally binding. The second is the accompanying Circular 12/91, which contains more detailed suggestions about how appraisal might be implemented in practice (DES 1991b). The aims of the scheme are contained in the Regulations and they state that:

1. Appraising bodies shall secure that appraisal assists:
   (a) school teachers in their professional development and career planning; and
   (b) those responsible for taking decisions about the management of school teachers.
2. . . . appraising bodies shall aim to improve the quality of education for pupils, through assisting school teachers to realize their potential and to carry out their duties more effectively.
3. Appraisal procedures shall in particular aim to:
   (a) Recognize the achievements of school teachers and help them to identify ways of improving their skills and performance.
   (b) Help school teachers, governing bodies, and local education authorities to determine whether a change of duties would help the professional development of school teachers and improve their career prospects.
   (c) Identify the potential of teachers for career development, with the aim of helping them, where possible, through appropriate in-service training.
   (d) Help school teachers having difficulties with their performance, through appropriate guidance, counseling and training.
   (e) Inform those responsible for providing references for school teachers in relation to appointments.
   (f) Improve the management of schools.

Regulations 4 and 14 state that though appraisal procedures should not form part of any disciplinary or dismissal procedures, relevant information from the appraisal statements may be used by the headteacher, Chief Education Officer (CEO) or any officers or advisers specially designated by the CEO " . . . in advising those responsible for making decisions on the promotion, dismissal or discipline of school teachers or on the use of any discretion in relation to pay" (DES 1991a). The wording of these clauses is sufficiently ambiguous to cause concern to the teacher associations. For instance, what constitutes "relevant information" in an appraisal statement and exactly how might it be used?

The stated purposes of the appraisal scheme replicate, to a large degree, the principles for appraisal agreed to by the ACAS Working Party in 1986 and subsequently endorsed by the pilot schemes. However, the references to the managerial purposes of appraisal were strengthened and

the suggestion that information from appraisal statements might be used
when giving advice about promotion, salary, or disciplinary procedures
was new. The role of the chair of the school governing body was also
strengthened; the headteacher's appraisal statement has to be sent to the
chair of governors, and he/she can also see, on request, the professional
development targets identified in the teacher appraisals. The scheme, as
defined by the Government, was intended to meet both accountability
and development goals. Thus, in practice, different stakeholders could
give priority to different purposes.

The components of the appraisal process are those recommended in
the NSG report on the six pilot schemes. The teacher's appraiser should
be either the headteacher or another teacher in the school designated by
the head. The recommended ratio of appraiser to appraisees is 1:4. The
appraisal cycle is a continuous period of two years and the model has
three main components: data collection, an appraisal interview, and a follow-up stage. The data collection includes two periods of classroom observation, collection of information from relevant others with the
permission of the teacher being appraised, and self-appraisal by the
teacher. The interview is a one-to-one discussion between the teacher and
her appraiser which is intended to review the teacher's work; identify
achievements and aspects in which further development would be desirable; identify training and development needs; and agree to targets for future action. At the end of the appraisal interview, a written statement is
produced which summarizes the conclusions reached and the agreed to
targets. This is to be treated as a confidential document, signed by both
parties and kept on file by the headteacher. The Chief Education Officer
has access to the statement on request and the Chair of the School Governing Body can be informed of the development targets agreed to for
teachers if he/she requests such data. Following an appraisal, teachers
should receive on-going support from their appraiser and through appropriate professional development activities. Each school now has its
own in-service budget so that, in principle, some limited resources are
available to support teacher growth.

The Implementation of the Appraisal Scheme

Appraisal is being phased in over a four-year period and to date the information submitted by the LEAs to the DFE shows that the interim target of having approximately 50 percent of the teacher force appraised by
July 1993 has been met. An informal telephone survey of teacher associations and the relevant officials at the DFE revealed that no significant
problems have been identified with the implementation; LEAs and

schools are quietly going ahead setting up teacher appraisal schemes. This is surprising because when Kenneth Clarke introduced appraisal he did not allocate the resources that had been considered essential. He rejected the carefully worked out costing estimates and said that the only expenses that the Government was prepared to fund, and then only in the introductory phase, were " . . . teacher substitution during observation and the costs of organising appraisal" (DES 1990b). Although the NSG had recommended that all teachers should be trained for the introduction of appraisal, he argued that the need for training had been overstated and that he was not prepared to fund it at the recommended level. Despite this, there is evidence that LEAs are continuing to train teachers before introducing appraisal, finding additional money in their own budgets to support this.

Future Development

Currently two agendas for appraisal appear to be existing side by side. In so far as it is possible to judge, given that no detailed evaluation of the implementation of appraisal has been funded, the schemes that are being introduced into schools emphasize professional development and appear to be broadly faithful to the recommendations contained in the NSG report. This is in no small measure due to the teacher unions that are monitoring the development of local schemes and are signing local agreements on appraisal with LEAs. By April 1993, the unions had signed agreements with 112 of 117 LEAs in England and Wales (Young 1993). In 1991, the six teacher associations produced joint advice on the implementation of appraisal which was distributed to all their members and which underlined the professional development purposes of the process (Six teacher organizations 1991). Despite this, the educational context has changed significantly, and this will almost certainly influence the future development of appraisal. Some of the many factors that are likely to impact on the scheme are detailed below.

1. The pressure on resources had continued; schools are still faced with numerous centrally imposed innovations; and they are realizing that a professional development model of appraisal is demanding of time. Without any resources to support implementation, there is concern that the process might be scaled down and so become less meaningful for teachers.

2. Recent Government reforms (e.g. the new system for school inspection) have seriously weakened the power of the LEAs. The majority of them have had to cut back on central staffing so they no longer have

teams of advisers and inspectors who can visit schools to monitor and support their work, including the practice of appraisal.

3. The majority of schools now control their own budgets, and little or no funding is held centrally by the LEA. If the school chooses not to make appraisal training a priority, then there is little the LEA can do.

4. Beginning teachers in their probationary year were initially specifically excluded from appraisal, but the Government has since abolished the requirement for probation. Beginning teachers are now to be included in the appraisal scheme and, since schools now have the sole responsibility of deciding whether a teacher should be recommended for qualified teacher status, the distinction between assessment and development is inevitably blurred.

5. Since September 1993, the school governors have been charged with the responsibility of annually reviewing every teacher's salary with a view to assessing whether they should be given an additional allowance. Though governors currently appear to be ignoring this provision, since a survey indicated that only 1 percent of teachers had received an "excellence" point from the new pay structure (TES 17/12/93), teacher associations are concerned that, in the long term, appraisal statements will be used to guide decision making.

6. The Government has chosen to put the issue of performance related pay back on the agenda and seems determined to introduce a scheme for teachers despite a risk that it might have a negative impact on the implementation of appraisal.

This last point needs to be elaborated because it represents another significant policy choice. The drive to introduce performance related pay is being led by John Patten, who succeeded Kenneth Clarke as Secretary of State for Education in April 1992. In its evidence to the pay review body (DFE 1992), the Department argued strongly for performance related pay which it sees as " . . . an essential component of the Government's strategy for raising standards in the public sector." Moreover, it has argued that this should be introduced at no additional cost: " . . . it believes that it is realistic and desirable to work towards arrangements whereby any increase in the pay of an individual teacher is triggered solely by his or her performance and achievements. It proposes that teacher performance should be assessed against a number of annual targets which have been agreed to in the context of the overall objectives for the school and that this could be done as part of the appraisal system. "In setting objectives for individual teachers, and in assessing performance against them, governing bodies will be able to make use of the processes of statutory school teacher appraisal." In response to the argument that this process might make teachers less willing to engage openly and honestly in their appraisals, the DFE has maintained that the professional development purposes of appraisal could still be sustained. The pay review body has not responded enthusiastically to these arguments. In the 1993 report (School Teachers' Review Body 1993), three strong counter arguments were put forward. First, " . . . that it would be quite wrong for the new appraisal arrangements to be diverted from their prime function of assisting teachers' professional development": second, given the differences in school intake, that any performance indicators would need to take account of the 'value added' by schools; and third, that the effective introduction of performance related pay would require additional funds. The Review Body recommended that pilot studies should be set up to explore how performance related pay might work in schools, and a small study is currently underway. In contrast to the appraisal pilot studies, it is being conducted in virtual secrecy and the findings are being reported only to the Review Body. The teacher unions have expressed their reservations about performance related pay, but they are not being consulted about the pilot study.

Conclusions

What can this study tell us about the reality of the educational policy-making process in Britain? Has the Government successfully maintained a coherent, strategic policy to introduce performance related pay over more than ten years despite numerous changes of education ministers and civil servants? Is the apparent success of the policy due almost to chance— the outcome of a series of relatively unconnected positive decisions in favor of appraisal at critical points over the years or is it the result of skillful political action? Why has there been no significant opposition to appraisal at a time when teachers have been outspoken in their criticism of many other government reforms and indeed have refused to implement some of them?

Stone (1988) has persuasively argued that policymaking is essentially political and involves a struggle over ideas. The development and introduction of teacher appraisal in England and Wales seems to illustrate and support her hypothesis. Certainly, the development of the policy has not followed a linear, rational model; rather it seems to have been the outcome of a struggle between two contrasting viewpoints about the purposes of teacher appraisal and about how to motivate teachers and achieve school improvement; different views supported by different groups have gained ascendancy at particular points in the process of policy formulation and implementation.

One central theme is the power of a strong and consistent political ideology. While teacher appraisal was mooted in the 1970s, pressure to introduce it built up in the 1980s after the election of Prime Minister Margaret Thatcher and the appointment of Secretary of State for Education Keith Joseph. During this period the Government's commitment to a market philosophy was at its height and, though there have been changes in personnel, Ministers remain faithful to the ideology. The attempt to introduce market principles into the education system has impacted upon Government thinking about the purposes and content of a teacher appraisal policy. This can be seen in their statements about the benefits of competition, about the motivating power of performance related pay, and in the support for managerialism and teacher accountability. Individual school governing bodies have been given much more responsibility for the management of their institutions; the power of the LEAs has been substantially reduced, and the position of the unions, particularly their national pay bargaining role, has been weakened. Performance related pay is increasingly seen by Government as a key means of raising standards in that it should give the governors of the school power to decide how individuals should be rewarded. "The Government has repeatedly made clear its belief that regular and direct links should be established, across all public services, between a person's contribution to the standards of service provided and his or her reward" (DFE 1993). The Conservative Government has now been in power for fifteen years; its commitment to the market philosophy has remained largely unchanged, and consequently it has been able to sustain a relatively coherent policy on appraisal and performance related pay.

Following the 1988 Education Reform Act, three more education acts have entered the statute book, all containing substantial reforms that teachers are required to implement. Although its attitude has softened recently, following widespread opposition from the teachers in 1993 to national testing, the Government's style of policymaking remains fairly autocratic. It has virtually abandoned the practice of holding regular consultative meetings with the teacher unions; consultation takes place by asking the educational community on short notice to send in written responses to draft documents; innovations are not piloted before being introduced nationally. Recent education Ministers (e.g. Kenneth Clarke and John Patten) appear as conviction politicians, clear that they know what to do, and not inclined to listen to any criticism of policy from teachers.

Second, whereas the personnel in the teacher unions remained fairly consistent over a number of years, the reality of political life has meant that the ministers and the civil servants dealing with the issue of teacher appraisal have all changed frequently. There have been six secretaries of state for education since 1979; none of the civil servants who now deal with teacher appraisal were involved in the ACAS discussions or with the pilot appraisal schemes. This is not necessarily a disadvantage when a political party has a clear ideology on which to base its thinking. A new group of ministers can reassess the policy and adjust its emphasis if they judge that it has swung too far in the wrong direction.

Viewed from this perspective, the Government has successfully sustained a coherent policy on appraisal but, even though our knowledge of events can only be partial, this explanation of events seems too simplistic; much may be due to chance and opportunism. At certain critical points action was taken, either by the Government or by the teachers, which swung events in a particular direction. Keith Joseph's 1985 statement, which reassured teachers that he was not proposing a direct link between appraisal and merit pay, paved the way for discussions between the teacher unions, the employers, and the DES about what might be the components of an appraisal scheme. His statement seems to have resulted from his listening and talking to teachers rather than from any cynical desire to dupe them by making concessions that would later be revoked. The ACAS agreement on appraisal was a further significant point—had the Government not felt that this was a good foundation for action they need not have accepted it as the basis for pilot work. Though the notion that innovations should be piloted prior to their introduction has now all but been abandoned, the teacher unions would certainly have objected if the DES had attempted to introduce a national appraisal scheme without this prior stage. The decision by the NUT to rejoin the NSG in January 1988 permitted appraisals to take place in schools and was a critical point where teachers took the initiative. The recommendations in the NSG report emphasized the professional development purposes of appraisal; this could be interpreted as a victory for a particular set of ideas which had been championed by the teacher unions. Had Kenneth Baker still been secretary of state for education in July 1989 a national appraisal scheme, based on the NSG recommendations, might have been introduced on the time-scale originally planned. John McGregor's decision to consult on the recommendations marked the beginning of a period when the Government began to take back the agenda. Now that national regulations on appraisal are in place and teacher and headteacher appraisal is being quietly implemented, the Government can seek to alter the emphasis of the policy without the need for further legislation.

There are several possible explanations for the lack of teacher opposition to appraisal. First, and probably most significant, there was no mention of performance related pay during the period when appraisal was being piloted; the NSG report emphasized the professional development purposes of appraisal; and the regulations on appraisal made no explicit reference to merit pay. The teachers agreed to the introduction of appraisal for professional development purposes, and this appears to be how it is being implemented in schools. Many teachers who have participated in appraisal for development purposes value the experience. The Government's early attempts to introduce an element of performance related pay have been widely ignored, not least because schools have been expected to introduce this change within their existing budgets. The future direction of the policy is uncertain. If a Conservative Government remains in power it seems likely that schools will be pressured to introduce performance related pay. However, given that the schools now control their own budgets, it seems unlikely that governors could be made to enforce this without being given additional funds. If the Labor party were to win the next election, the notion of performance related pay might be dropped altogether. The issue for schools will be whether they can sustain teacher appraisal for professional development when the future direction of the policy is unclear.

References

ACAS. (1986). *Teachers' Dispute ACAS Independent Panel: Report of the Appraisal/Training Working Group*. London: Advisory, Conciliation and Arbitration Service.

Baker, K. (1993) *The Turbulent Years: My Life in Politics*. London: Faber and Faber.

Becher, T., and Maclure, S., ed. (1978). *Accountability in Education. Windsor: NFER*.

Bolam, R. (1981). Evaluative Research: A Case Study of the Teacher Induction Pilot Schemes. *Journal of Education for Teaching* 7(1):70–83

Bradley, H., Bollington, R., Dadds, M., Hopkins, D., Howard, J., Southworth, G., and West, M. (1989). *Report on the Evaluation of the School Teacher Appraisal Pilot Schemes*. Cambridge: Cambridge Institute of Education.

Cox, C. B., and Boyson, R. ed. (1977). *Black Paper 1977*. London: Maurice Temple Smith Ltd.

DES. (1972). *Teacher Education and Training*. London: HMSO.

———. (1977). *Education in Schools: A Consultative Document*. London: HMSO.

———. (1983). *Teaching Quality Cmnd 8836*. London: HMSO.

———. (1985). *Better Schools*. London: HMSO.

———. (1988). Letter to all CEO's from J Wiggins 12/8/88.

———. (1989a). *School Teacher Appraisal: A National Framework*. London: HMSO.

———. (1989b). *Press Notice 303/89: Government Policy on Teacher Appraisal*. London: DES.

———. (1990a). *Press Notice 389/90: Teacher Appraisal to be Compulsory— Kenneth Clarke*. London: DES.

———. (1990b). Letter to CEOs from R Horne 10/12/90.

———. (1991a). *The Education (School Teacher Appraisal) Regulations 1991*. London: DES.

———. (1991b). *Circular 12/91 School Teacher Appraisal*. London: DES.

DFE. (1992). *School Teachers' Review Body: Written Evidence from the Department for Education*. London: DFE.

———. (1993). *School Teachers' Review Body: Written Evidence from the Department for Education*. London: DFE.

HMI. (1989). *Developments in the Appraisal of Teachers*. London: DES.

Evans, A., and Tomlinson, J. eds. (1989). *Teacher Appraisal: A Nationwide Approach*. London: Jessica Kingsley Publishers.

Joseph, K. (1985). The Role and Responsibility of the Secretary of State in DES (1986). *Better Schools Evaluation and Appraisal Conference Proceedings*. London: HMSO.

McGregor, J. (1990). Developments in the 1990s: Speech to the BEMAS Conference September 1990. *Educational Management and Administration* 19(2):72–77.

Maclure, S. (1988). *Education Re-formed*. London: Hodder and Stoughton.

Morris, B. (1991). School Teacher Appraisal: Reflections on Recent History. *Educational Management and Administration* 19(3):166–171.

NUT. (1981). *A Fair Way Forward*. London: National Union of Teachers.

———. (1984). *Teaching Quality: The Union's Response to the White Paper*. London: NUT.

Rafferty, F. (1993). New Merit Rise Paid to Only 1 in 100 Staff. *Times Educational Supplement*, 17 December 1993.

School Teachers' Review Body. (1993). *Second Report 1993*. London: HMSO.

Stone, D. (1988). *Policy Paradox and Political Reason.* USA: Harper Collins Publishers.

Suffolk LEA. (1985). *Those Having Torches . . . Teacher Appraisal: A study.* Suffolk LEA.

————. (1987). *In the Light of Torches . . . Teacher Appraisal: A Further Study.* Suffolk LEA.

The Six Teacher Organisations. (1991). *Appraisal—Report of Six Teacher Organisations.* London: NUT, Hamilton House.

Young, S. (1993). Left-wing Notches Up Appraisal Victory. *Times Educational Supplement,* 16 April 1993.

8

Conflict and Consensus in the Reform of Teacher Evaluation

Daniel L. Duke

The preceding case studies capture the complexity of the process by which teacher evaluation policy has been developed and revised in recent years. Jeffrey Pfeffer's (1992, p. 7) observation regarding the difficulty of organizational change applies equally well to policy formulation:

> Accomplishing innovation and change in organizations requires more than the ability to solve technical or analytic problems. Innovation almost invariably threatens the status quo, and consequently, innovation is an inherently political activity.

In this chapter, a cross-case analysis is undertaken in order to understand better the politics of teacher evaluation. Conflict resides where politics prevails, as the case studies demonstrate. While the context in which teacher evaluation policy emerged has been unique in each case, a comparison of the cases reveals similar types of conflict as well as a surprising degree of agreement about how to reconcile differences of opinion. The latter may indicate a nascent consensus regarding how to handle teacher evaluation in an era of school reform and restructuring.

The chapter opens with a discussion of four areas where conflict frequently arose during the course of policy formulation and implementation. These areas cover the purposes of teacher evaluation, the structure of teacher evaluation, the relationship between teacher evaluation and pay for performance, and resources for teacher evaluation and related activities. Compromise was required to resolve disputes in each area. The next section looks at some of the compromises that were reached, particularly those where outcomes were similar across cases. In most instances, for example, policymakers eventually agreed that teacher evaluation should (1) serve professional development as well as accountability purposes; (2) differentiate between new and experienced teachers; (3) include training for teacher evaluators; (4) provide extended periods for professional development; (5) be shaped by local school systems; and (6) avoid direct links to pay for performance schemes.

The cases also reveal similarities concerning how the policies themselves were formulated and initially implemented. The next section of the chapter addresses aspects of the policy formulation process, including the roles played by teacher organizations, vanguard school districts, pilot testing, and consultants. The chapter closes with a brief review of some of the general lessons offered by the case studies.

Sources of Conflict

The process of formulating teacher evaluation policy can be contentious and protracted. Among the issues that generated the most controversy and debate in the case studies were the purposes of teacher evaluation, the structure of teacher evaluation, the relationship between teacher evaluation and pay for performance, and the resources required to support teacher evaluation and related activities. This section reviews these controversies.

Why Evaluate Teachers?

In some parts of the United States teachers have been evaluated for so long that it is difficult to imagine public schools where the ritual does not occur. It is instructive, therefore, to note that England and Wales only recently introduced teacher evaluation. For decades, English and Welsh teachers performed admirably in the absence of mandated teacher evaluation. Why, then, formulate policies requiring periodic teacher evaluation? What causes policymakers to insist that scarce resources be used to monitor teacher performance?

M. L. Armiger (1981, pp. 292–293) points out that the history of teacher evaluation can be understood in terms of a tension between two primary purposes, variously described as summative and formative, or accountability-based and growth-oriented. When she wrote her chapter for the first *Handbook of Teacher Evaluation* in 1981, Armiger saw a trend away from the growth purpose and toward accountability. Criticism of public schools was escalating, and politicians placed much of the blame on poor teaching. The impetus for teacher evaluation reform in Connecticut, Washington State, and Great Britain reflected this politically based concern. In Louisiana and North Carolina, politicians argued that if they were going to improve teachers' salaries, they would need a rigorous system of evaluation to make sure that the money was well spent. Business officials supported these moves toward accountability-based evaluation, arguing that such evaluation was a key to the success of all enterprises.

As the 1980s progressed and teacher organizations began to play an active role in formulating teacher evaluation policy, pressure mounted for greater attention to professional development. That the leaders of these organizations reflected the sentiments of rank and file teachers is indicated by a recent survey of approximately 1,000 elementary teachers across the United States. Asked their preferences regarding the purposes of teacher evaluation, most teachers favored formative or professional development purposes (National Center for Education Statistics 1994, p. 11). Among the specific purposes associated with professional development were (1) to guide improvement of teaching skills (81 percent); (2) to recognize and reinforce teaching excellence (70 percent); (3) to help teachers focus on student outcomes (62 percent); and (4) to plan in-service education activities (51 percent). Much smaller percentages of teachers supported accountability purposes: (1) to make tenure and promotion decisions (33 percent); (2) to discharge incompetent teachers (45 percent); (3) to help teachers define standards for their peers (23 percent); (4) to determine teachers' pay levels (14 percent); and (5) to give administrators greater control over teacher job performance (11 percent).

The desire of teachers to focus more evaluation effort on professional development has received considerable support from educational researchers. While acknowledging that accountability is a legitimate and legally required purpose of teacher evaluation, researchers have been unable to offer much evidence that the accountability purpose has been well-served by conventional teacher evaluation practices (Stiggins and Duke 1988).[1] Duke and Stiggins (1986) reasoned that, if relatively few teachers are incompetent, too great a focus on accountability and getting rid of poor teachers actually can have a negative impact, destroying morale and syphoning off scarce resources that could be used more productively to promote growth. Interestingly, W. Edwards Deming, the famous business consultant, has made a similar point with regard to private sector operations. Deming (Walton 1986) noted that too much emphasis on the evaluation of individuals for accountability purposes fosters an unproductive climate of fear and detracts from the establishment of collective responsibility. Additional weaknesses with accountability-based evaluation include the tendency to stress mastery of minimum competencies, rather than more challenging goals, and the heavy demands such evaluation places on overworked school administrators.

Elmore (1990, p. 7) observes, "As long as the accountability argument is kept at a high level of abstraction, it has strong political appeal." As efforts to achieve greater specificity are undertaken, he goes on, the potential for conflict increases. The cases in this book offer support for

Elmore's observation. As politicians and teacher representatives, along with other stakeholders, tried to clarify the nature of accountability, disagreements surfaced. Should performance standards or student outcomes serve as the focus of accountability. Who should be held accountable, individuals or teachers collectively? If professional development is a purpose of teacher evaluation, how should it be evaluated?

How Should Teacher Evaluation Be Structured?

Deciding how to implement teacher evaluation proved no less disputatious than determining its purposes. The case studies suggest a variety of structural issues, ranging from the frequency of teacher evaluation to the sources of data upon which evaluation should be based. Perhaps no issue engendered greater debate, though, than whether or not to approach teacher evaluation in a differentiated manner. Traditionally, teacher evaluation tended to entail a unitary system. While multiple purposes may have been addressed, they were addressed as part of a single evaluation system. For example, teachers might have been observed and assessed according to a list of accountability-based performance standards and simultaneously required to set annual professional development goals.

The commingling of purposes in the same system began to be challenged in the early 1980s (McNeil 1981, p. 284). Teacher advocates and some researchers complained that, while accountability and professional development might be jointly pursued in theory, actual practice presented a number of difficulties. Teachers often feared taking the risks associated with genuine growth because they knew they were also being evaluated for summative purposes. Administrators admitted paying less attention to the professional development purpose because the accountability purpose required so much time and energy. To deal with these problems, reformers advocated the development of differentiated teacher evaluation systems (Stiggins and Duke 1988). In some cases, the basis for differentiation derived from the purpose of evaluation. In other cases, separate systems were proposed for nontenured and tenured teachers or competent teachers and teachers in need of intensive assistance.

Another structural issue concerned the timing of teacher evaluation. In the past, teachers in many school districts were subjected to accountability-based evaluation annually, regardless of whether they had amassed years of satisfactory evaluations. Recent efforts to revise teacher evaluation policy have found teachers and administrators challenging this practice, noting its high costs and questionable benefits. They wondered whether teachers with strong records might be freed from annual accountability evaluation in order to focus on professional development. Proposals were made to move to multiyear, multistage evaluation systems in which individual teachers would only experience accountability-based evaluation every three years or more. Such proposals caused some politicians to grow nervous. They wondered how administrators would know whether or not teachers had encountered problems if they were not conducting regular observations and writing up formal evaluations. Reformers countered that classroom observations are only one source of data concerning teaching performance, and an unreliable source at that. If teachers were experiencing difficulties, administrators were as apt to learn about them from students, parents, other teachers, or their own wanderings around school as from formal observations.

Data for teacher evaluation and who is responsible for gathering it were two other issues around which considerable debate took place. Probably the most sensitive issue concerned what role, if any, should be played by student achievement data. In Washington State, for example, business leaders argued that student achievement was the "bottom line." They cared little about how teachers got students to learn as long as intended learning outcomes were accomplished. Teacher representatives countered that students are not randomly assigned to teachers and that students, not teachers, ultimately determine that learning will take place.

Disagreements also surfaced concerning who should be involved in evaluating teachers. In several of the case studies, the use of external evaluators was considered. The value of local peer evaluators was debated as well. The principal's role in formative evaluation became a touchy issue in Washington State, where teacher representatives challenged the authority of administrators to veto teachers' growth goals. In Florida, Brandt noted that the roles of data collector and evaluator were separated in the hopes of reducing concerns over subjectivity.

The role of data from the formative evaluation process in summative evaluation prompted concerns in Washington State and Great Britain. Teacher representatives expressed fear that teachers might be reluctant to participate in professional development activities if their performance could be used for accountability purposes. Why would a teacher choose an ambitious growth goal if failure to achieve it might contribute to an unsatisfactory summative evaluation? Those who disagreed with the teachers' position claimed that public funds were used to support formative activities, the implication being that the public was entitled to know that its money was well-spent.

Should Evaluation and Pay Be Linked?

The June 8, 1994, issue of *Education Week* reported that approximately half of the states in the United States are funding some form of incentive pay plan. Plans cover career ladders, mentor-teacher programs, and projects tied to school improvement. For various reasons, most of these efforts stopped short of basing teachers' pay on the results of summative evaluations of teaching performance. Chapter 2 described some of the issues that can surface when policymakers consider performance pay schemes. They include the lack of valid measures of outstanding teaching, the lack of skilled evaluators, and the possibility of cheating. Confusion over the difference between incentives and rewards also can become an issue (Mitchell, Ortiz, and Mitchell 1987, pp. 188–190). While incentives are associated with anticipated performance, rewards supposedly are based on demonstrated performance. Teachers sometimes object to rewards because of perceived reliability problems among evaluators. Furthermore, they contend that some teachers may have less opportunity to earn rewards because they are assigned to teach more challenging students.

Conflict over performance pay figured in the formulation of teacher evaluation policy in North Carolina, Washington State, and Great Britain. In each case key legislators, backed by business leaders, argued that the quality of teaching would improve only when better teachers received better pay. Teacher organizations countered these arguments with questions about the technical details of performance evaluation and the practical impact on morale of differential pay. Despite the seeming success of these counteroffensives, performance pay proposals periodically reappear. In England and Wales, teachers fear that continued Tory leadership eventually will lead to a direct link between teacher appraisal and teacher pay, despite assurances to the contrary. In Washington State, those who believed the performance pay issue had been laid to rest with the passage of legislation moderating the accountability-based focus of teacher evaluation were surprised to see it resurface during meetings of the Governor's Council on Educational Reform and Funding. Connecticut implemented a career ladder, but did not tie it directly to teacher evaluation. North Carolina, on the other hand, pilot-tested a merit pay plan linked to the statewide Teacher Performance Appraisal Instrument. Despite some encouraging results, the plan was prevented from being expanded by the North Carolina Association of Educators and, interestingly, representatives of business and industry. The latter voiced fears about the loss of local control, though the price tag associated with the merit pay plan probably was a greater concern.

What Resources Are Needed?

North Carolina's experience with merit pay illustrates how resource issues impact the formulation of teacher evaluation policy. Economic conditions vary and, with them, attitudes toward policy initiatives requiring public funds. Business leaders who were only too willing to press for a link between pay and teacher appraisal during good times backed off in the face of an economic downturn. Agnes McMahon indicated that the Tories' interest in performance pay was not matched by a willingness to increase educational expenditures. The Government expected merit raises for top performing teachers to come from annual increments withheld from less deserving colleagues. In North Carolina, the General Assembly saw the 48 million dollar price tag for piloting the Career Development Program in sixteen districts, involving roughly 6,000 teachers (about one out of every ten teachers in the state), and decided it was too great to warrant further consideration.

Other problems related to the funding of teacher evaluation initiatives were noted in the case studies. In Washington State, for example, initial legislative enthusiasm for teacher evaluation reform cooled somewhat when funding was sought for pilot projects to test alternative schemes. Progress on implementing teacher appraisal in Great Britain slowed when politicians judged the cost of evaluation training and professional development for teachers to be too great. After providing liberal funding for the first year of implementation of its new teacher evaluation program, Connecticut's legislature suddenly halted further appropriations. Iwanicki and Rindone identified several possible explanations for the abrupt about-face, but they surmised that the major reason was the prospect of tight economic times.

Nowhere, perhaps, was the politics of teacher evaluation policy-making more apparent than deliberations over resources. Politicians critical of public schools, including many self-styled conservatives, were most willing to invest in teacher evaluation when the focus was accountability. They supported the idea of rewarding excellent teachers and training administrators to get rid of poor teachers. Resources for formative evaluation and related professional development activities were relatively low on their list of priorities, but high on the teachers' list. State department officials not surprisingly favored the allocation of resources to support statewide efforts to develop performance standards and train evaluators. Local educators meanwhile fought for funds that might be used at their discretion to assist in teacher evaluation and development. Perhaps because of these different priorities, a comprehensive, long-term funding program to support new teacher evaluation policy has yet to emerge in any of the case study sites.

A New Era for Teacher Evaluation?

After more than a decade of experimentation, policy formulation, and large-scale implementation, what are the prospects for a new era in teacher evaluation? Five case studies, of course, do not permit the degree of generalization necessary to answer this question with complete confidence, but they are sufficient to suggest whether or not thinking is shifting regarding the purposes and practice of teacher evaluation. It appears that policymakers and educators in Connecticut, Louisiana, North Carolina, Washington State, and Great Britain agree on some matters, but not others.

The most obvious focus of agreement, at least in the four case studies from the United States, concerns the need to change prevailing teacher evaluation practice. During policy deliberations, few voices were raised to defend traditional practice. Administrators, teachers, and legislators alike believed that teacher evaluation previously had accomplished relatively little, despite the investment of considerable time and energy. Little evidence was presented that past evaluation efforts had led to improved instruction, greater learning, better professional development, or fewer inadequate teachers.

The preceding section indicated that conflict accompanied efforts to determine a new direction for teacher evaluation. Interestingly, though, few major players in any of the case studies ever suggested abandoning altogether the evaluation of individual teachers. Such an idea will be explored in the concluding chapter, however.

Conflict typically gave way to compromise during policy formulation, and the compromises across the various sites were sufficiently similar to suggest the beginnings of a paradigm shift in teacher evaluation. In this regard, the most important area of emerging agreement concerned the purpose of teacher evaluation. Policymakers in every case acted to strengthen the link between teacher evaluation and professional development. How this link was forged, however, varied somewhat.

Table 8-1 summarizes some of the key reforms described in the five case studies. Teacher evaluation policy in the four U.S. states shared a tendency toward greater complexity. In place of traditional unitary teacher evaluation systems, new guidelines have enabled school districts to differentiate between evaluation for the purpose of accountability or dismissal and evaluation for the purpose of professional development. Policymakers have acknowledged, for the most part, that the vast majority of experienced teachers are unlikely to benefit greatly from annual evaluations based on a set of minimum performance standards. They have made it possible for local school systems to implement alternative teacher evaluation schemes. Individual districts have begun to encourage tenured teachers, for example, to pursue long-term professional development goals in lieu of routine annual observations and summative evaluation. Louisiana has gone so far as to mandate that all teachers set professional development goals.

New teacher evaluation policy in four U.S. sites also has differentiated between beginning and experienced teachers. A fundamental weak-

TABLE 8-1. Comparing Teacher Evaluation Policies

Reforms	North Carolina	Louisiana	Connecticut	Washington State	England & Wales
Separate evaluation systems for accountability and professional development	*	#	*	*	
Differentiated evaluation guidelines for tenured and non-tenured teachers	#	#	#	*	
Summative evaluation not required annually for competent, tenured teachers	*	*	*	*	*
Local control of teacher evaluation	#	#	#[1]	#	#
State-specified performance standards and/or guidelines for local summative evaluation	#	#	#	#	
Roles for peer and/or external evaluators		#	#		
Required training for evaluators	*	#	#	#	
Professional development component of teacher evaluation guided by teacher-initiated goals	*	#	*	*	*
Formative evaluation results excluded from consideration during summative evaluation	*	*	*	#	

Note:
= required by State policy
* = State policy allows local option
[1] = excluding intern teachers' evaluation

ness in many traditional policies was perceived to be their failure to recognize the need for separate approaches to evaluating novices and veterans. North Carolina, for example, decided to require districts to use the state performance appraisal system only for nontenured, out-of-state, and transfer teachers. Similar guidelines were developed in Connecticut, which opted to use external, state-trained evaluators to evaluate beginning teachers. Louisiana supported the training of external assessors to evaluate intern (first-year) teachers.

The complexity of the emerging teacher evaluation paradigm in the U.S. so far is absent in England and Wales, largely because the official purpose of evaluation is currently understood to be solely professional development. When this writer spoke with officials in the British Department for Education and the head of a leading Tory think tank in 1993, though, he learned that government leaders intended eventually to press for a link between teacher evaluation and accountability.

For now, policy in all five sites displays a commitment to local control of teacher evaluation. Decentralization, of course, has been a major theme of Tory education policymakers since the Reform Act of 1988. The commitment to local control in the U.S. is less comprehensive and ideological, with certain states retaining some central controls in the form of designated performance standards for nontenured teachers, training functions, resource allocation, and other aspects of teacher evaluation. Still, the case studies reveal that legislators insist on preserving a relatively high degree of local control, at least where teacher evaluation is concerned.

Given the discretion accorded local school systems, there will be a need to study the new policies implemented by individual school districts in order to determine the extent of variation. Will districts take advantage of new state policies to move away from annual accountability evaluation for all tenured teachers? Will some districts make greater use of evaluators other than principals? Will traditional reliance on classroom observation be reduced as new sources of data on teaching are tapped? Where teachers are encouraged to set goals for purposes of professional development, how will progress be assessed?

And how will local teachers and administrators react to these new developments? Will they accept greater complexity, given all the other demands on their time? Will formative evaluation eventually degenerate into a meaningless ritual just as summative evaluation did for many veteran teachers? In the Washington State case study, it was interesting to note that a substantial number of school districts failed to comply with the mandated deadline for revising teacher evaluation policy.[2] Will this pattern of differential compliance be repeated elsewhere? If so, will states take any action to force recalcitrant districts to cooperate? Such questions should keep researchers busy in the coming years.

Lessons about Policy Formation

The case studies offer insights not only into the nature of new thinking about teacher evaluation, but also the process by which teacher evaluation policy is formulated. For example, the initial impetus for changes in teacher evaluation has tended to come from political rather than professional sources. Motivated in most instances by concern for greater accountability, politicians had to moderate their initial goals in the face of teacher resistance. Teacher participation on advisory groups and intense lobbying by teacher organizations resulted in greater attention to professional development in all five case studies. Interestingly, special interest groups representing school administrators, with the possible exception of Great Britain, did not play a major role in policy formulation, despite the fact that administrators were legally responsible for teacher evaluation and greatly affected by the work demands placed on them by supervision and evaluation.

The reasons why teachers were able to influence the original policy agenda of politicians included tenacity and organization. In Washington State, for example, the Washington Education Association made certain to keep the same representatives on the Advisory Task Force on Evaluation over the course of its deliberations. Continuity of representation gave the teachers considerable clout, since participants representing other groups came and went. Another reason for the teachers' success was the unwillingness of politicians to stick with the teacher evaluation issue. Unlike teacher representatives, they quickly moved on to other policy concerns. Their lack of sustained interest in teacher evaluation reform may have been due to the unexpectedly high cost of implementing a new accountability-based evaluation system or the fact that teacher evaluation was a relatively low priority issue.

Another similarity in policy formulation across the case studies involved the key role played by vanguard districts, pilot testing, and consultants. Had it not been for South Kitsap in Washington State or Suffolk Local Education Authority in England, for instance, it is entirely likely that the push for growth-oriented teacher evaluation would never have gained momentum. In the former instance, South Kitsap tested a promising new model of teacher evaluation before the state initiative began. As a result, teacher representatives had at their disposal a concrete example of growth-oriented evaluation to help counter political pressure for accountability-based evaluation. Suffolk, on the other hand, was funded by the Government to investigate developments in appraisal in the United States, Germany, and private industry. The report of the Suffolk team failed to support a move to merit pay, thereby dampening Tory hopes that a link could be forged between teacher appraisal and pay for performance.

Pilot tests of new teacher evaluation systems were undertaken in North Carolina, Washington State, and England. In each case, the resulting field reports played a role in the policy formulation process. In Washington State, pilot programs were intended to test various models of teacher evaluation, the hope being to identify the best model and use it as a basis for drafting state guidelines. When most of the pilot projects turned out to resemble the South Kitsap model, a model that stressed professional development, the Office of the Superintendent of Public Instruction was compelled to change its strategy. The original desire to test a new accountability-based teacher evaluation system, perhaps one involving pay for performance, could not be satisfied, leaving OSPI little choice but to create guidelines granting local school systems broad discretion in developing new teacher evaluation policy.

Pilot tests of new teacher appraisal schemes in six English LEAs provided advocates of growth-oriented appraisal with an important opportunity to strengthen their case. At the time of the piloting, the Government was strongly committed to accountability-based appraisal, including pay for performance. The pilot schemes, each of which focused considerable energy on professional development, generated sufficient enthusiasm among participants that the National Steering Group became convinced that growth-oriented appraisal was the way to go.

In North Carolina, pilot testing occurred *after,* rather than prior to, the initial design of teacher evaluation guidelines. Once the North Carolina Teacher Performance Appraisal System was developed by the Department of Public Instruction, twenty-four school systems were funded to test the new process. An evaluation of the NCTPAS pilots revealed that instructional improvement was the primary focus in most localities. The legislature had expected accountability to be stressed. The DPI overlooked low ratings for the formative portion of the NCTPAS and recommended adoption of the new system to the legislature. The pilot tests convinced them, however, that the summative portion of the new system required extensive training for principals in order to succeed.

Consultants played key roles in policy formulation in all five case studies. For the most part, these individuals were university-based researchers specializing in teacher evaluation. Almost without exception, they believed that teacher evaluation should serve two purposes—accountability *and* professional development. In Connecticut, an in-state consultant was instrumental in convincing State Department of Education officials to merge teacher evaluation with professional development and school improvement. The same individual also played a pivotal role in moving Louisiana officials in the direction of growth-oriented teacher evaluation. Consultants helped North Carolina develop the performance standards for the NCTPAS and evaluate pilot tests of the new system as well as the Career Development Program. In Washington State, two consultants working with the Northwest Regional Educational Laboratory helped design the South Kitsap model as well as several other pilot projects and subsequently worked with the Washington Education Association and various school systems to develop local teacher evaluation policy. Consultants from the University of Bristol served as coordinators for the National Steering Group that made recommendations to the British government regarding teacher appraisal policy. In their efforts to build awareness among NSG members of various approaches to teacher evaluation, they contributed greatly to the case for formative appraisal.

The process of policy formulation across the five sites shared several other features. Substantial delays in implementing new policy were experienced in four cases, suggesting that politics may not cease upon initial approval of a new policy. Resistance, in fact, sometimes surfaces only when special interest groups actually see what a new policy looks like. Policymakers, for their part, often wondered why it took so long for concerns to surface. Delays were attributed as well to the fact that local officials invariably required more time to respond to new policy than policymakers anticipated. Funding for training also can become an issue once policy has been adopted, thereby causing implementation efforts to be postponed. Postponement, of course, increases the likelihood that circumstances will change and support for the new policy will erode.

Interpreting the Case Studies

Now that some of the similarities and differences across the case studies have been reviewed, it is appropriate to consider what these cases might mean to those concerned with teacher evaluation and related matters.

That people have grown dissatisfied with traditional teacher evaluation there can be little doubt. When the reasons for this dissatisfaction are examined, however, it becomes clear that teacher evaluation means different things to different people. For politicians critical of public schools, and their allies, teacher evaluation symbolizes a "get tough" strategy to ensure that incompetent teachers are removed from classrooms. For teachers and, to some extent, school administrators, teacher evaluation reform constitutes an opportunity to improve school climate, promote professionalism, and provide constructive feedback to teachers as they undertake ongoing professional development.

The wave of reform efforts in teacher evaluation that began during the 1980s was launched by politicians and state officials. When their efforts, which often included attempts to link teacher evaluation and teacher pay, bogged down in complex negotiations with teachers, they backed off their original "hard-line" position. Policy compromises tended to endorse both the professional development and the accountability purpose of teacher evaluation. Instead of extensive state controls, local discretion over most decisions related to teacher evaluation was affirmed.

The primary focus of accountability-based evaluation apparently has shifted to beginning teachers. Their evaluation is the only area where states have retained a relatively high degree of oversight and control. Such a course of action comes as no surprise. It is always easier politically to concentrate on newcomers than on veterans, as Louisiana learned. Baldwin speculated that teacher evaluation reform would have proceeded much more smoothly had veteran Louisiana teachers been grandfathered under the new policy instead of being threatened with loss of tenure.

Concentrating accountability-based evaluation efforts on non-tenured teachers makes sense for other reasons besides politics. There is little evidence, for example, that teachers who were outstanding early in their careers become incompetent as time goes by. School administrators often observe that the least capable teachers are typically those who started off with major problems. If such individuals can be remediated early or removed before tenure, the need for subsequent accountability-based evaluation presumably would diminish greatly.

Teacher evaluation policy that stresses the accountability purpose early in teachers' careers is premised on the existence of a steady supply of capable teachers. If the labor pool is shallow and school systems cannot afford to dismiss teachers with marginal competence, such policy becomes harder to defend. It is likely, for example, that many urban and rural districts do not have the luxury of being able to enforce high performance standards for new teachers.

The willingness of politicians to accede to teachers' wishes for greater emphasis on professional development may mean several things. Teacher evaluation reforms, for instance, could be interpreted as an indication of a maturing profession. Teacher groups have been pressing for years for greater recognition of their status as professionals. Most highly experienced professionals outside of teaching, nursing, and social work (traditional female professions) are not subjected to annual accountability-based performance evaluations. Requiring such evaluation for competent, highly experienced professionals constitutes a form of institutionalized distrust, one which fails, by almost everyone's admission, to contribute much to good instruction or improved student achievement.

An alternative interpretation holds that many politicians no longer regard the evaluation of individual teachers as an effective and relatively cheap accountability mechanism. If this view is correct, it would be reasonable to expect to see new accountability initiatives filling the gap once occupied by teacher evaluation. Clearly, politicians cannot afford simply to walk away from the issue of educational accountability. Chapter 9 provides a discussion of what some alternative means for holding teachers accountable might look like.

Notes

1. A possible exception to this generalization is Carol Furtwengler's evaluation of North Carolina's Career Development Pilot Program (1988). She found that many teachers felt their skills had improved as a result of the evaluation process associated with the trial project. David Holdzkom speculates that these teachers' judgments probably were influenced by the substantial financial rewards that could be earned by participation.

2. David Holdzkom reported that many of the school districts that applied for waivers under North Carolina's 1989 teacher evaluation law (GS 115C–283) sought to reduce the number of annual classroom observations or spread observations over more years without offering alternatives to promote greater professional development for veteran teachers.

References

Armiger, M. L. (1981). The Political Realities of Teacher Evaluation. In J. Millman, ed., *Handbook of Teacher Evaluation*. pp. 292–302. Beverly Hills: Sage.

Duke, D. L., and Stiggins, R. J. (1986). *Teacher Evaluation—Five Keys to Growth*. Washington, D.C.: National Education Association.

Elmore, R. F. (1990). Introduction. In R. F. Elmore and Associates, *Restructuring Schools*. pp. 1–28. San Francisco: Jossey-Bass.

Furtwengler, C. (1988). Evaluation of North Carolina's School Career Development Pilot Program. Raleigh: North Carolina General Assembly.

McNeil, J. D. (1981). Politics of Teacher Evaluation. In J. Millman, ed. *Handbook of Teacher Evaluation*. pp. 272–291. Beverly Hills: Sage.

Mitchell, D. E. Ortiz, F. I. and Mitchell, T. K. (1987). *Work Orientation and Job Performance*. Albany: State University of New York Press.

National Center for Education Statistics. (1994). Public Elementary Teachers' Views on Teacher Performance Evaluations. Washington, D.C.: U.S. Department of Education.

Pfeffer, J. (1992). *Managing with Power*. Boston: Harvard Business School Press.

Stiggins, R. J., and Duke, D. L. (1988). *The Case for Commitment to Teacher Growth: Research on Teacher Evaluation.* Albany: State University of New York Press.

Walton, M. (1986). *The Deming Management Method.* New York: Putnam.

9

Speculations on the Future of Teacher Evaluation and Educational Accountability

Daniel L. Duke

The context in which educational policy is crafted constantly changes. By the time one wave of policies strikes the schools, another storm offshore promises to launch a new wave. I believe that the conditions are building for new thinking about educational accountability and, with it, a new round of changes in teacher evaluation. This concluding chapter briefly summarizes the new thinking and its possible implications for schools.

The reforms in teacher evaluation that have been described in the preceding chapters represent an historic shift from a relatively exclusive focus on individual accountability to a combination of individual accountability and professional development. Initially, however, many of the reform initiatives attempted to improve the technical quality of accountability-based teacher evaluation. Brandt earlier described how Florida separated the functions of coding and evaluating teacher behavior in order to enhance objectivity. Elsewhere efforts were made to utilize multiple data sources instead of relying exclusively on classroom observation. Careful training of observers was a key element of most statewide programs.

Many of the efforts to improve the technical quality of teacher evaluation failed to yield convincing evidence of better teaching or greater student achievement.[1] In the absence of such data, arguments by teacher organizations for more attention to growth-oriented evaluation gained strength. I predict that the evaluation of individual teachers, especially veteran teachers, will continue to concentrate on professional development. The goal of accountability, on the other hand, increasingly will be addressed in ways other than the summative evaluation of individual teachers.

One reason for these predictions derives from the realities of contemporary school administration. Principals face too many other demands on their time to permit careful evaluation of all teachers. This fact may help explain why training large numbers of school administrators to be expert evaluators has proven to be very difficult. It is all many principals can do to concentrate on a few teachers who require intensive assistance.

Contemporary reforms in public schools and private businesses constitute another reason for my predictions. Innovations such as site-based management, shared decision making, teacher empowerment, and expanded parental choice of schools are indirectly exerting considerable influence on thinking about educational accountability. Interestingly, these reforms often have been inspired by developments in the private sector. Many businesses have reached the conclusion that efforts to hold individuals accountable are not particularly productive. Following the advice of gurus like W. Edwards Deming, they increasingly rely on self-managing teams and shared responsibility (Barker 1993).

Efforts to decentralize educational decision making and encourage greater teacher participation are altering relations between teachers and school administrators. Hierarchy is giving way to collegiality. The traditional command-and-control model of school management hardly seems compatible with the spirit of collaboration that undergirds reforms like site-based management. To the extent that teachers perceive accountability-based evaluation to be associated with traditional, top-down management, they are unlikely to welcome its continuation. The role confusion that results when administrators are expected to evaluate *and* share authority with teachers can undermine the effectiveness of both teacher evaluation and shared decision making.

The rise of school choice, meanwhile, raises questions about the very need for teacher evaluation in the first place. Is it necessary to focus on holding individual teachers accountable when parents in many school districts are free to withdraw their children from one school and enroll them in another? Perhaps unfettered consumer choice—the free market—represents the ultimate form of accountability (Gerstner 1994, pp. 46–47). Of course, to work in a manner consistent with the goals of a liberal democracy, a free market system of schools requires an informed public. If some parents have greater access to information about school quality than other parents, for example, school choice simply may serve to perpetuate destructive divisions in society. Policymakers currently are grappling with how to increase school choice in a fair and equitable manner.

If the evaluation of individual teachers is growing less tenable as an instrument of accountability, and if a completely free market in public education is still far from reality, what is likely to be the next initiative designed to satisfy the public's desire for accountability. The following section offers a discussion of some possibilities.

The Range of Accountability Options

One way to think about accountability options involves differentiating on the basis of that for which individuals are held accountable. Raymond Bolam, for example, speaks of the bureaucratic, professional, and market models of accountability.[2] The bureaucratic model holds teachers accountable for complying with policies, regulations, and contractual obligations. The professional model is based on the expectation that teachers will demonstrate certain proficiencies or competencies associated with effective practice. The market model meanwhile is based on student outcomes and customer satisfaction. Compliance and competence are largely irrelevant as long as students learn what they are expected to learn.

The three options described by Bolam are based on holding individual teachers accountable. Is there another way to think about accountability options, one that recognizes the possibility of collective accountability?

Diagram 9-1 illustrates four possible configurations of accountability. The two basic dimensions are (1) the source of accountability judgments, and (2) the focus of accountability. Sources of judgments encompass individuals, such as principals and supervisors, and groups, such as evaluation teams and consumers in general. The focus of accountability, or that about which accountability judgments are made, include the performance of individuals and the performance of groups. Let us look more closely at each of the four possibilities in Diagram 9-1.

Option 1 represents traditional teacher evaluation. Individual teachers are evaluated by individual evaluators, typically a principal or assistant principal. Frequently the evaluator is guided by a set of performance standards and indicators, usually in the form of a checklist. The checklist may be developed collaboratively by teachers and administrators or, in some school systems, by administrators alone. In a number of states, local performance standards must conform to state guidelines.

The weaknesses of the traditional teacher evaluation model are well-known. Performance standards, for example, tend to represent "minimum" competencies. They often are perceived to have little capacity to promote excellence. Basing teacher evaluation on the same standards year in and year out has led many capable teachers to discount the value of evaluation. Another problem concerns the ability of evaluators to conduct meaningful assessments. Teachers believe that evaluators lack adequate time and training to undertake effective evaluations. While some evalua-

DIAGRAM 9-1.

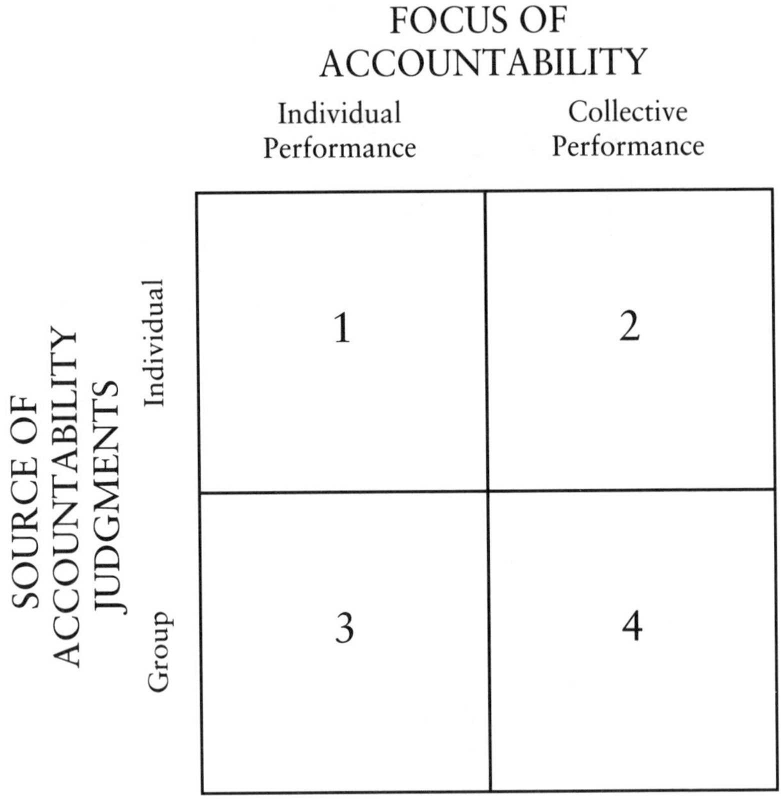

FOCUS OF
ACCOUNTABILITY

	Individual Performance	Collective Performance
Individual	1	2
Group	3	4

SOURCE OF ACCOUNTABILITY JUDGMENTS

tors are unable to provide anything more than gratuitous praise, others purposefully go out of their way to note minor concerns. The latter tack is justified on the grounds that a "paper trail" full of glowing evaluations may come back to haunt evaluators in cases where teachers subsequently encounter problems.

Option 2 is illustrated by the evaluation of principals in some school systems. Principals often are evaluated by one supervisor, typically the superintendent or assistant superintendent. Supervisors base their assessments not just on what the principal does, but on the collective performance of those in the principal's school. Aggregate student achievement, teacher evaluations, and surveys of parents may be reviewed in order to determine how good a job was done. The assumption is that one administrator is somehow responsible for all that goes on in a school.

The basic weakness of this administrative evaluation model is its unfairness. One person cannot determine alone what students learn or teachers teach. Maintaining the pretense of an omniscient leader may discourage capable individuals from seeking administrative positions and drive incumbents from office, while simultaneously inhibiting the development of shared leadership.

Examples of the kind of accountability found in Option 3 are becoming more common, though they still are far from typical. In this option, small teams of evaluators focus their assessment on the performance of one individual. The intention is to reduce the likelihood that evaluator bias or lack of expertise will undermine the efficacy of the evaluation. Multiple evaluators mean more data and more opportunities to corroborate findings. Team-based evaluations are currently undertaken in some school systems for beginning teachers and teachers on plans of assistance.

While team-based evaluation in many ways represents an improvement over traditional models, it, too, has some shortcomings. Logistically, it is less easy to coordinate a team evaluation than an evaluation by one person. In addition, disagreements may arise among members of a team, particularly when they are selected for different reasons. For example, some evaluation teams include a person chosen by the local teacher organization. This individual's function is to protect the due process rights of the teacher in question, an undertaking that may conflict with the responsibilities of other members.

Option 4 is characterized by collective judgments of collective performance. Perhaps the best traditional example of this option is an accreditation review. Typically, teams of evaluators visit schools, review various sources of data, and draw conclusions regarding overall school performance. Individuals rarely are singled out for blame. Collective accountability is intuitively appealing. Many educators, as well as policymakers, acknowledge the wisdom of the African saying, "It takes a whole village to raise one child." If such a statement is valid, then it is equally defensible to argue that it takes an entire faculty to educate a cohort of students.

Collective accountability is not without problems, of course. As with Option 3, scheduling evaluation activities for groups of people is difficult. Arriving at consensus poses a challenge when the focus is collective performance, as does determining the parameters of the assessment. Should the evaluation of school performance, for instance, include assessments of parental support and the community's willingness to fund schools adequately?

In developing Diagram 9-1, I must confess to some uncertainty regarding where to place the "free market." In a sense, when parents choose schools for their children, they are conducting accountability-based evaluations of schools. The choice made by any one parent may fit Option 2, in the sense that an individual makes a judgment in which an entire school is held accountable. On the other hand, if all parents are presumed to exercise choice, the situation may be closer to Option 4. The problem is that the parents typically arrive at their judgments independently rather than as a result of systematic sharing of information.

What Does the Future Hold?

If the literature on the reform of schools and businesses is any indication, consensus regarding one best model of accountability is lacking. While attracted to the idea of collective accountability, many reformers seem unwilling to abandon some provisions for holding individuals accountable (Gerstner 1994; Osborne and Gaebler 1993). They insist that organizational success is a function of group initiative, while still clinging to systems of individual reward and sanction.

Of all the states in the case studies, Connecticut may provide the best glimpse of the future. As a result of the Systemic Reform Initiative of 1993, Connecticut is attempting to integrate individual and collective accountability. Individual educators are expected to develop professional growth plans which include specific goals. These goals are intended to serve as the basis for the evaluation of individual performance. In order to receive a satisfactory evaluation—at least in theory—each tenured teacher must set goals which contribute to overall school improvement and demonstrate progress toward that end. Beginning teachers continue to be subject to state-directed, accountability-based evaluation based on specified performance standards.

What constitutes school improvement for Connecticut policymakers? Edward Iwanicki, in Chapter 4, refers to language from the reform act:

> Educators, working with each other, parents, the community and supporting agencies, create a learning environment that enables each student to perform at high levels.[3]

In other words, the Connecticut vision is a system in which professionals and the public assume collective responsibility for individual student performance. In order to reach this lofty goal, coalitions of educators, parents, and community members first must create appropriate learning environments, certainly an outcome that only can be achieved through collective effort.

Connecticut is not alone in exploring the possibility of collective accountability. Under John Murphy's leadership, Charlotte-Mecklenburg Public Schools require every school to set improvement targets based on such indicators as student test scores, attendance, enrollment in particular courses, and parent surveys. The walls of Murphy's "war room" are lined with charts for every school in the system. Charts contain graphs noting progress toward each school's goals. Each year bonuses are awarded to all staff members in schools that reach designated percentages of their targets.

The shift to collective accountability can be linked, in part, to efforts in many states to collect and share data on school performance (Wohlstetter 1991). Virginia's Outcome Accountability Project is a case in point. Each year the Virginia Department of Education collects data from school divisions. Most of the data is reported for individual schools. The state distributes reports of these data every spring, making it possible for the news media and interested parents to obtain comparative information on local schools. Some school divisions have begun to use the annual reports on school performance to set targets for school improvement. Suggestions have been made that rewards or bonuses should be linked to the achievement of these targets.

While interest in collective accountability is growing in public education, this option has a longstanding tradition in certain fields. Perhaps the most dramatic example is the bomb disposal unit in the military. While members of such units may hold different ranks, no one would consider shirking their responsibilities. To do so would be to put everyone in the unit, including themselves, in jeopardy. Self-interest merges with collective interest.

The challenge for school systems, in my judgment, is to foster the kind of collective accountability present in a bomb disposal unit. Lack of educational success may not threaten the lives of educators, but students certainly can be placed at risk. How can teachers and administrators be encouraged to regard the success of *all* students as their collective responsibility? Shared responsibility need not mean equal contributions by every educator to each student's education. Obviously, particular students would continue to have more contact with some teachers than others. Collective accountability simply requires that all staff members do whatever they can to assist all students, or their teachers, to reach school goals. Acceptance of such responsibility would lead teachers to intervene to reduce disorder, even when they are not officially "in charge." Regular education teachers would begin to welcome instructional advice from special education teachers, regardless of whether or not their students have disabilities. Individual teachers no longer would dwell on reducing the size of their own classes, since such action would mean that other teachers' classes would have to grow. Achieving school goals would become more meaningful professionally than pursuing one's own "thing."

That the world of tomorrow's schools will be consumer-driven is beyond doubt. The days of public school monopolies and little parental choice are waning. In the new world of public education, consumers will expect competent service, no matter which teachers are assigned to their children. Faculties that protect weak members or that regard teacher remediation as solely the responsibility of administrators are unlikely to fare well in direct competition with faculties that accept collective accountability as a worthy foundation for school culture.

While I predict increasing interest in collective accountability in schools, I do not foresee a complete abandonment of the traditional individual accountability model. Some states like Maryland, for example, have begun to link the evaluation of individual teachers to recertification. Teachers must produce a specified number of satisfactory evaluations, along with other requirements, in order to renew their teaching license. Some veteran teachers will opt to sit for examinations offered by the National Board for Professional Teaching Standards. High scores could lead to advancement and salary improvement.

In the coming years, however, I believe the primary focus of individual accountability initiatives will be beginning teachers. The trend was evident in three of the case studies. It reflects the belief among many experts that traditional evaluation, guided by performance standards and informed by announced observations, diminishes in value as teachers gain experience and expertise. Unless a compelling case can be made that large numbers of competent teachers lose their skills and effectiveness over time or collective accountability experiments produce disappointing results, I doubt that interest in individual accountability models for experienced teachers will be revived.

Little (1993) makes the case that most of today's school reforms require a focus on collective rather than individual effort. MacKinnon and Brown (1994) support this position with regard to meeting the needs of special students. Inclusion, they argue, cannot succeed in schools where teachers continue to work alone and think as independent agents. No one teacher, they contend, can address effectively the diverse needs of all of today's students. What are required are collaborative professional cultures, sometimes referred to as communities of learners or adhocracies. I believe that individual accountability models of teacher evaluation, with the possible exception of those aimed at new teachers, are largely incompatible with such school cultures. Collective accountability appears to be much more likely to foster the kind of cooperation necessary to reform public education.

Notes

1. An exception to this trend may have been North Carolina, where at least one study of Career Development Program pilot projects indicated a relationship between the new evaluation system and student achievement. See Richard M. Brandt, *Incentive Pay and Career Ladders for Today's Teachers* (Albany: State University of New York Press, 1990).

2. The author is indebted to Professor Raymond Bolam of the University of Wales for sharing these models of accountability. A similar framework for thinking about accountability has been developed by Linda Darling-Hammond in "Accountability for Professional Practice," *Teachers College Record,* Vol. 91, no. 1 (Fall, 1989): pp. 59–80.

References

Barker, J. R. (1993). Tightening the Iron Cage: Concertive Control in Self-managing Teams. *Administrative Science Quarterly,* 38(2): 408–437.

Brandt, R. M. (1990). *Incentive Pay and Career Ladders for Today's Teachers.* Albany: State University of New York Press.

Darling-Hammond, L. (1989). Accountability for Professional Practice. *Teachers College Record,* 91(1): 59–80.

Gerstner, L. V. (1994). *Reinventing Education.* New York: Dutton.

Little, J. W. (1993). Teachers' Professional Development in a Climate of Educational Reform. *Educational Evaluation and Policy Analysis,* 15(2): 129–151.

MacKinnon, J. D., and Brown, M. E. (1994). Inclusion in Secondary Schools: An Analysis of School Structure Based on Teachers' Images of Change. *Educational Administration Quarterly,* 30(2): 126–152.

Osborne, D., and Gaebler, T. (1993). *Reinventing Government.* New York: Plume.

Wohlstetter, P. (1991). Accountability Mechanisms For State Education Reform: Some Organizational Alternatives. *Educational Evaluation and Policy Analysis,* 13(1): 31–48.

Index